IMAGES
of America

AGAWAM AND FEEDING HILLS

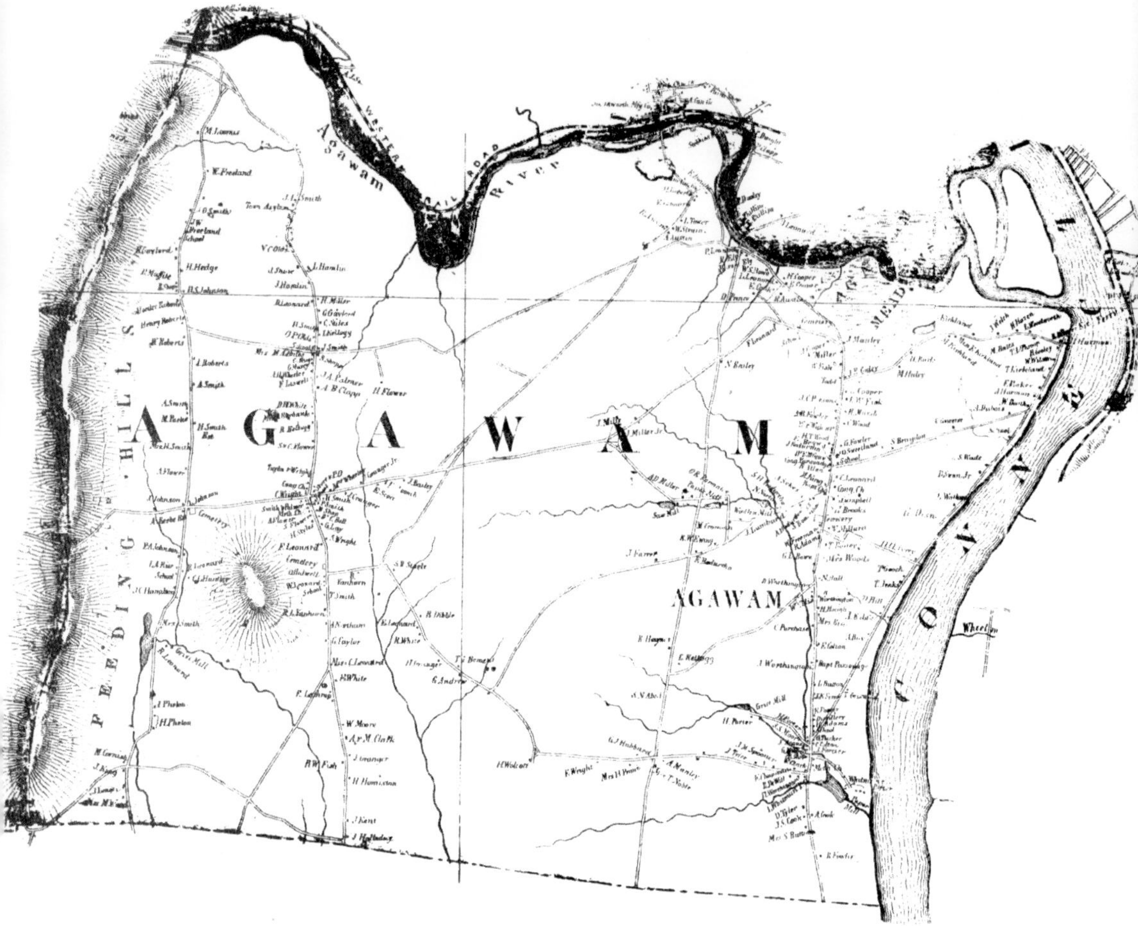

This map shows Agawam, Massachusetts, at the time of its incorporation as a town in 1855. Previously, Agawam had been part of Springfield until 1774. It was then part of West Springfield until 1855. (Agawam Historical Association collection.)

IMAGES
of America

AGAWAM AND FEEDING HILLS

David Cecchi for the Agawam Historical Association

ARCADIA
PUBLISHING

ISBN 978-0-7385-0469-8

Published by Arcadia Publishing
Charleston, South Carolina

Printed in the United States of America

Library of Congress Catalog Card Number: 00-104067

For all general information contact Arcadia Publishing at:
Telephone 843-853-2070
Fax 843-853-0044
E-Mail sales@arcadiapublishing.com
For customer service and orders:
Toll-Free 1-888-313-2665

Visit us on the Internet at www.arcadiapublishing.com

For Joseph and Bailey,
may they someday share my love of their hometown,
and to Laurie,
whose patience, understanding, and support allow me to be who I am.
Love, David

On the cover: A.K. Fuller's store and the Feeding Hills Methodist Church were both in Feeding Hills Center. This photograph was taken long before these structures at 14 and 18 South Westfield Street were destroyed by fire on February 14, 1899. The church, which had been built in 1851, was replaced by the one shown on page 59. E.A. Kellogg, who had been operating his store from the Fuller building by 1899, built his new store shown on page 52. (Agawam Historical Association collection.)

Contents

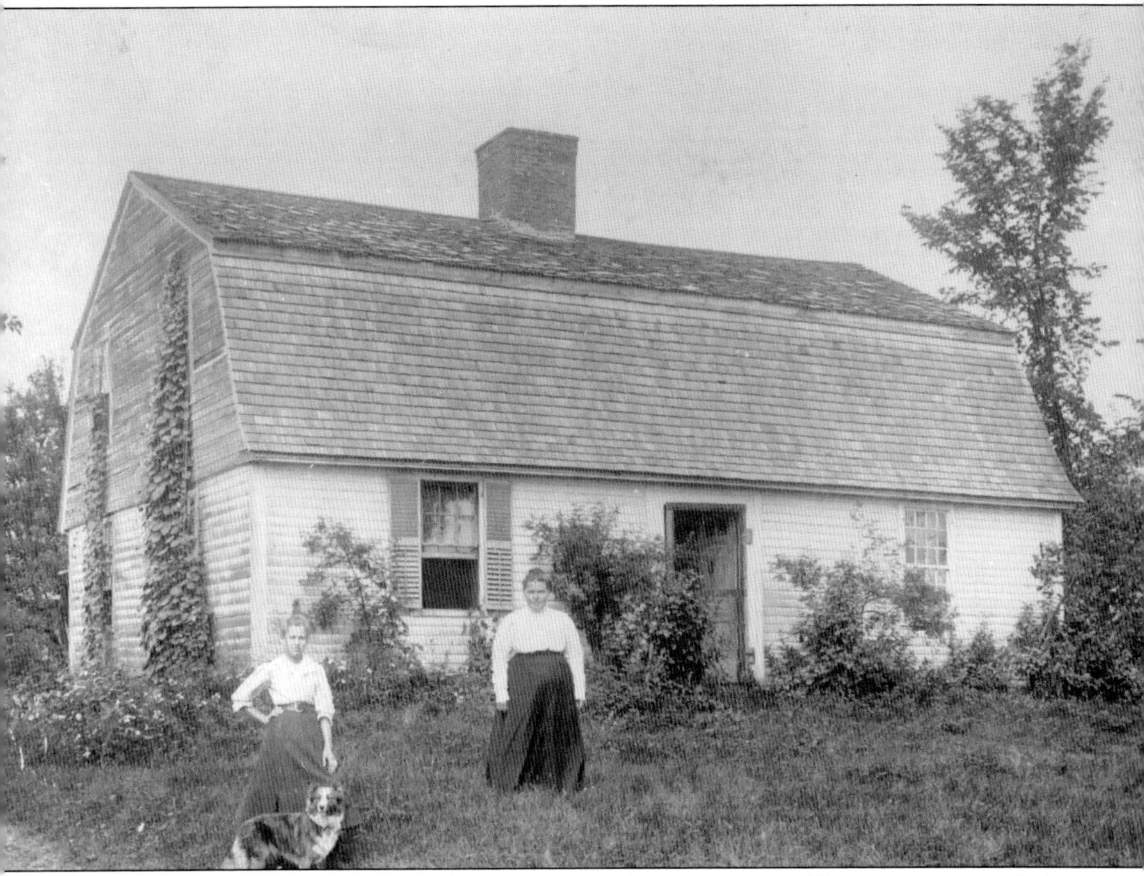

The oldest house in town is the Noble-Rosenberg House on North West Street. It was built in 1715 by Mathew Noble, the son of the founder of Westfield, Massachusetts, Thomas Noble. No heating or indoor plumbing was ever added, and the house remains much as when it was built nearly three centuries ago. Oscar Parks (see page 58) owned the home at the turn of the 20th century, when this photograph was taken. The two women are most likely members of Parks's family. (Courtesy John Rosenberg.)

INTRODUCTION

As you look at the photographs on the following pages, you will see an Agawam and Feeding Hills you probably never knew existed. But it did exist until just a short time ago. As early as 1905, the board of selectmen reported that "the Town is changing from a distinctly rural to a suburban community." However, it was not until after World War II that development in this town got into high gear. Actually, high gear is an understatement: buildings were moved, landmarks demolished, and hundreds of acres of farmland were lost to development. This still happens today, unfortunately. Through it all, however, Agawam has retained a sense of its small town roots. Even as our population approaches 32,000, and the town is now technically a city by virtue of its form of government, Agawam and Feeding Hills remain, whether you moved here last year or last century, our hometown.

If there is one thing this book hopes to accomplish, it is to show the importance of saving our historical resources. Many of the buildings featured are now gone. When we demolish a Betty's Town House or a Hamilton House, or throw away an old photograph or artifact, they are gone forever. Please support the Agawam Historical Association and the Agawam Historical Commission in their efforts to protect the town's historical resources.

ACKNOWLEDGMENTS

I would especially like to thank the following people for their contributions to this book, through material, conversation, information or photographs: Anna Cecchi; Robert Cecchi Sr.; Frank Chriscola Jr.; Marilyn Curry; Marilyn Gable; Donald Goss; Mr. and Mrs. Everett Hodge; Mr. and Mrs. Russell Jenks; Hollis Kane; Mr. and Mrs. Alvin Kellogg Jr.; Dale Melanson; Dorothy Morris; Clyde Pomeroy; Raymond Pond; Esther Reynolds; Jeffrey Reynolds; Mr. and Mrs. Norman Roberts; the family of the late Walter T. Kerr; and everyone listed within who loaned photographs.

I must also give credit to those who have come before me and done so much to preserve the history of this town. Charles Hull, Edith LaFrancis, Jean Taylor, the Van Heusens, the Thorpes, and Marilyn and Dick Curry all cast a long shadow when it comes to this town's history. I hope this book meets the standards set by them.

My gratitude also goes to Rick Bellico, president of the Agawam Historical Association, and the Agawam Historical Association Board of Directors for the opportunity to work on this project. Your faith and support means a lot. It was a privilege to work on this book for the association and for the people of this town.

Special thanks also to Marilyn Curry for all her help.

—David Cecchi, Agawam, Massachusetts
July 2, 2000

Author's note: Unfortunately, not every photograph submitted for this project was able to be used, so if you do not see yours in this edition, it may appear in a future volume. If you have photographs you would like to share with us, please contact me, care of the Agawam Historical Association, P.O. Box 552, Agawam, Massachusetts, 01001. All photographs will be returned upon request.

Every effort was made to be as accurate as possible, but as Michael K. Miller, author of *Images of America: Enfield* writes, "Errors and disagreement are inevitable in any historical composition. Much written history can only be traced to secondary sources. Even primary sources can be contradictory—when they can be found." Like Mr. Miller, we "welcome any information that our readers have that proves or contradicts any information in this book."

One

Not the Howes Brothers

More than 30 years ago, Marilyn and Dick Curry purchased a box of glass negatives taken in Agawam at the turn of the century, assuming the photographs were the work of the Howes Brothers of Ashfield, Massachusetts. The negatives sat in that box until well after Dick's death in 1991, when Marilyn donated the negatives to the Agawam Historical Association. The association had prints made of the negatives in preparation of this book, and during research, Kimball Howes of the Ashfield Historical Society (and grandson of Walter Howes) revealed that the photographs were probably not taken by the Howes Brothers. The size of the negative was different, and none of the photographs included people—a Howes Brothers trademark. Later, an old photograph album bought at a tag sale in Southwick, Massachusetts, was offered by Sylvia Deliso for use in this book. The inscription on the opening page read, "Views of Agawam, Massachusetts taken by Rev. Hollis A. Campbell, 1895–1896." The two incidents were unrelated until it was discovered that the photographs in the album had been made from the Curry's glass negatives a century ago. The album contains many of the Curry's photographs. Unless otherwise noted, the images in this chapter are from the collection of Marilyn and the late Richard Curry. The words that appear in boldface are the original captions of the photographs.

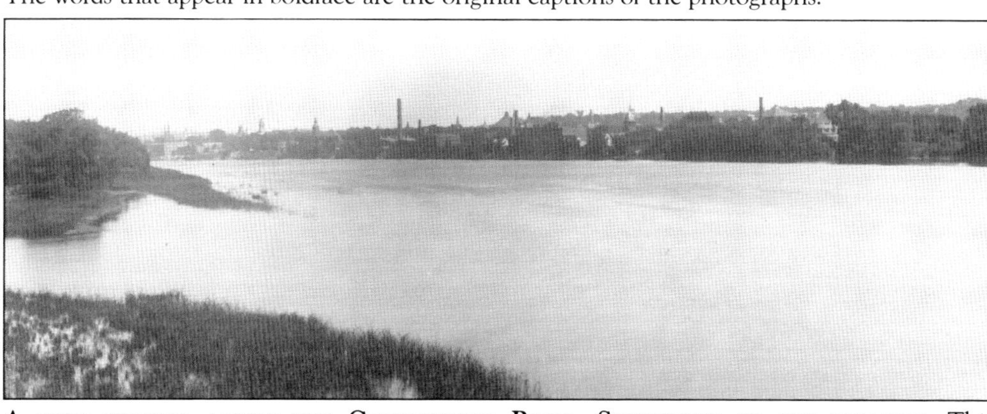

A view looking across the Connecticut River. Springfield in the distance. This photograph was taken from near the South End Bridge, near Pynchon Point at the Agawam and Connecticut Rivers. Agawam was part of Springfield upon its founding by William Pynchon in 1636. It remained so until 1774, when the town of West Springfield was created. Agawam was a parish of West Springfield and did not become an independent town until May 17, 1855.

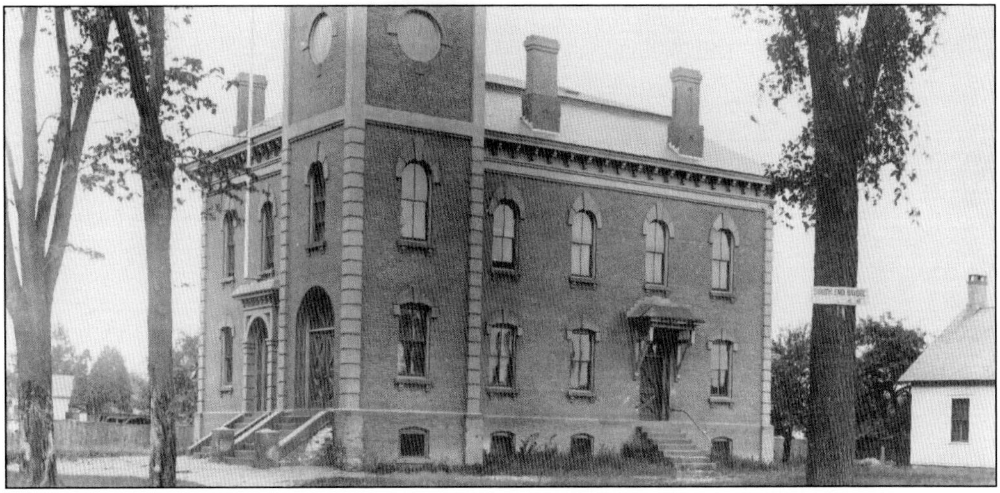

THE CENTER PUBLIC SCHOOL. BUILT IN 1874 UNDER THE SUPERVISION OF ALANSON L. CHAPIN, ARCHITECT. Located at the corner of Main and School Streets, this building served as Agawam's town hall and schoolhouse for upper elementary grades. Grades one through three attended class in the building at right. The brick building was demolished in 1938. The white wood building was moved to Monroe Street and is still in use as a home. Benjamin Phelps elementary school now occupies this location. The sign on the tree points the way to the South End Bridge. (Courtesy of Sylvia Deliso.)

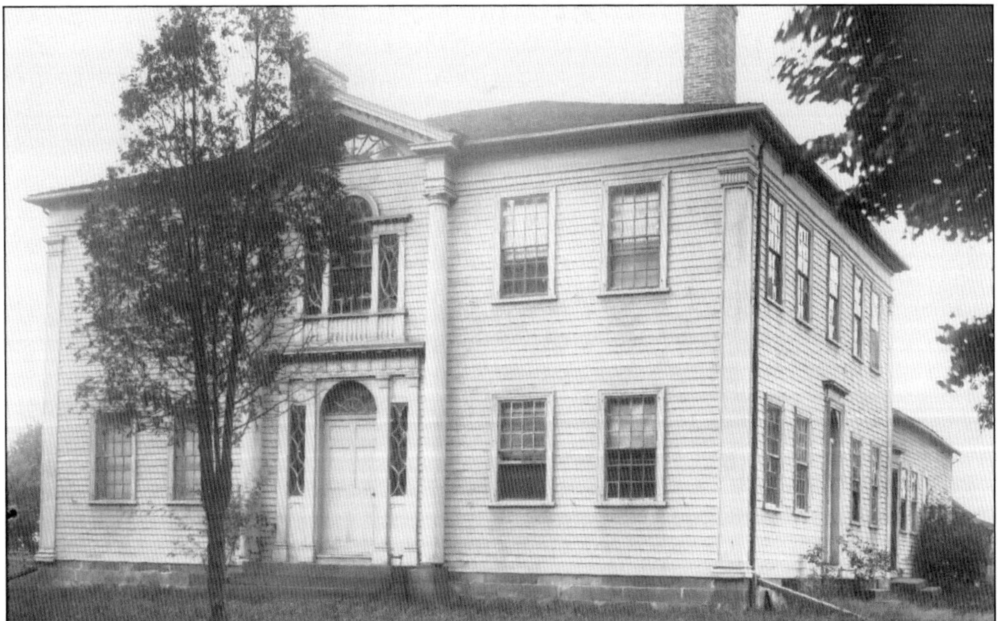

THE FOWLER HOMESTEAD, JUST NORTH OF CENTER PUBLIC SCHOOL, BUILT IN 1807 [*SIC*] BY CAPTAIN CHARLES LEONARD AND FOR A TIME USED AS A TAVERN. Built in 1805 and attributed to Asher Benjamin, this exceptional Federal-style home has been owned by Charles and Mercy Leonard, Lewis Warriner, Rev. Ruben Hazen, Daniel Austin, Kasson Freeman, George Fowler, Jessie Bowley, Dr. Carpenter, Nelson Lewis, Edwin T. Davis, and his son, W.W. Davis. It was later purchased by Mrs. Minerva Davis and opened as the Captain Charles Leonard House for use as a community house (see page 89).

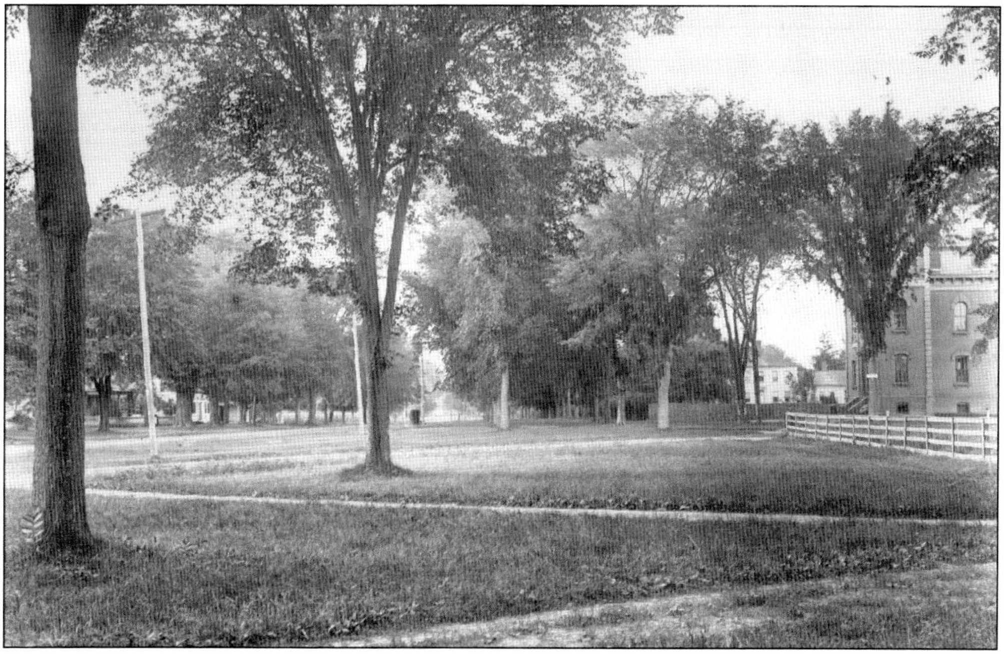

MAIN STREET, THE CENTER SCHOOL ON THE RIGHT. Looking north on Main Street, the Captain Charles Leonard House is visible just to the left of the brick school building on the right. Note the double row of trees on either side of the street.

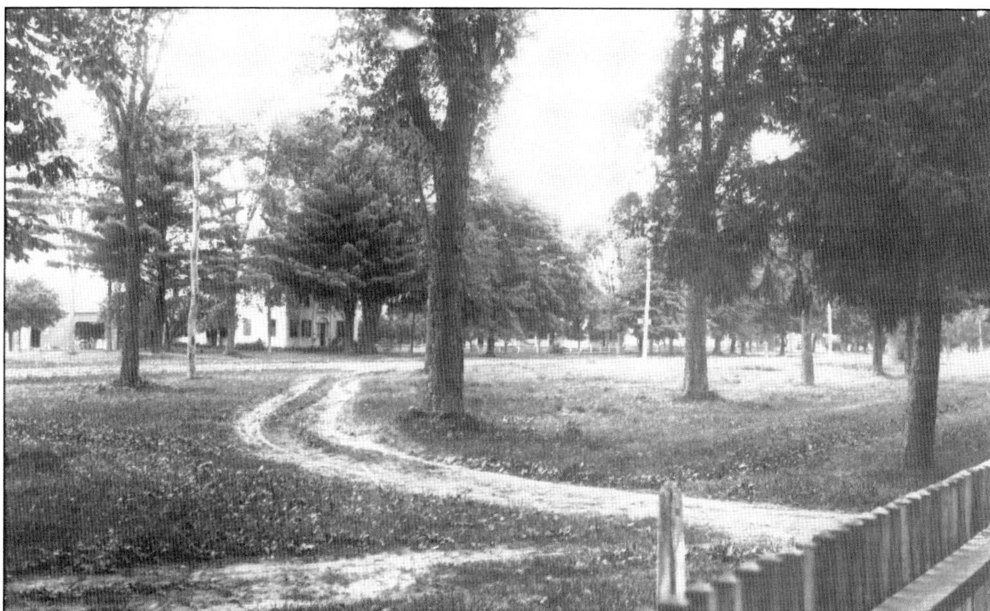

IN ITS UNDISTURBED QUIET; THE LORD PLACE ON THE CORNER OF THE CENTER. OLD MARTIN KING PLACE. Located at the corner of Main and Elm Streets, this outstanding Federal-style home was built by Rufus Colton in 1806. Legend has it that he used part of the $5,000 prize he won from a $5 lottery ticket to finance its construction. In the 1830s, it was known as Martin King's Tavern. Asher Benjamin's Hollister House in Greenfield, Massachusetts, may have been the inspiration for its facade.

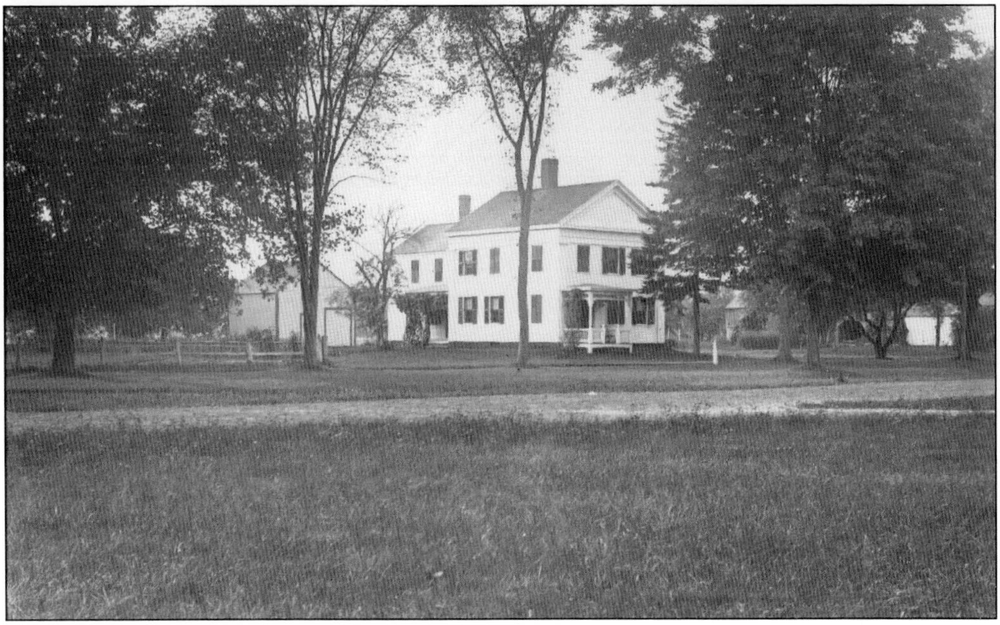

The Congregational Church Parsonage. Built in the mid-19th century, this home is located at 706 Main Street. It served as the parsonage for the Congregational Church on the opposite side of Main Street for many years.

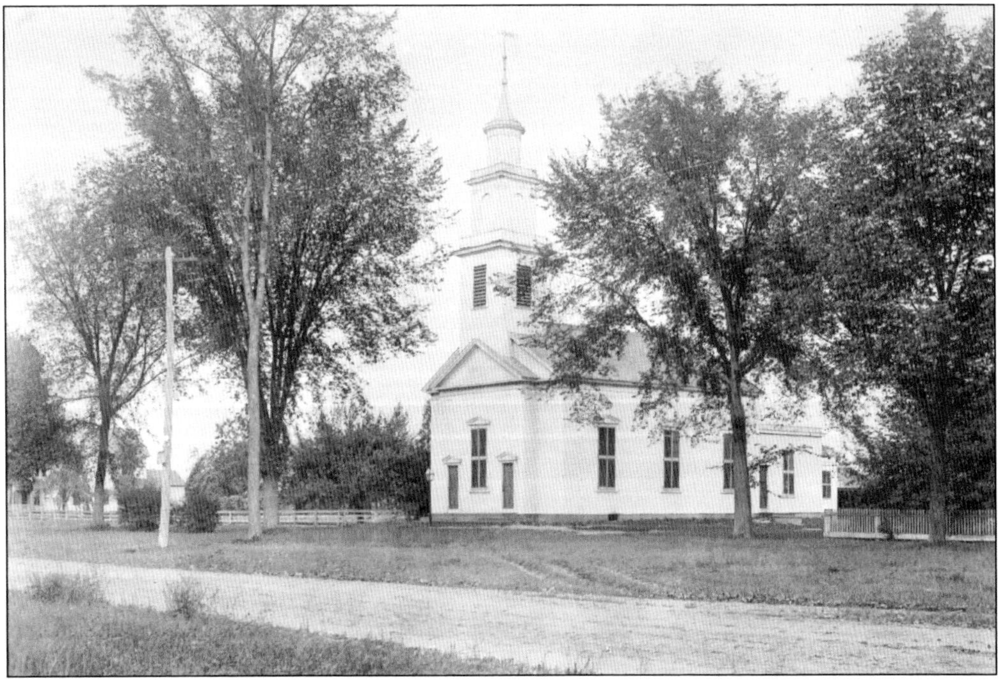

The Congregational Church, 1895. Built in the early 1800s and originally shared by the Baptists and Congregationalists on alternating Sundays until 1830, this structure stood for more than 100 years until it was demolished in the late 1960s, when the current church was built. Before the Elm Street fire station was constructed in 1918, fire apparatus was stored in a shed on the property. (Courtesy of Sylvia Deliso.)

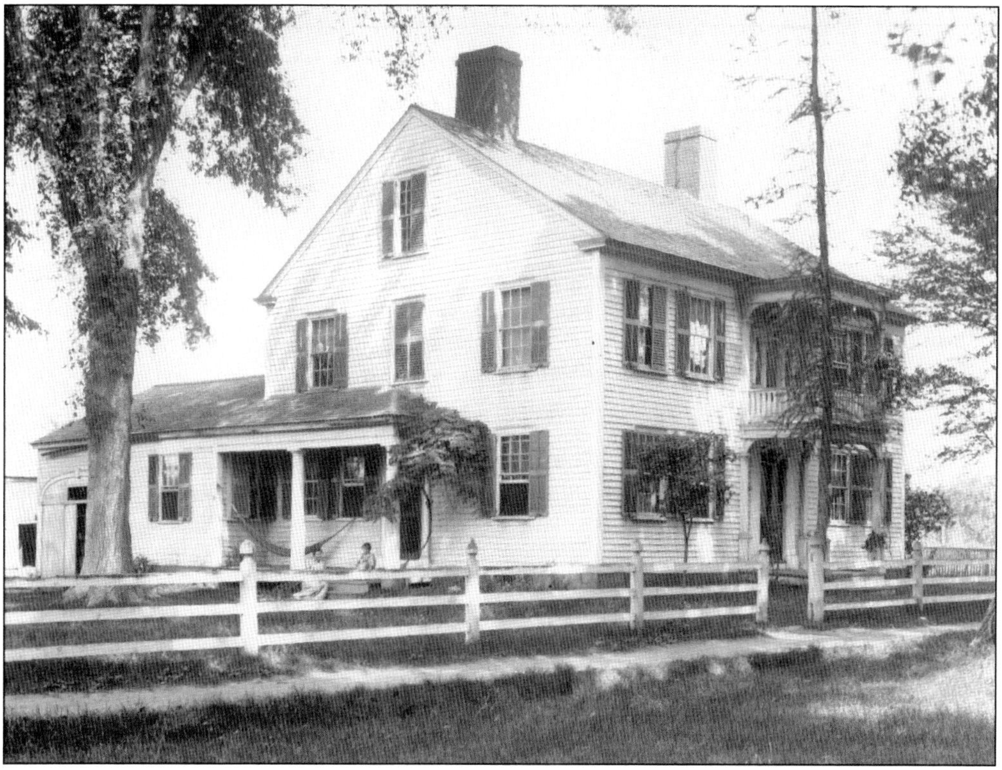

THE LYMAN ALLEN HOMESTEAD. IN 1896 THE RESIDENCE OF FRANK E. CAMPBELL. Still standing at 722–726 Main Street, this home is thought to have been bought from Asahel Adams by Roderick Allen and finished in 1801. It was the home of the Campbell family for many years. The front porch shown here has been removed, but the side porch and graceful arch with keystone remain. Roderick Allen's son, Agawam postmaster Lyman Allen, was killed in 1886 on the grade crossing of the New York, New Haven & Hartford Railroad tracks on the old South End Bridge (see page 26).

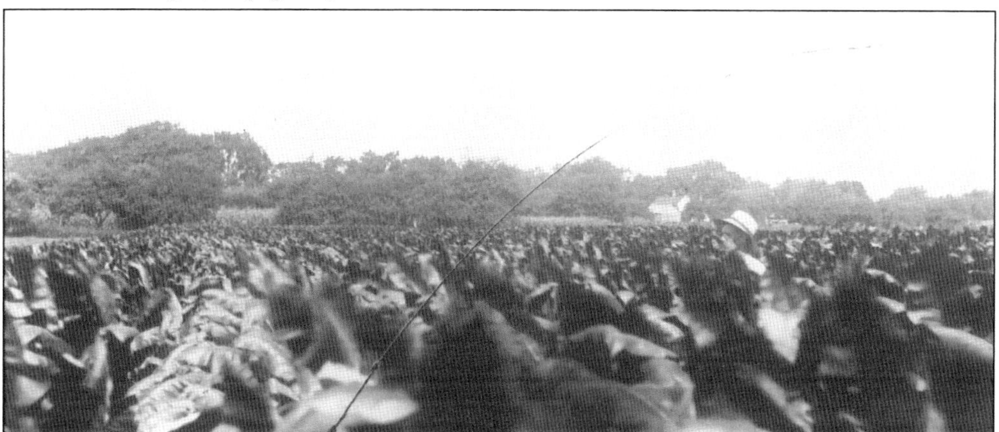

TOBACCO FIELD OF FRANK E. CAMPBELL. Tobacco had been raised in this area since the 1600s. By 1915, Frank Campbell's farm was one of 15 in town that were larger than 100 acres. In addition to his Main Street farm, consisting of what is now Raymond Circle, Campbell owned 156 acres on South Street. The line across the photograph is a crack in the glass negative.

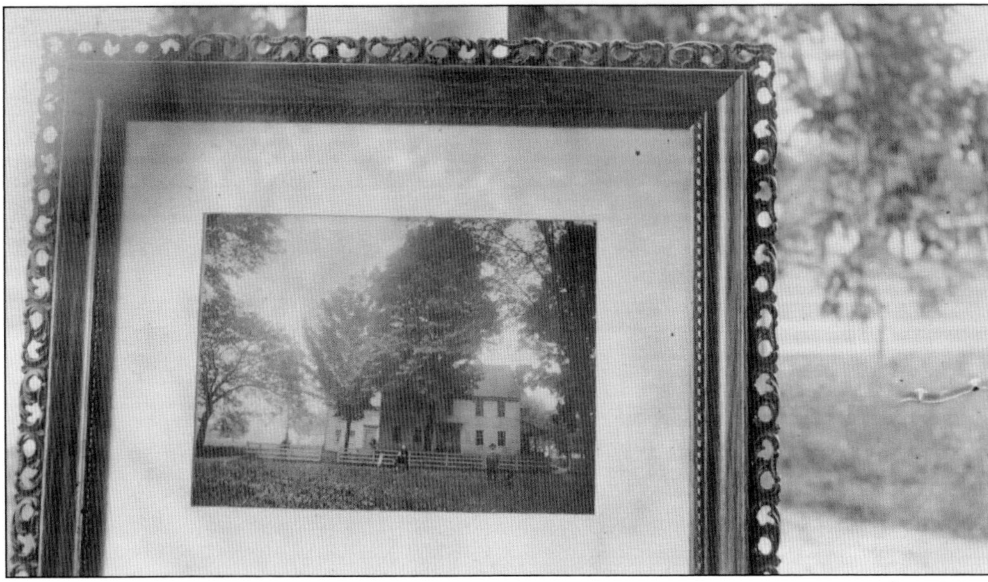

THE OLD LEONARD HOMESTEAD. AN OLD LANDMARK, REMOVED IN 1893–4. Located on Main Street between School and Monroe Streets, this home was demolished to make way for the building shown in the photograph below. (Courtesy of Sylvia Deliso.)

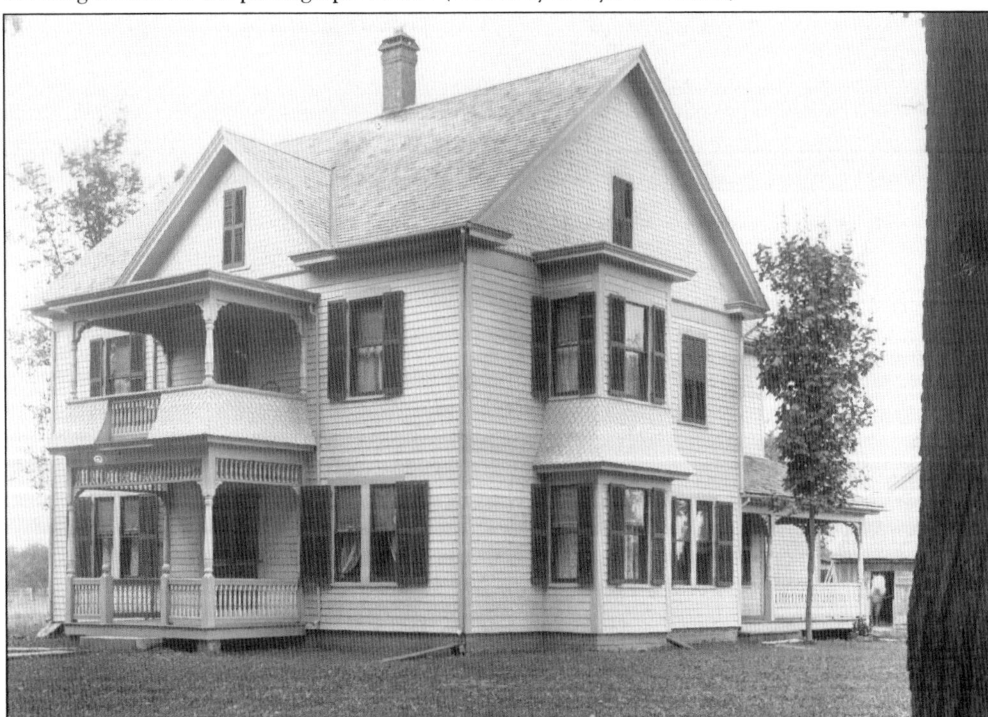

THE LEONARD HOMESTEAD, THE NEW HOUSE BUILT IN 1893 AND 1894, THE HOME OF CARRIE S. LEONARD. MAY 2, 1894 IT BECAME THE HOME OF MONROE AND CARRIE LEONARD HAYWARD. This house, which replaced the one shown above, stood on Main Street between School and Monroe Streets until it was demolished to make way for the shopping center now occupying that location.

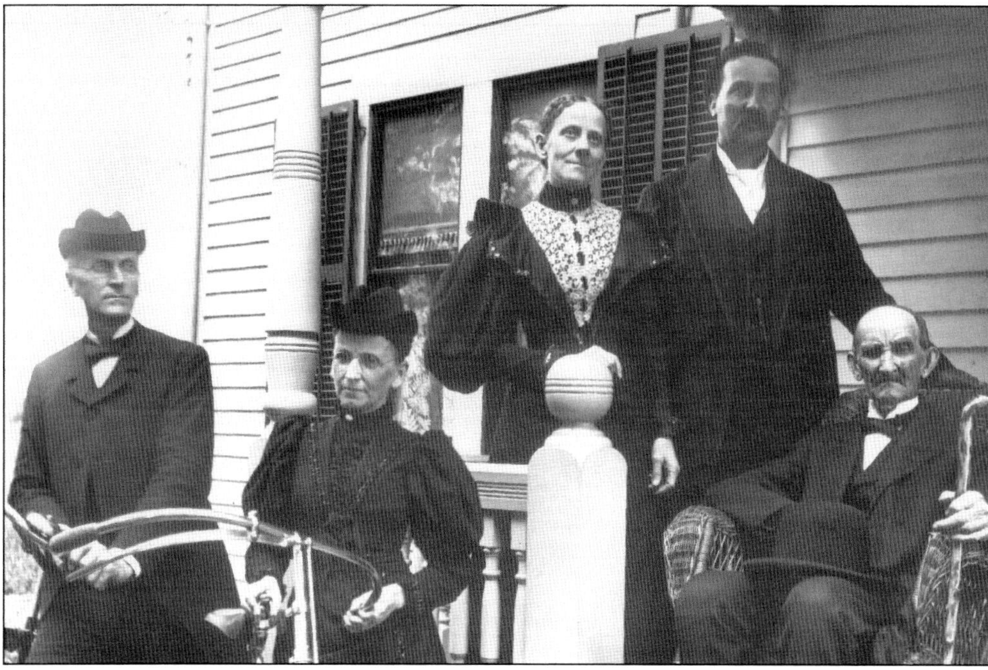

At the home of Mr. and Mrs. Hayward., Rev. Mr. King and wife, Mrs. Hayward, Mr. Hayward, and Ralph Adams, left to right. This is the porch of the house pictured on the previous page. Ralph Adams lived in the house seen on page 19.

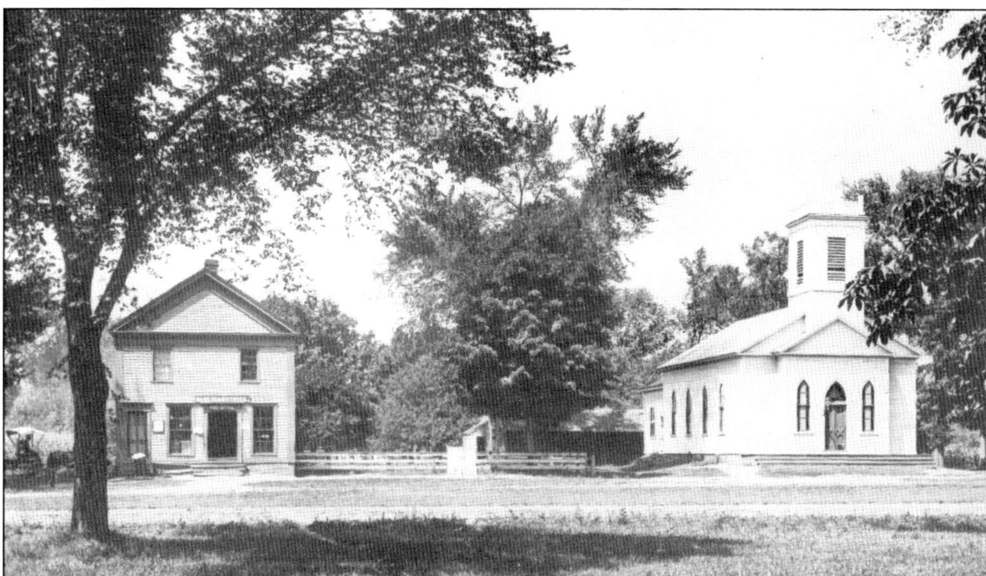

The Baptist Church and the Store and Post Office, 1895. The First Baptist Church of Agawam was built in 1830 at the corner of Main and Elm Streets. C.W. Hastings's store, at left, served the community for many years as a general store and post office. The building shown was later moved to Central Street, where it still serves as a residence. Charles William Hastings served as postmaster for nearly 50 years and died in 1936. The Agawam Public Market now stands on the site. (Courtesy of Sylvia Deliso.)

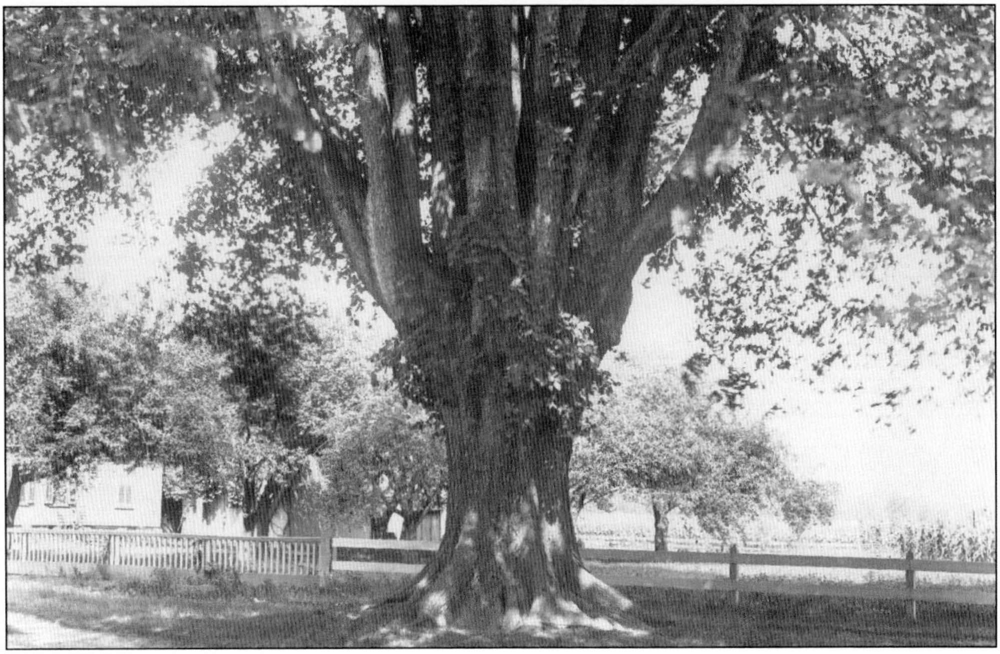

The Beautiful Elm, West Street. Just west of 44 Elm Street, this elm measured 17 feet in circumference and survived into the 1930s. At one time, North and South West Streets in Feeding Hills were also known as West Street. In 1905, a list of new street names was brought to a town meeting to end the confusion. Elm Street was no doubt named after this majestic specimen.

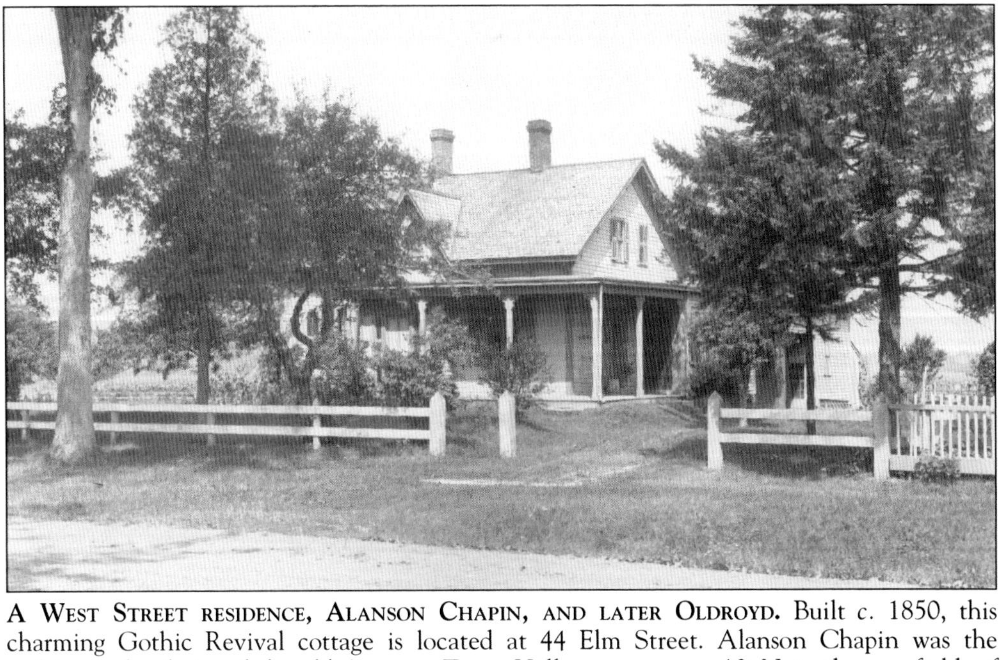

A West Street residence, Alanson Chapin, and later Oldroyd. Built c. 1850, this charming Gothic Revival cottage is located at 44 Elm Street. Alanson Chapin was the architect who designed the old Agawam Town Hall, seen on page 10. Note the cornfields of the Frank Campbell farm the background (see page 13). The homes located on Raymond Circle now occupy that location.

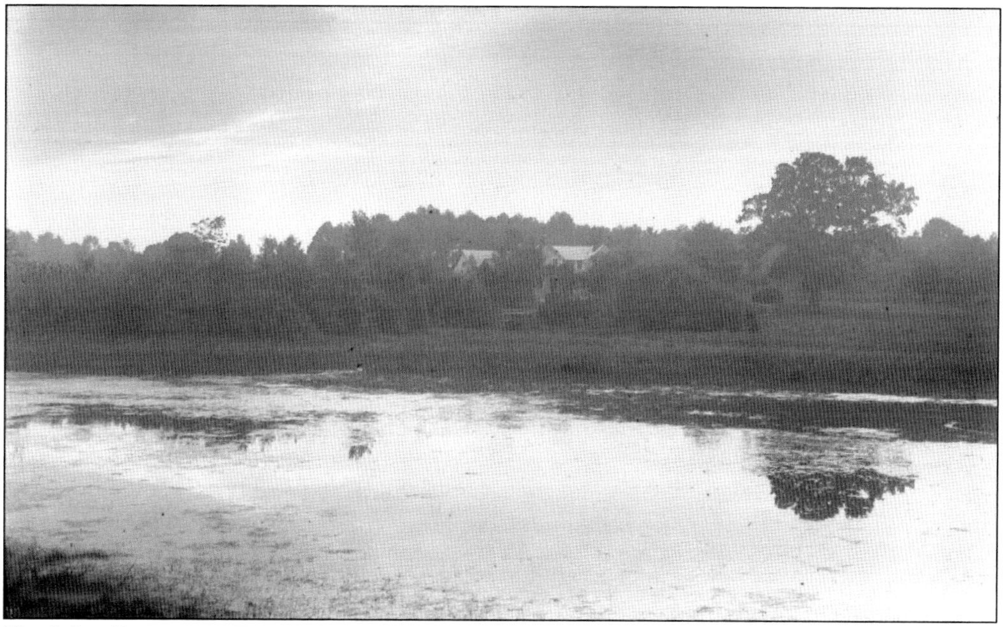

The Mill Pond, the Factory water supply. The home across the pond was the residence of Reverend Perry and son Ralph Perry. This pond was located behind the woolen mill on Elm Street and supplied power to the mill (see pages 34–35). The Perry home, after which Perry Lane was named, was destroyed by fire.

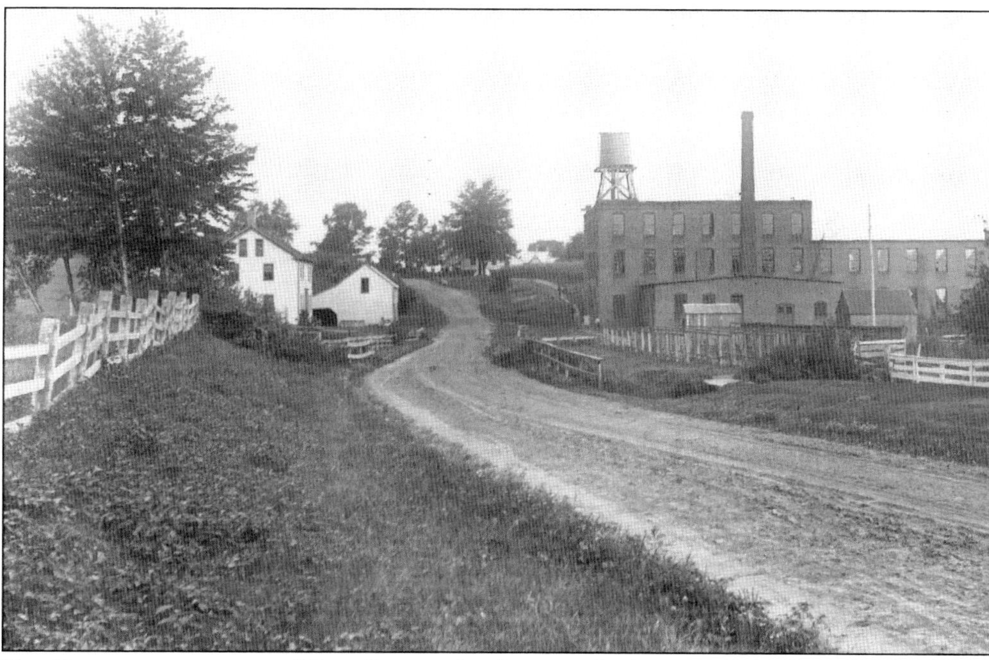

The Factory, so called, West Street. In this view looking west on Elm Street, the new Agawam Company woolen mill, built after the 1889 fire (see page 34) can be seen on the right. Mill workers are walking down the dirt path from the boardinghouse at the top of the hill in the center of the photograph. An addition was built onto the home on the left, and it later served as the Agawam Company's offices (see page 36).

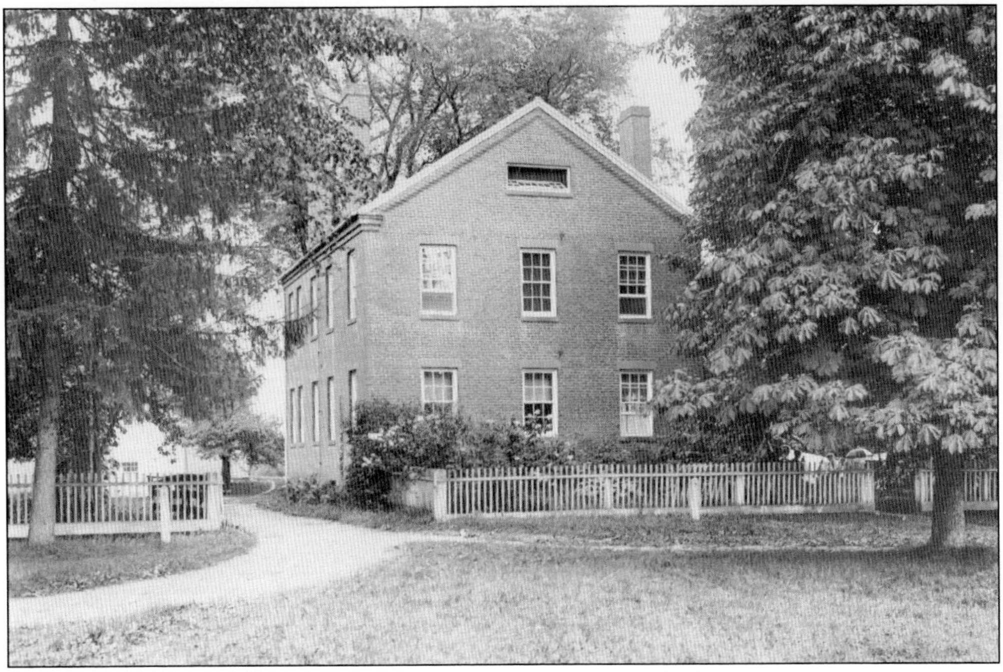

NORTH VIEW OF THE CHARLES CAMPBELL HOUSE, BUILT IN 1841 FROM BRICKS MADE ON THE PLACE. LATER WAS RESIDENCE OF CHARLES L. CAMPBELL, SON OF CHARLES AND STILL LATER THE RESIDENCE OF ELBERT L. CAMPBELL, SON OF CHARLES L. At the time this photograph was taken, it was one of two brick homes in Agawam Center. Located at 769 Main Street, this home is an excellent example of the Greek Revival style. (Courtesy of Sylvia Deliso.)

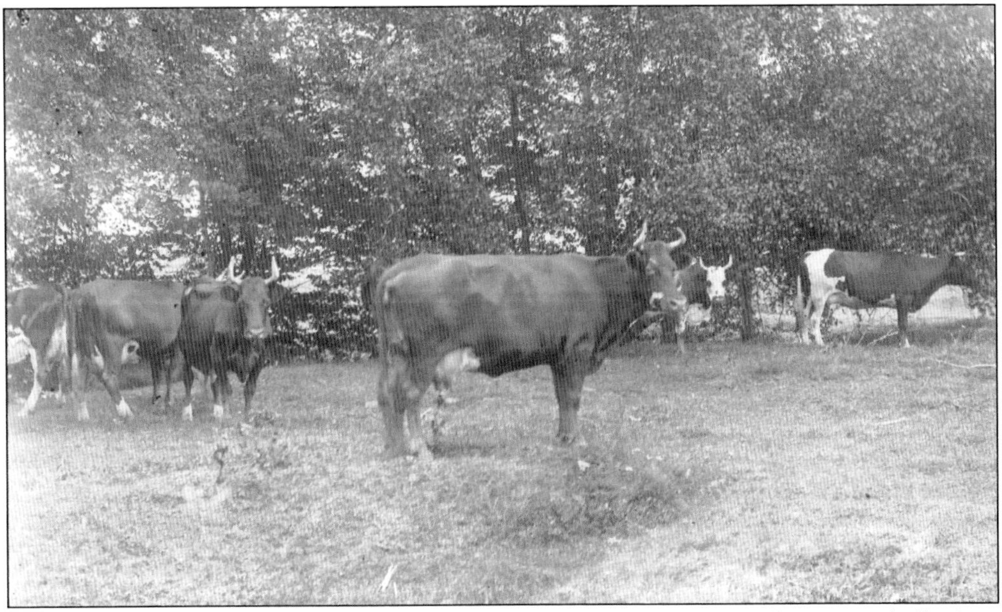

MORE COMBS IN THE ROUGH, A PORTION OF THE HERD, E.L. CAMPBELL. Elbert Campbell's farm occupied land that is now Elbert Road off Main Street. The author was unable to determine what the term "combs in the rough" means. It may refer to hair combs, which were once made from the horns of cows.

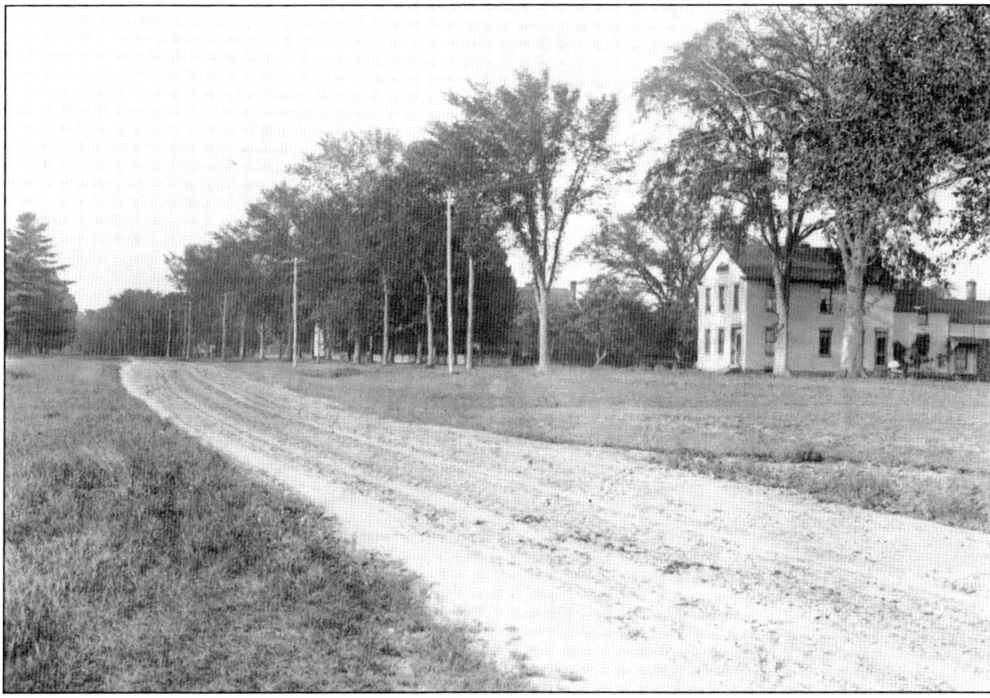

MAIN STREET AND THE OLIVER HILL HOUSE, BUILT IN 1826. THE BRICK WAS MADE ON THE CAMPBELL ESTATE NEAR THE CLAY BANK, LOCATED UNDER THE HILL. This home, known as the Parsons Hill House, is a late Federal-style building. It still stands, painted white, at 789 Main Street. The Campbell House at 769 Main Street can be seen in the distance. The wires strung along the street were then newly installed telephone wires. Agawam received telephone service in 1895 and electricity service in 1900. (Courtesy of Sylvia Deliso.)

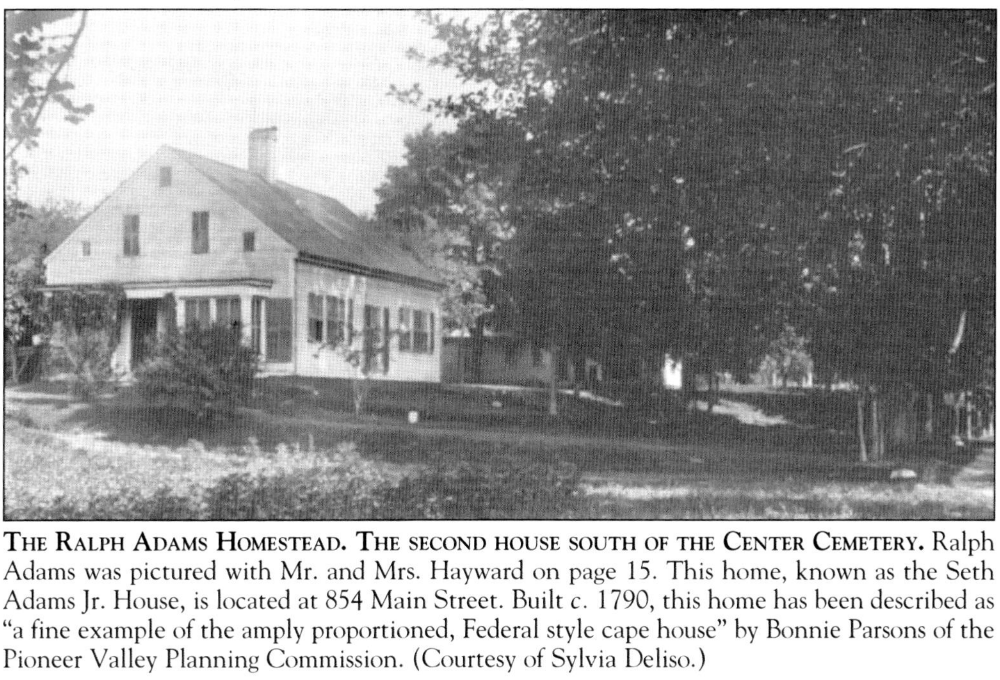

THE RALPH ADAMS HOMESTEAD. THE SECOND HOUSE SOUTH OF THE CENTER CEMETERY. Ralph Adams was pictured with Mr. and Mrs. Hayward on page 15. This home, known as the Seth Adams Jr. House, is located at 854 Main Street. Built c. 1790, this home has been described as "a fine example of the amply proportioned, Federal style cape house" by Bonnie Parsons of the Pioneer Valley Planning Commission. (Courtesy of Sylvia Deliso.)

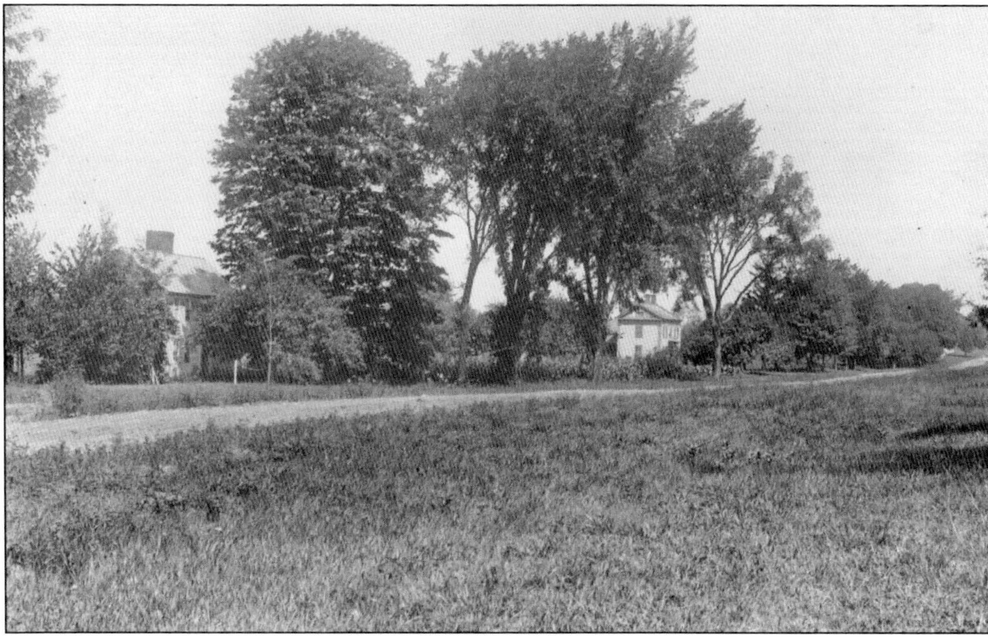

The Old Bowe Homestead, one of the oldest on Agawam Street. It is not known exactly where or when Main Street was known as Agawam Street, but this Georgian-style saltbox, known as the Bliss Tavern, still stands at 940 Main Street. It was built in 1745 and remains the oldest home in Agawam proper. Only the Mathew Noble House in Feeding Hills, built in 1715, predates it (see page 4). The home in the distance also survives; it is located at 914 Main Street on the corner of Main Street and Meadowbrook Manor. (Courtesy of Sylvia Deliso.)

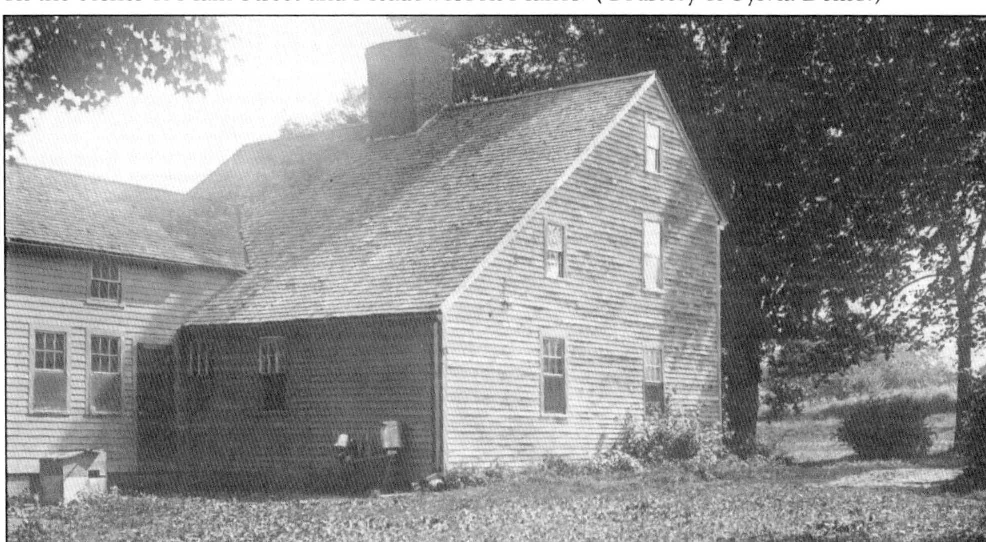

Rear view of Bowe Homestead. The saltbox style of the Bliss Tavern is clearly shown from this angle. Believed to date back to Joseph Leonard, the Bliss Tavern is the town's only surviving early house built in the saltbox style. The town's 75th anniversary program from 1930 lists an H.B. Craig Florist at this address, specializing in "perennials for Hardy Borders and Rockeries; Annuals, Potted or from Flats; Potted Plants, Ferns and Bulbs. Also Vegetable Plants and Cut Flowers."

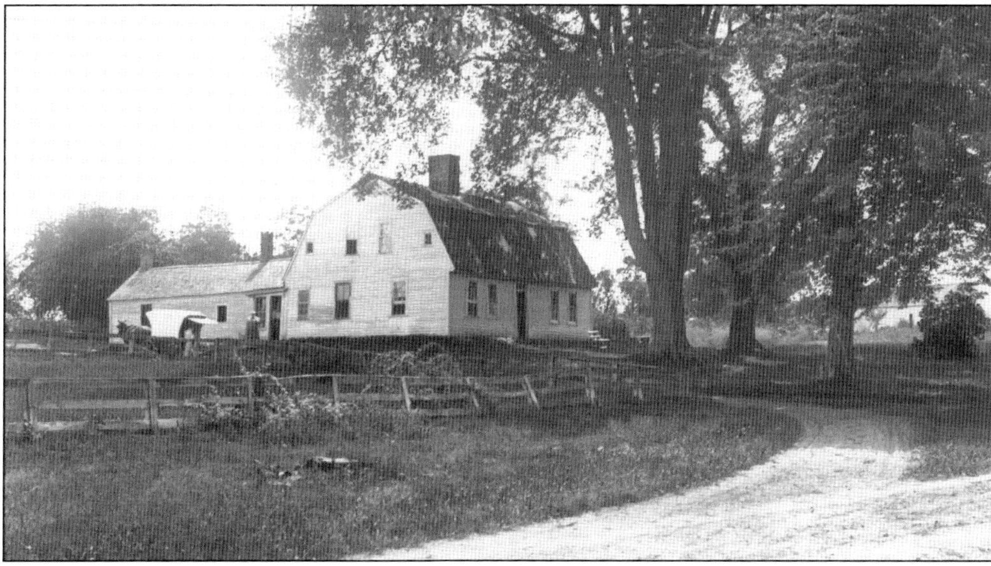

THE LOMBARD BUTTON HOUSE ON SOUTH MAIN STREET, BUILT EARLY IN 1800. ONCE OCCUPIED BY ELDER JESSE WHITMAN. Lombard Button served in the 30th Company unattached heavy artillery during the Civil War and was one of the signers of the petition for the incorporation of Agawam. Built c. 1775 and located approximately at 1255 Main Street, the Lombard Button house was destroyed by fire in 1917. Mrs. Minerva Davis bought the property and built her home on the site in 1924.

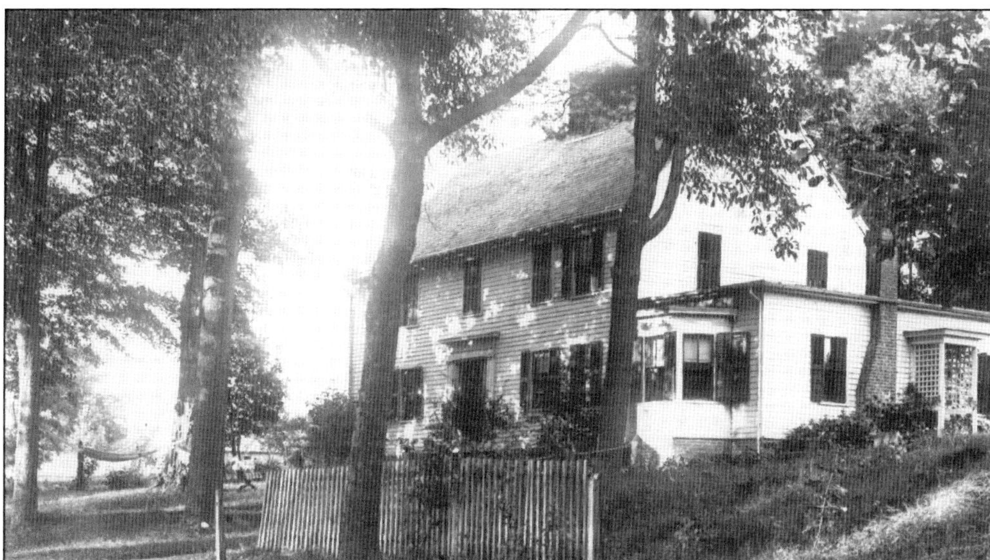

THE FERRE HOMESTEAD ON SOUTH MAIN STREET BUILT BY JONATHAN PURCHASE IN 1764. BOUGHT BY MOSES FERRE IN 1799. This magnificent Colonial end-gable structure still stands at 1289 Main Street. The original property extended eastward to the Connecticut River. According to local legend, the house was part of the Underground Railroad, and a passage led from the basement to the river. The home is listed on the National Register of Historic Places and is currently protected by preservation restrictions through the Society for the Preservation of New England Antiquities. It is now known as the Purchase-Ferre House.

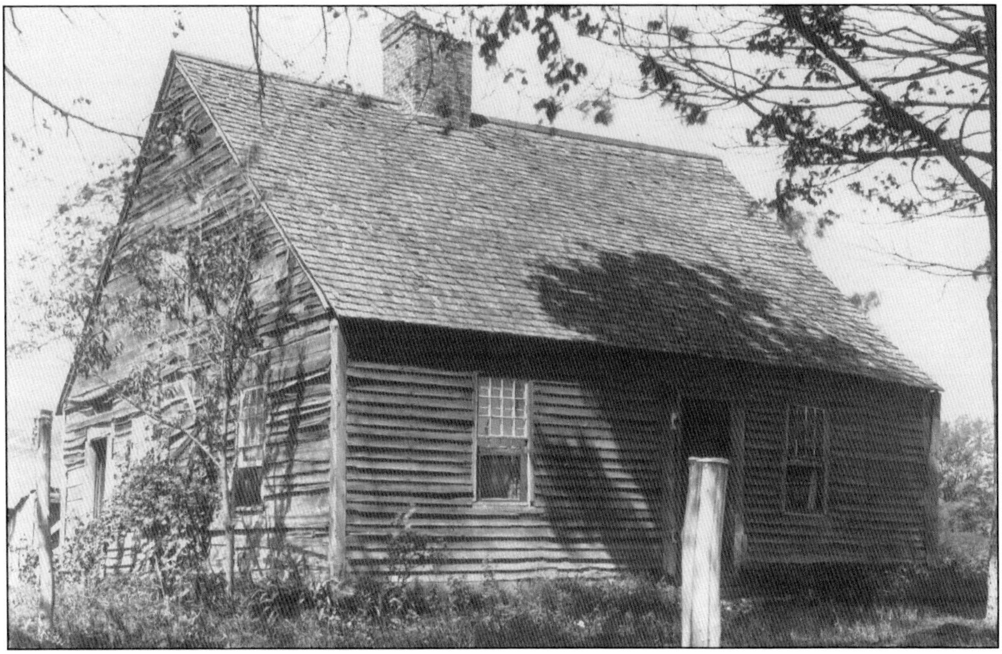

THE PURCHASE HOUSE. LOCATED ON SOUTH MAIN STREET, WEST SIDE OF THE ROAD AND NEAR THE BROOK. IT WAS THE MANLEY HOME. MRS. PURCHASE WAS A REGULAR AT CHURCH, MORE OFTEN LATE TO HEAR THE CLOSE OF THE SERMON, OR JUST AT THE BEGINNING. This home on the west side of South Main Street no longer stands.

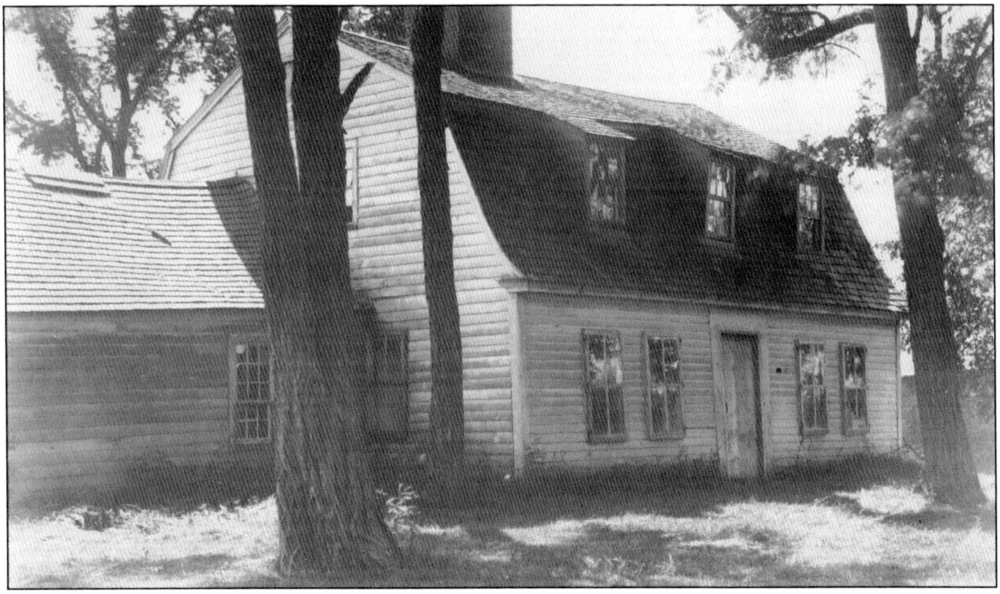

THE OLD PORTER HOUSE, LOCATED NORTH OF THE DISTILLERY. This house is believed to have stood on the east side of Main Street, just south of the Purchase-Ferre House. The house Minerva Davis built on the Lombard Button property in 1924 seems to be a combination of the Lombard Button house and this former family home. Mrs. Davis was a descendent of John Porter, who founded the distillery. She was the daughter of Harvey Porter and the wife of Charles Palmer Davis, founder of *Current Events* magazine.

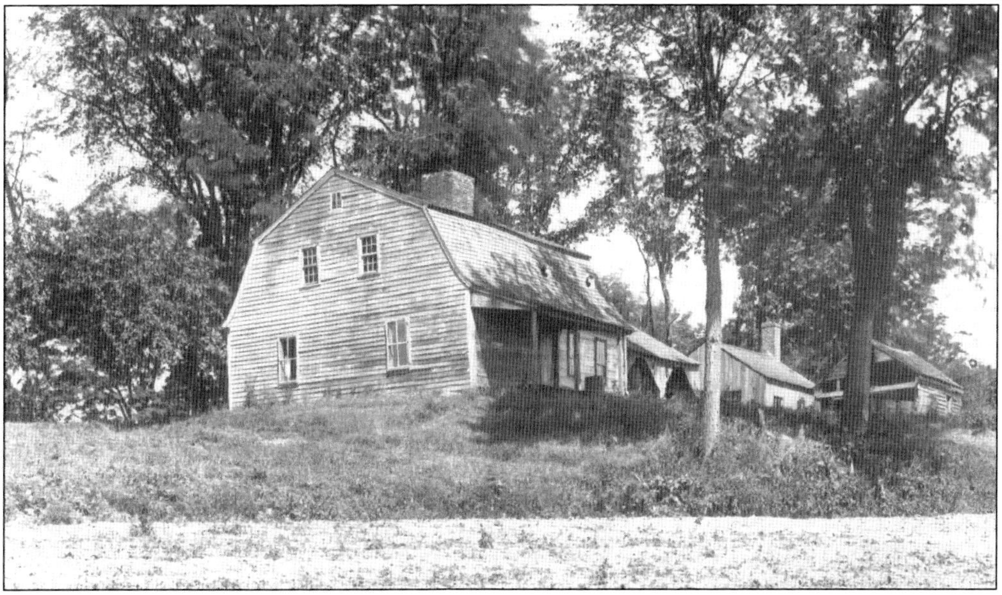

The Elijah Porter House built by Horace Stiles about 1800 located on South Main Street. Elijah Porter was the son of John Porter, who founded the distillery on Main Street, and the father of Harvey Porter, who ran the business in later years as the H. Porter Distilling Company. This house was demolished many years ago.

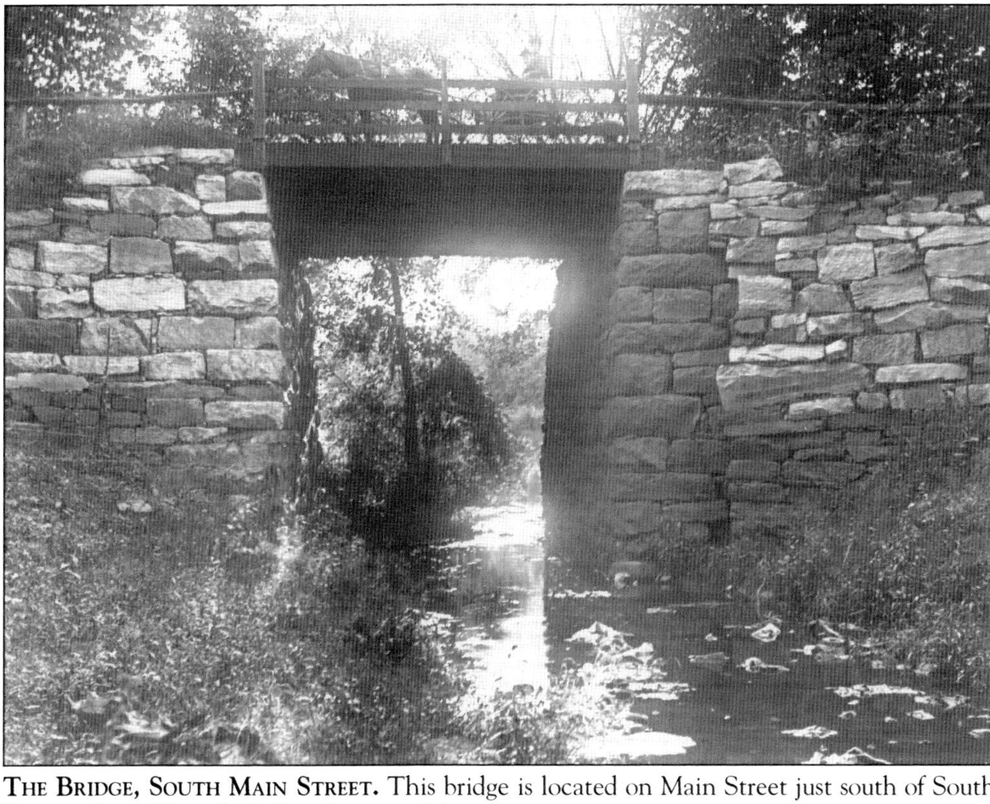

The Bridge, South Main Street. This bridge is located on Main Street just south of South Street, where Three Mile Brook crosses Main Street.

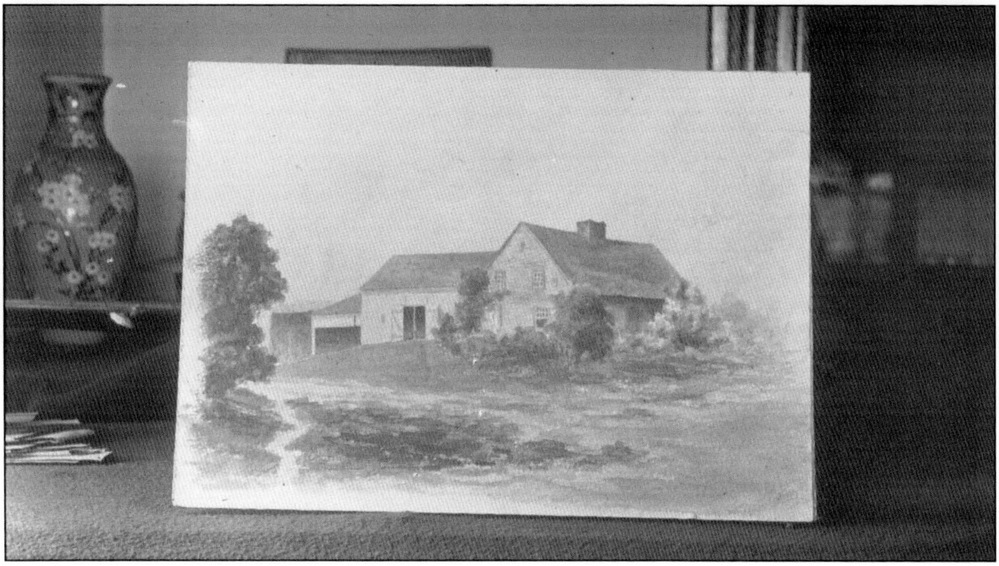

THE OLD RED HOUSE, RESIDENCE OF COMMODORE PERRY. MR. PERRY WAS DROWNED IN THE RIVER WHILE DRAWING WATER FOR HIS STOCK AND OTHER PURPOSES. This house was replaced with the house in the following photograph. The 1869 map of Agawam lists an H.H. Perry at the corner of Leonard Street and River Road; for a time, Leonard Street was known as Perry Street.

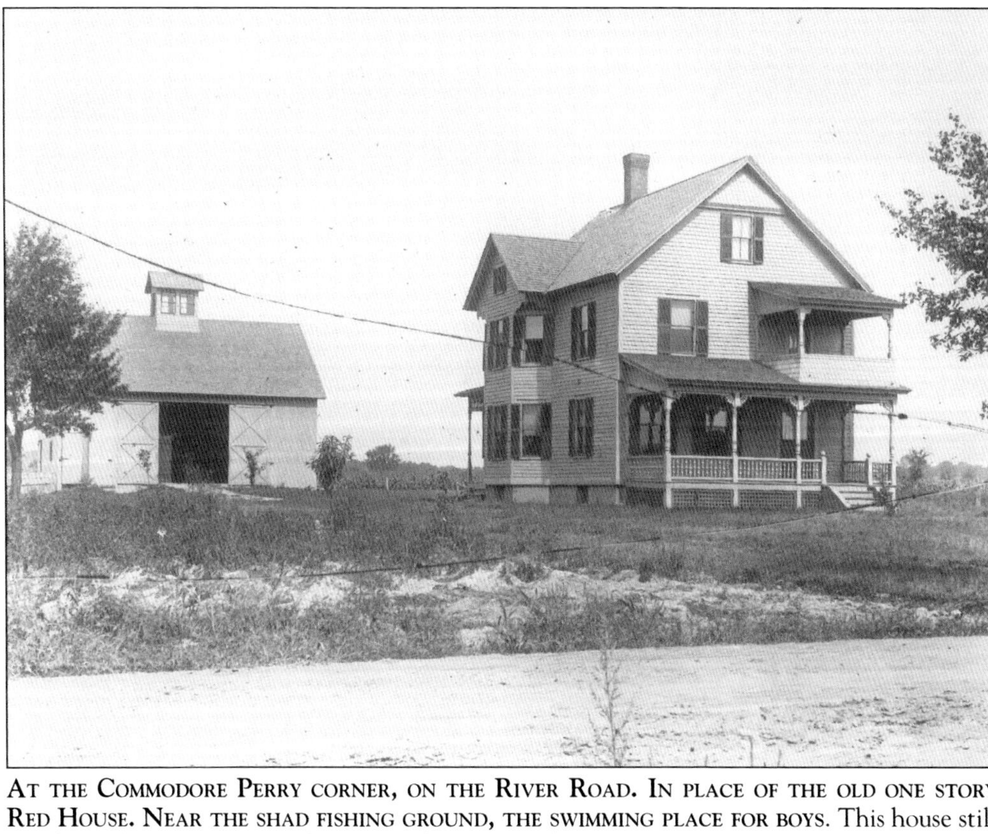

AT THE COMMODORE PERRY CORNER, ON THE RIVER ROAD. IN PLACE OF THE OLD ONE STORY RED HOUSE. NEAR THE SHAD FISHING GROUND, THE SWIMMING PLACE FOR BOYS. This house still stands on the corner Leonard Street and River Road.

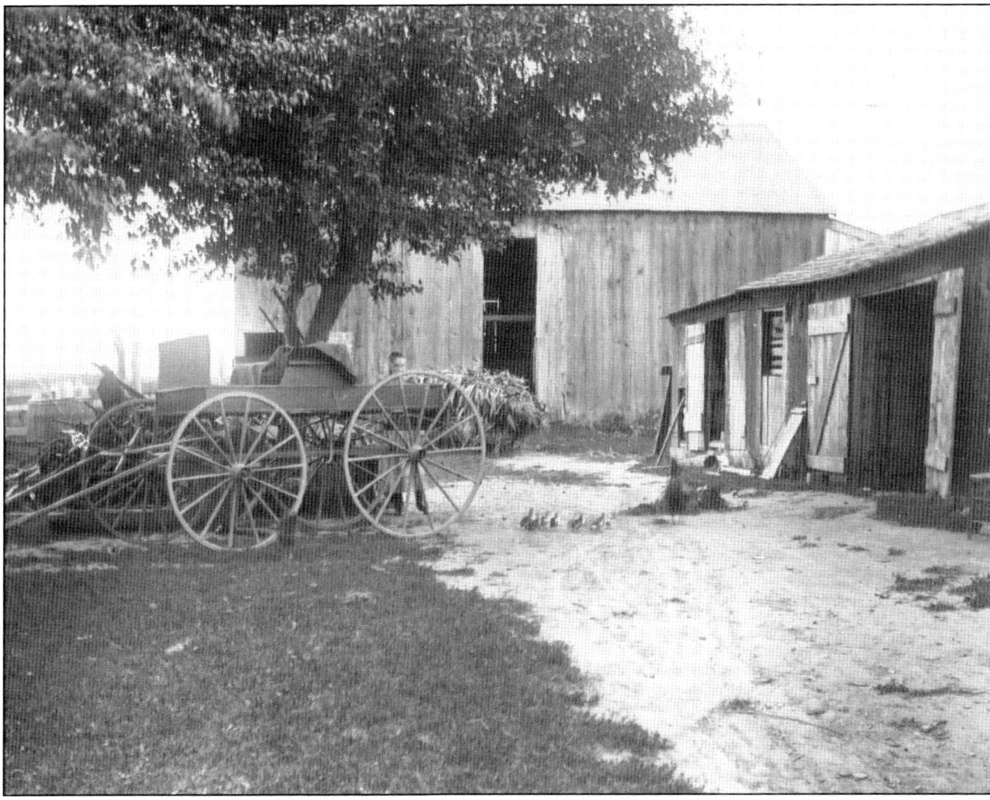

EDMUND POWER BARN, RIVER ROAD. NOW THE GREEN HOUSE. This farm was located on River Road just south of Leonard Street. The "green house" referred to was the large greenhouse range owned by Aitken Florist's of Springfield, which was used to grow geraniums and potted holiday plants. They have since been demolished.

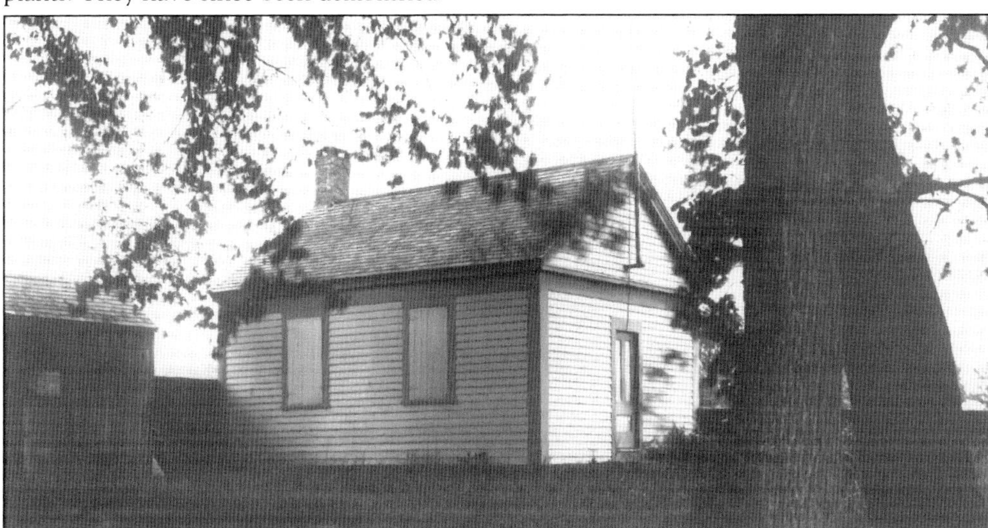

THE RIVER ROAD SCHOOLHOUSE ABOVE ALDEN PLACE. LATER TURNED INTO A CLUB HOUSE. This schoolhouse has survived numerous floods and now serves as a residence. It is located at 914 River Road.

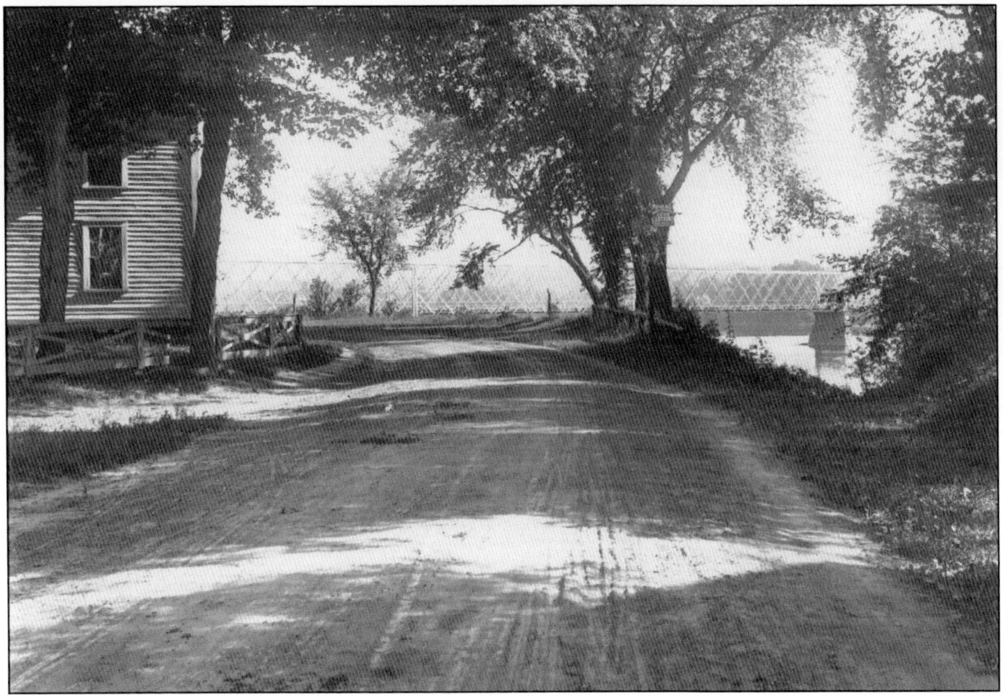

THE OLD FERRY LANDING AND THE NEW BRIDGE IN THE DISTANCE. This photograph was taken from about where the current South End Bridge crosses River Road. The sign in the tree advertises, "Meigs & Co., makers and retailers of good clothing. 395 and 401 Main Street, Springfield." Note the gas lamp in front of the tree.

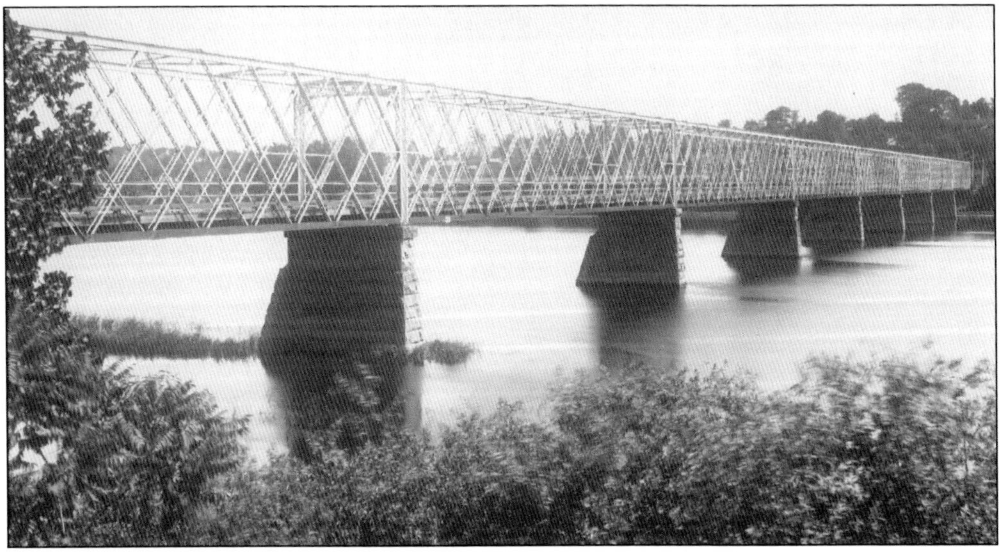

THE SOUTH END BRIDGE OPENED FEBRUARY 1, 1879. This bridge was built to replace a seasonal ferry service that operated between Agawam and Springfield. The bridge crossed at grade on the Springfield side (see page 13). At the town meeting on April 6, 1903, it was voted to "appropriate and raise by taxation" $1,000 for the raising of the South-end bridge. The bridge was then raised to go over the railroad tracks on the Springfield side and to allow boat traffic to pass beneath (see page 46).

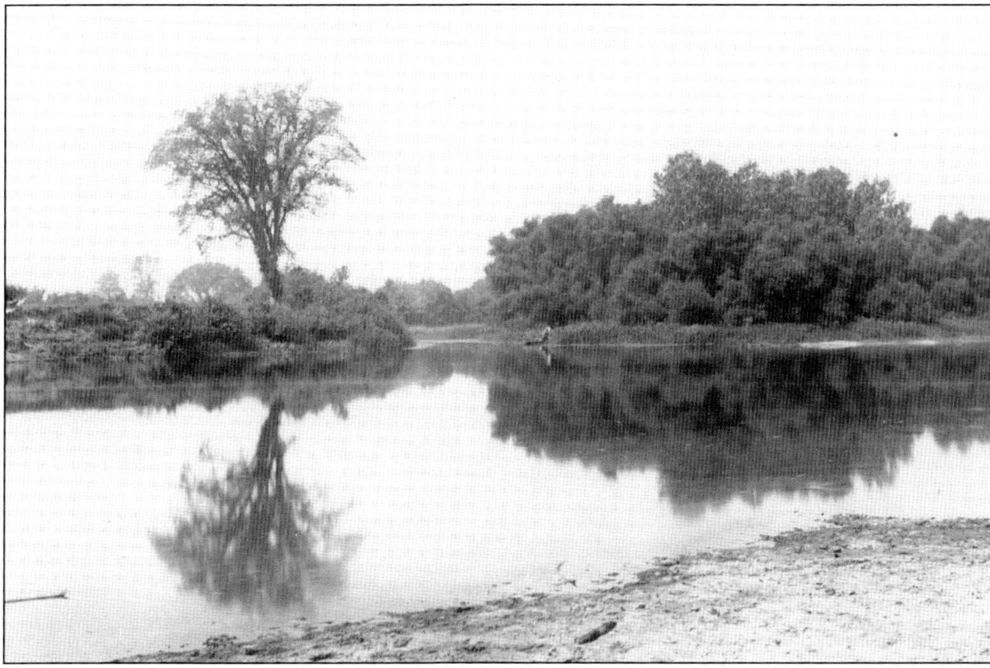

AGAWAM MEADOWS, NEAR THE WIRE FERRY, THE AGAWAM RIVER. LOCALITY OF THE FIRST SETTLEMENT IN 1635. WARNED BY THE INDIANS OF THE SPRING FLOODS THEY RETURNED TO THE BOSTON SECTION AND SETTLED SPRINGFIELD IN 1636. William Pynchon, along with John Cable and John Woodcock, visited Agawam on a scouting trip in the summer of 1635. Pynchon returned to Roxbury, but it is believed that Cable and Woodcock spent the winter in a crude hut on the South Bank of the Agawam River.

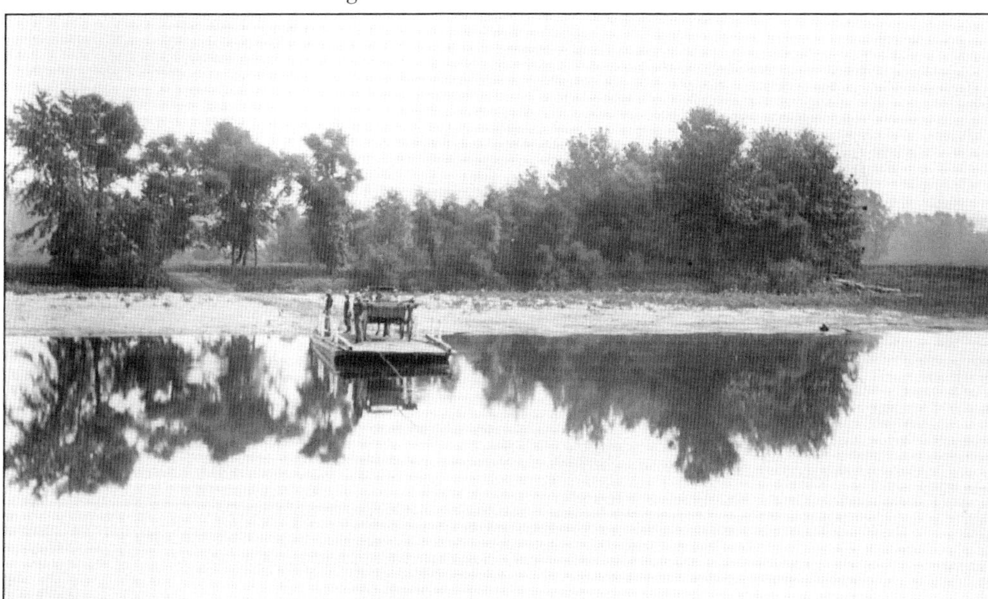

THE WIRE FERRY NEAR THE MOUTH OF THE AGAWAM RIVER, GOING NORTH TO THE SMALL ISLAND. The Agawam Meadows have long been the location of some very fertile soil. Many farmers, including Albert Christopher (see page 76) have braved the spring floods to plant fields there.

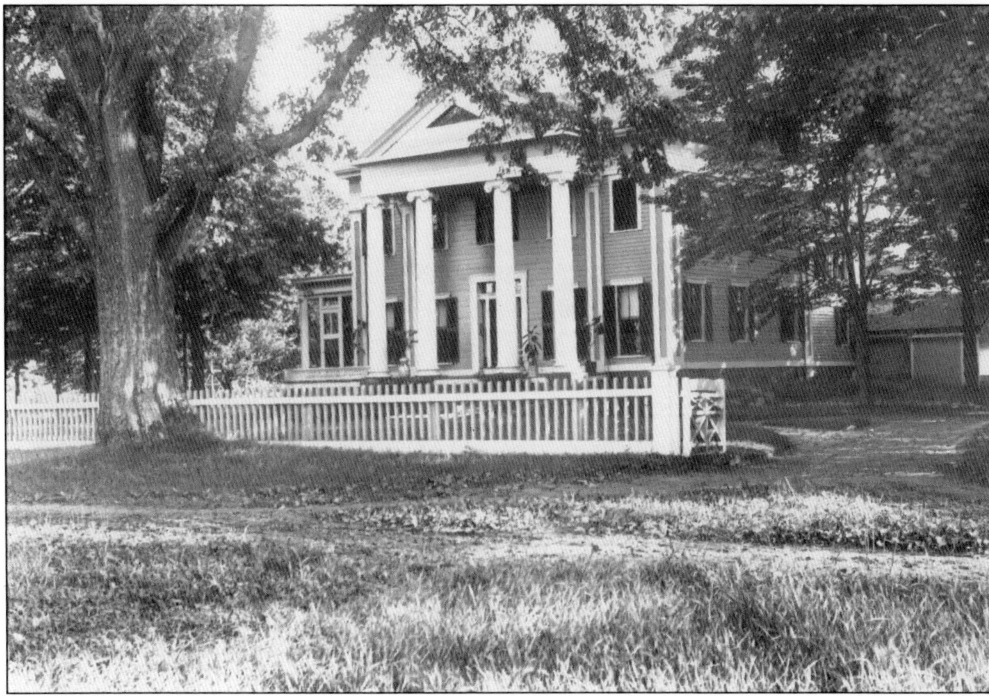

THE BEEMIS PLACE ON THE HILL. This home was built by Samuel Converse c. 1862 and is located at 135 Cooper Street at the top of Federal Street. It was home of the Federal Hill Club for many years and still serves as a restaurant.

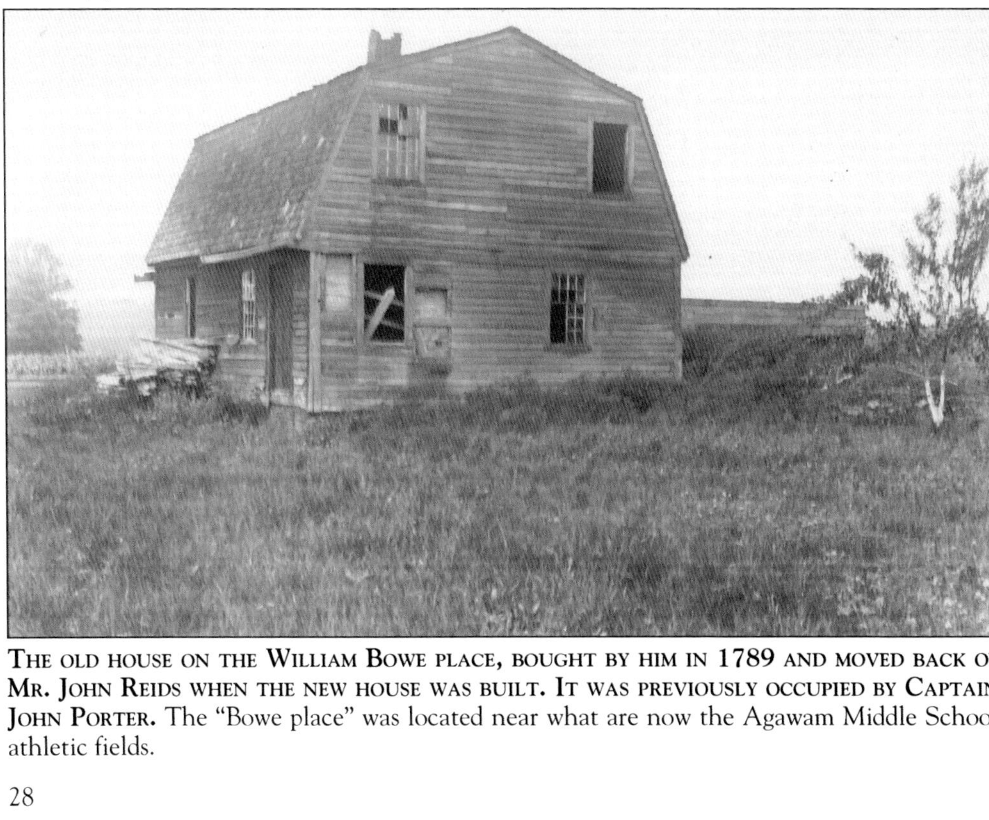

THE OLD HOUSE ON THE WILLIAM BOWE PLACE, BOUGHT BY HIM IN 1789 AND MOVED BACK OF MR. JOHN REIDS WHEN THE NEW HOUSE WAS BUILT. IT WAS PREVIOUSLY OCCUPIED BY CAPTAIN JOHN PORTER. The "Bowe place" was located near what are now the Agawam Middle School athletic fields.

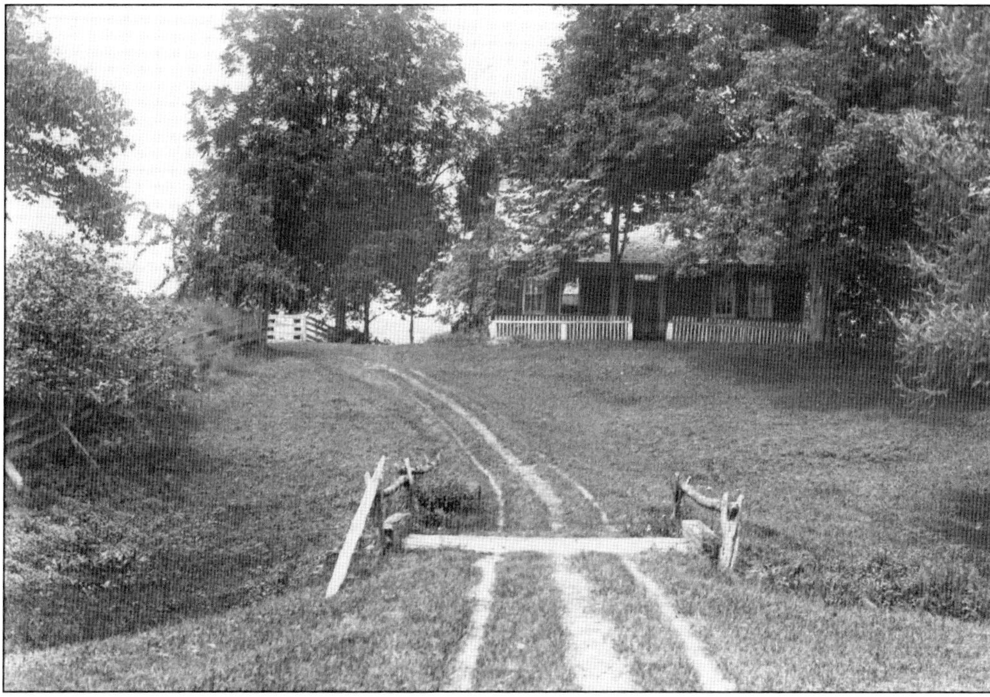

THE PRINCE HOME. Located on Prince Lane, off Federal Street and south of Reed Street, this home was demolished many years ago. Samuel Leonard farmed near here during the early 1800s (see below.).

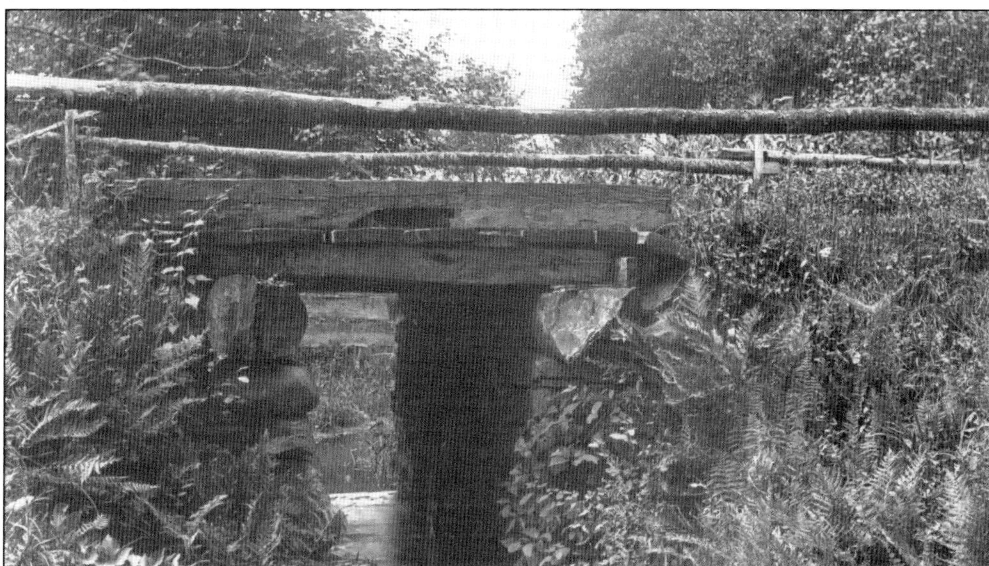

APPROACH TO THE PRINCE PLACE. THE BRIDGE AND THE FERNS. Samuel Leonard's wife was caught up in the religious revivals of the 1820s. Unable to share his wife's enthusiasm, Samuel became depressed and began drinking. In fear of her husband's rages, she left her children in Samuel's care and went to stay with friends. When the youngest became sick, she returned home to attend the child, then set about to leave again. Samuel killed her with an ax and then killed himself.

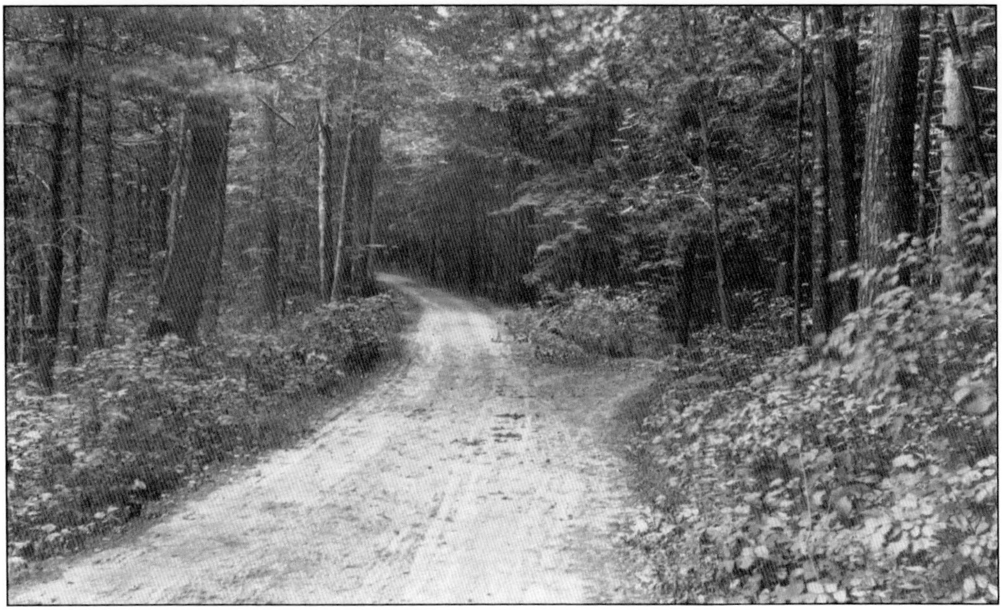

On the way to Feeding Hills, entering the Fowler woods beyond the Hitchcock home. The 1894 L.J. Richards map of Agawam lists a William Hitchcock on Mill Street, near where Mill Street crosses Route 57. Unfortunately, there are few places remaining in town that look like this.

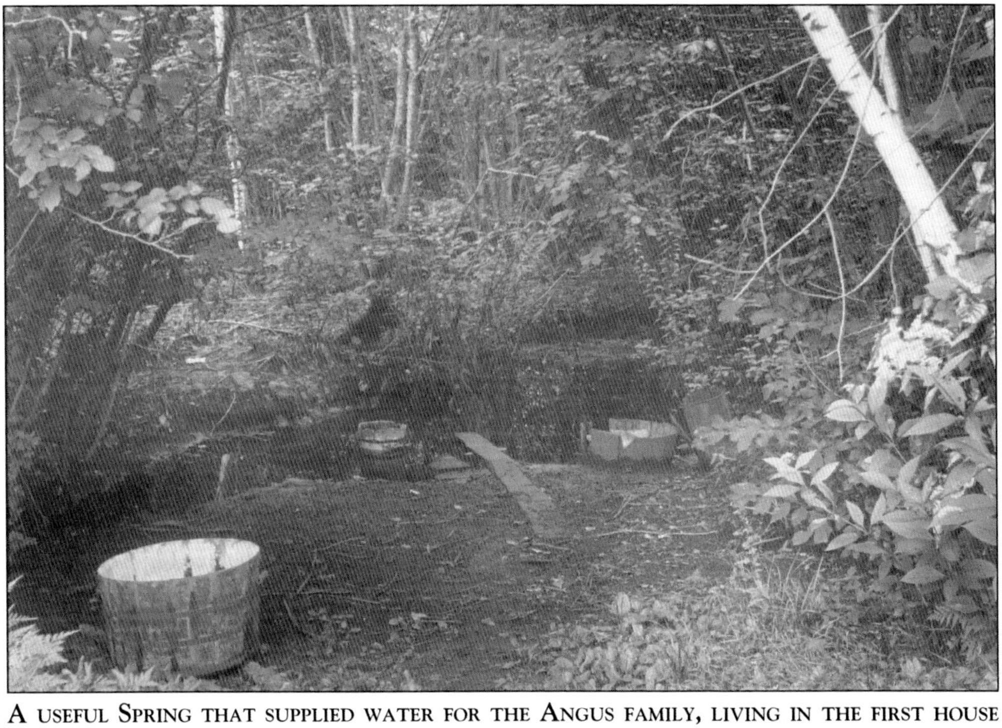

A useful Spring that supplied water for the Angus family, living in the first house on the left approaching the Plains, near two miles west of the Center. This spring was probably located somewhere in the area of Tennis Road, just south of Route 57. The Plains section of town received its name due to the sandy soil and flatness of the area.

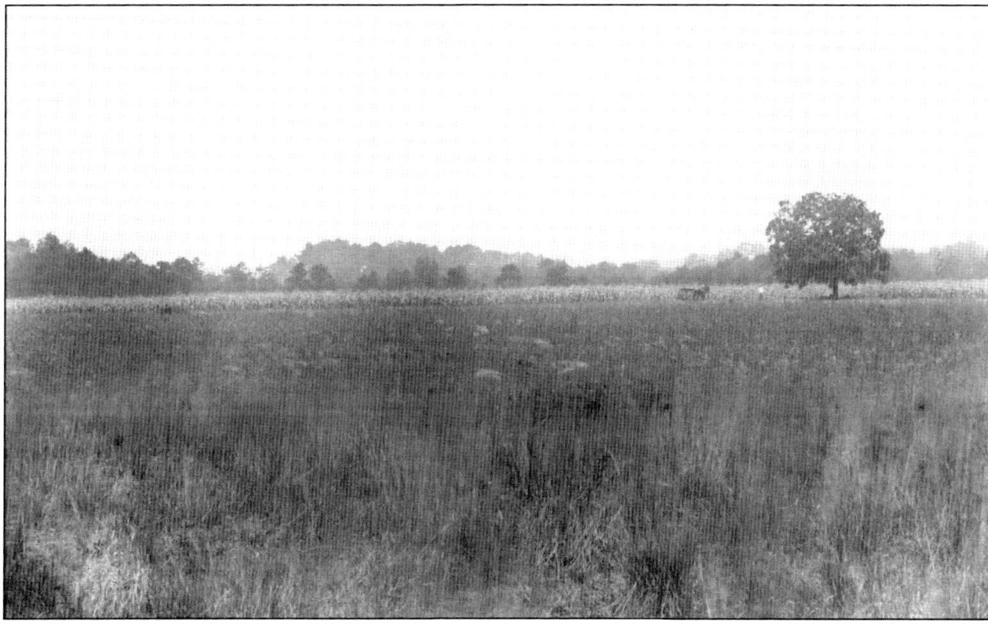

The Plains and how they looked, near two miles west of the Center. The Plains section of Agawam extends more or less from just east of the industrial park north to just past the police station on Springfield Street. In 1895, two roads left Agawam Center for Feeding Hills: Silver and Mill Streets, from the end of Elm Street. This photograph was most likely taken on Mill Street just west of the high school.

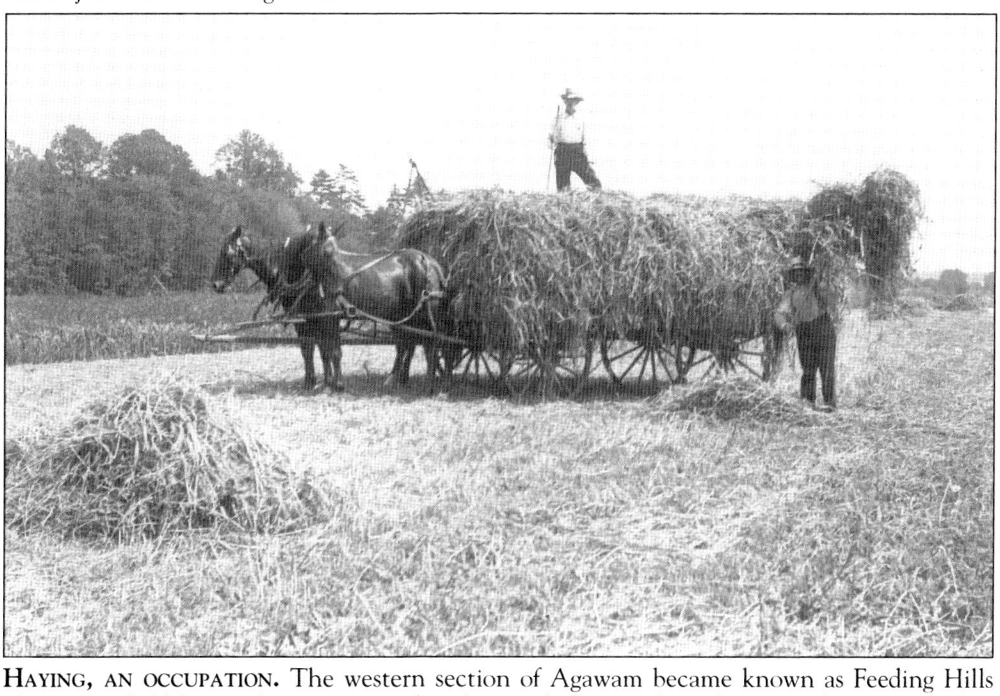

Haying, an occupation. The western section of Agawam became known as Feeding Hills after Springfield farmers began grazing their livestock there early in the town's history. The first cattle drives in the nation began when farmers drove their stock from Feeding Hills to Boston in the late 17th century.

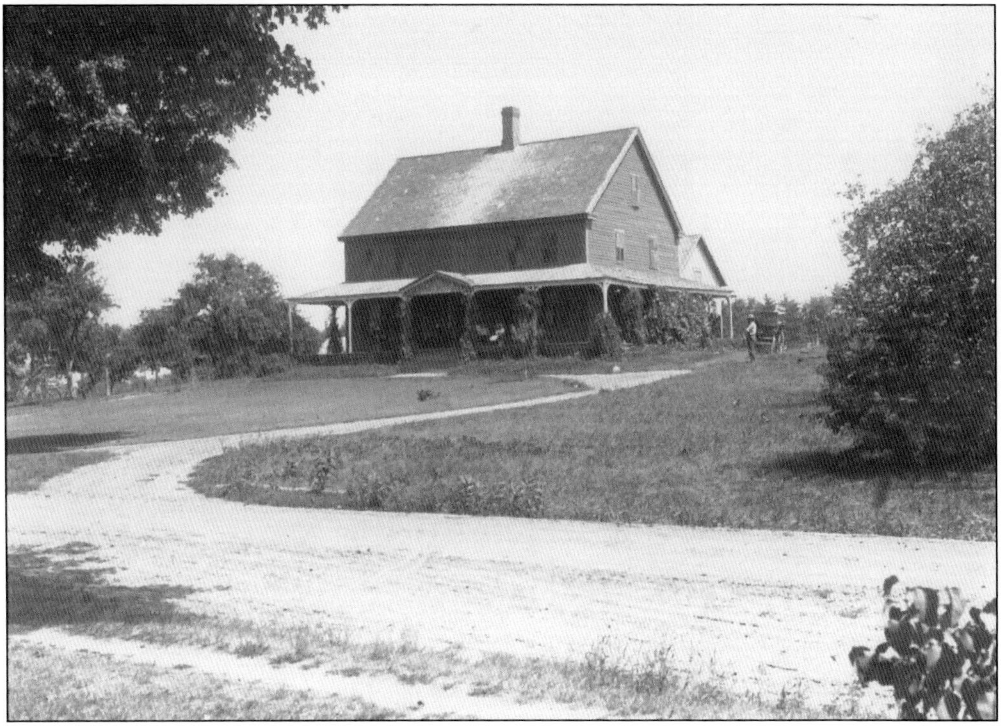

The old Gallup Homestead, at the Gallup Grove. In 1870, John Gallup opened Gallup's Grove at the site of Riverside Park. It was a popular place for picnics and clambakes, necessitating construction of the steamboat *Mayflower* to transport customers from Springfield to Agawam. Gallup sold the grove and the *Mayflower* to Harvey Porter in 1881. This home was built in 1752 and was later moved to River Road, where it became the Green Gables bar and grill (see page 101). It is no longer standing.

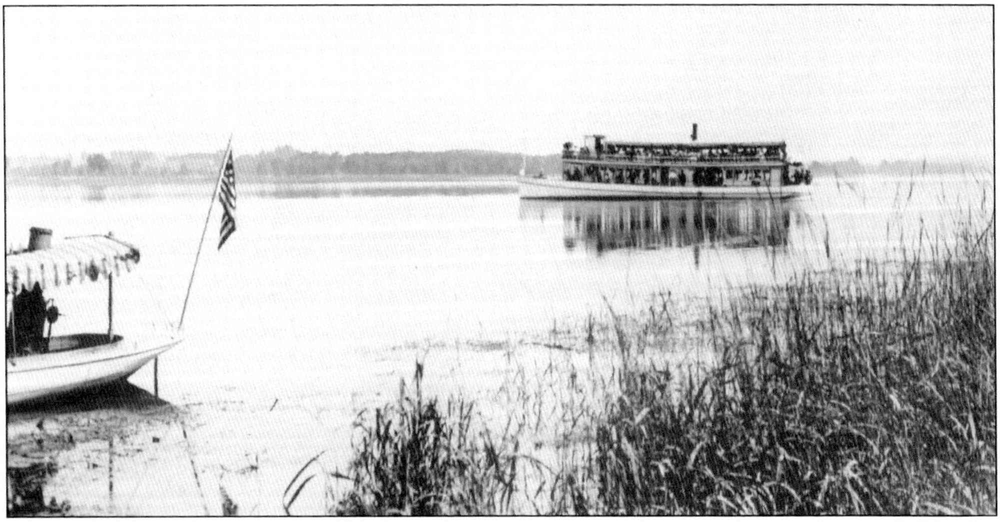

A later steamer for pleasure parties to Gallup's Grove. This vessel is probably the steamer *Sylvia*. By the late 1800s, Harvey Porter had sold Gallup's Grove to Elmer Smith, and attendance had increased to the point where a vessel larger than the *Mayflower* was needed. The *Sylvia* was nearly 92 feet long and could carry 350 people. (Courtesy of Sylvia Deliso.)

Two

The Agawam Woolen Mill

There has been a mill on Elm Street at Three Mile Brook since the early 1800s. Justus and Calvin Bedortha established a mill there that did only custom work until 1812. The mill began to produce broadcloth during the War of 1812, only to see demand for that product fall once the war ended and foreign imports were again available. The business was reorganized in 1840 as Norton, Bedortha, and Company. The new owners rebuilt and enlarged the original mill and resumed custom work at that time.

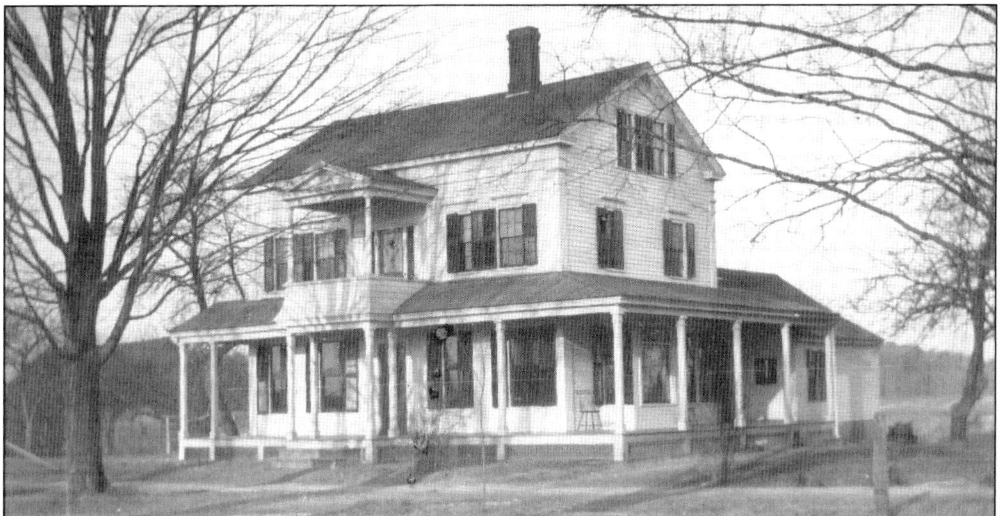

Frederick Worthington ran the Agawam Company's woolen mill for many years from his office in the corner of the building at 159 Elm Street. His former home still stands, minus the elaborate porches, at 70 Elm Street. Frederick Worthington's grandson, Percival Hastings Jr., provided several of the photographs on the following pages. This photograph was taken on December 23, 1903. (Courtesy of Donald Goss.)

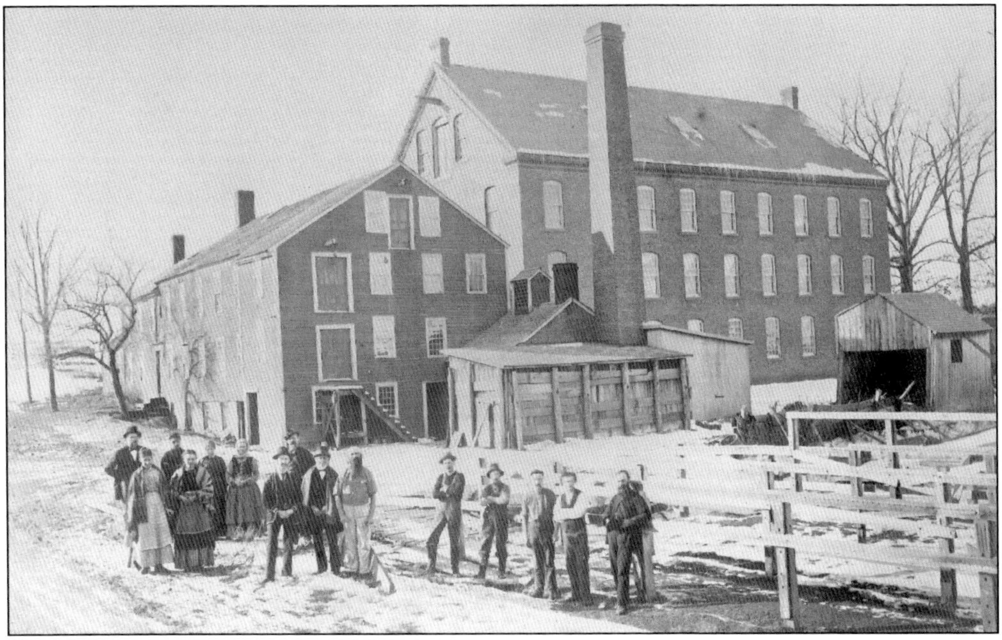

On May 12, 1857, the Agawam Company was incorporated by Ashbel Sykes and Newbury Norton. In addition to the Elm Street mill, they bought a mill in South Hadley, Massachusetts, to make wool prepared in Agawam into cloth. The cloth was returned to Agawam and finished there. In 1875, a new brick mill was built in Agawam and the entire operation consolidated there. This photograph was taken before the complex burned down in 1889, after a fire broke out in the dye house. (Courtesy of Mr. and Mrs. Percival Hastings Jr.)

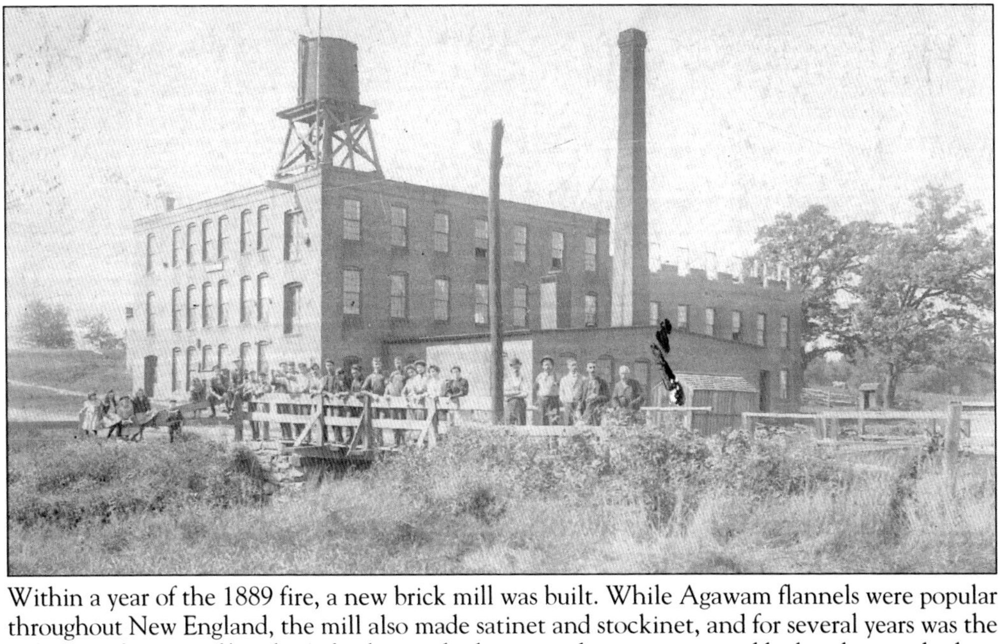

Within a year of the 1889 fire, a new brick mill was built. While Agawam flannels were popular throughout New England, the mill also made satinet and stockinet, and for several years was the only manufacturer of butcher's frocking, which was made into coats used by butchers and others working in cold storage. By 1901, when this photograph was taken, demand necessitated the first of several additions to the mill, seen here under construction. (Courtesy of Donald Goss.)

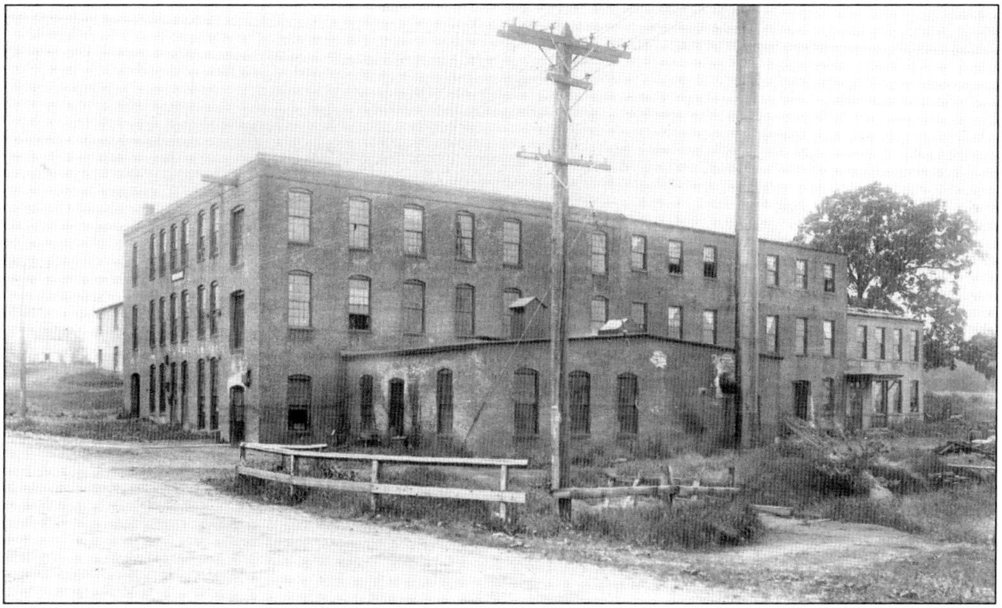

Another small addition was added to the rear of the mill *c.* 1910. The mill was powered by water from the "Factory Pond," or "Mill Pond," created by a dam located directly behind the mill. In 1918, A.B. Emery and A.G. Harris bought the Agawam Company. In addition to the Agawam mill, the Harris-Emery Company operated mills in New Hampshire and Vermont until the deaths of the two owners. At that time, the Agawam Company was reorganized as the Agawam Woolen Company. (Courtesy of Mr. and Mrs. Percival Hastings Jr.)

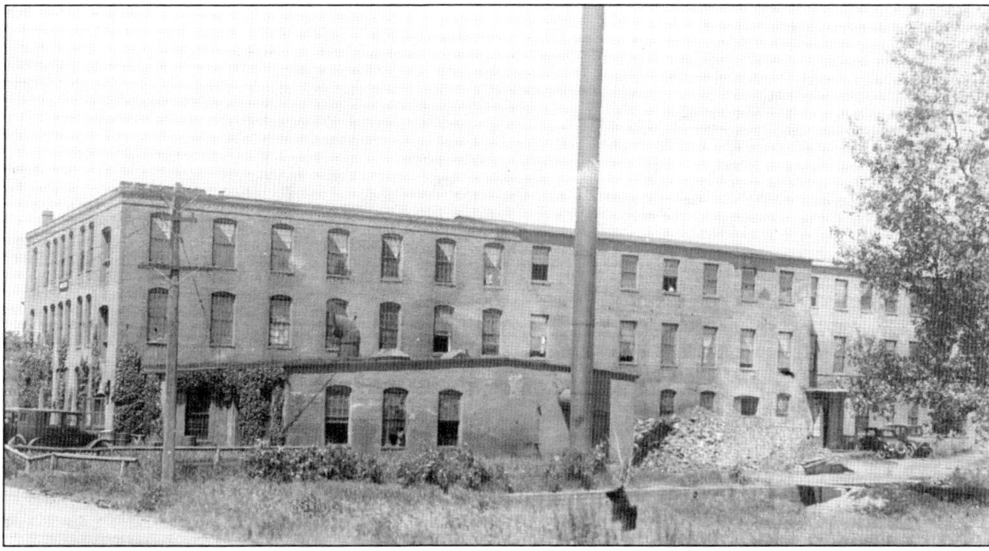

This photograph from the late 1920s shows the final configuration of the mill. The Agawam Woolen Company operated into the late 1940s, when cheaper imports and synthetics made it impossible to stay in business. The company was reorganized in 1952 as the Agawam Manufacturing Company. By 1954, however, nothing could save the mill, and the entire plant was sold. In 1955, a flood washed away the Mill Pond dam, symbolically ending almost 150 years of textile work on Three Mile Brook. The dam was never rebuilt. (Courtesy of Mr. and Mrs. Percival Hastings Jr.)

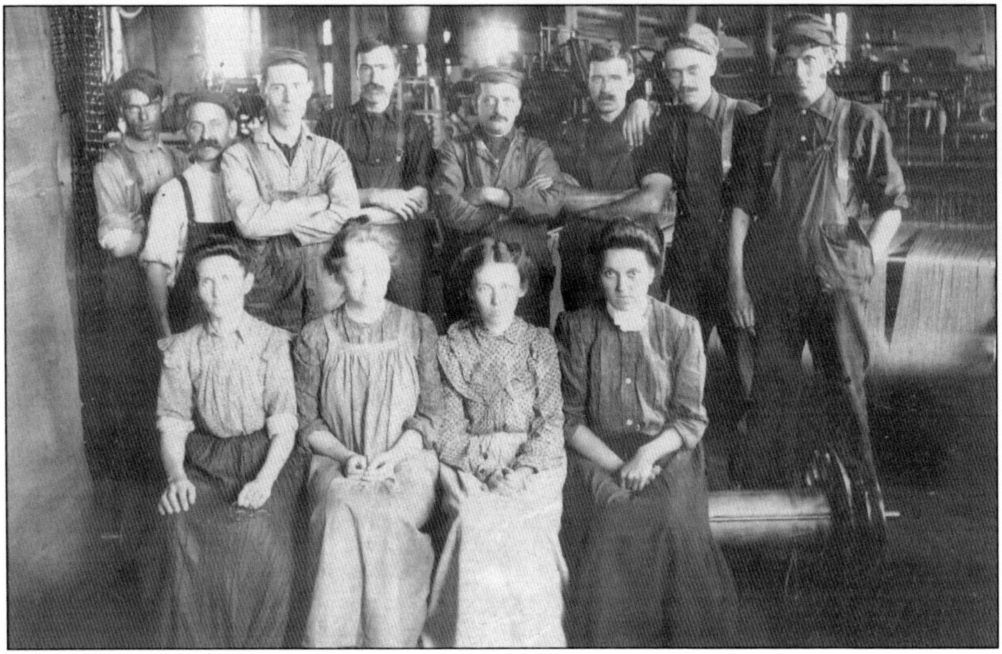

Shown in the main weaving room at the Agawam Company woolen mill *c.* 1915 are, from left to right, the following: (front row) Charlotte Milne, unidentified, Elizabeth Wheeler, and Maude Randall; (back row) unidentified, Larry Cirillo, John Bitgood, Paul Maynard, William Duncan (boss weaver), Walter Goss, Frank Goss, and "Shy" Randall. The Agawam Company mill produced broadcloth and tweeds; after World War I, the company was a leading producer of capcloth. In the 1920s, the mill produced mainly women's dress cloth. (Courtesy of John Bitgood, son of the Mr. Bitgood pictured here.)

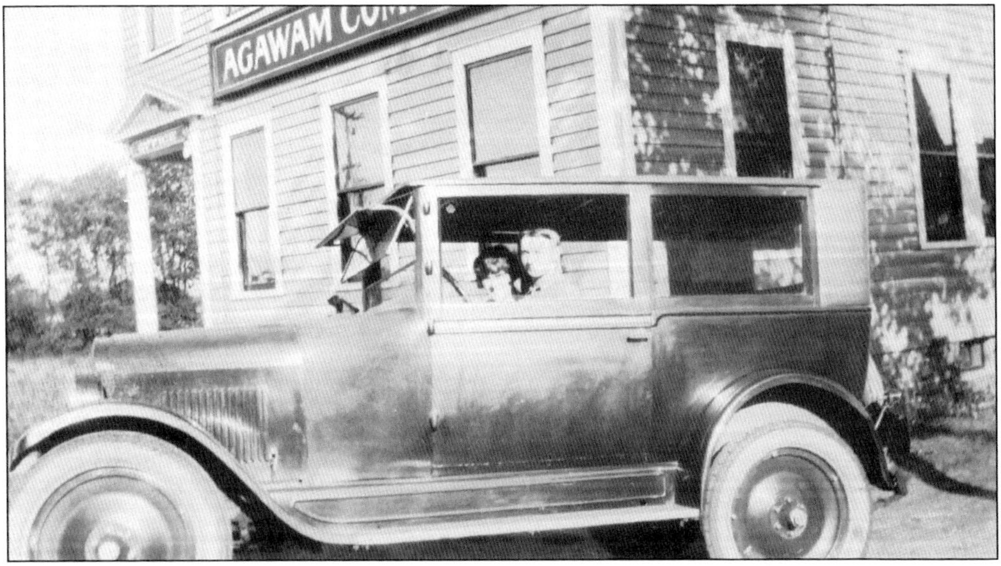

On July 15, 1924, Mr. and Mrs. Leonard Johnson are shown in front of the Agawam Company offices. The offices, located at 159 Elm Street, were housed in an addition built on the home in the bottom photograph on page 17. The porch and pediment detail remains. Frederick Worthington's office was in the right corner of this building. (Courtesy of John Y. Hess.)

Three

AGAWAM

While the "town of Agawam" encompasses both Feeding Hills and Agawam, Agawam proper is what was formerly the Second Parish of West Springfield, roughly from Line Street east to the Connecticut River. When Agawam was incorporated as a town in 1855, its population was 1,000. The 20th century brought explosive growth to town. In 1905, just 50 years after its incorporation, the town's population it had nearly tripled to 2,795; by 1930, it had more than doubled again to 7,092. By 1967, nearly 20,000 people were living in town. Trolley service along Main Street and the automobile helped spread development along Main Street and throughout Agawam.

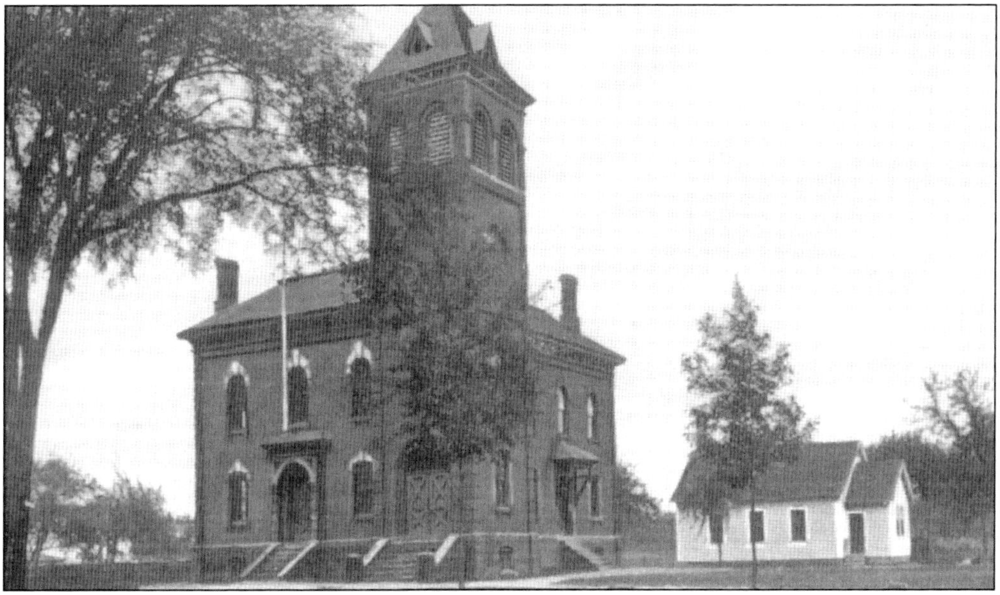

The Agawam Town Hall was built in 1874 at the corner of Main and School Streets. It served as town hall and a school building for grades three through six. The small white building at right housed grades one through three. Before the building of the Agawam Center Library, the library was housed in the Tower Room of the town hall. The building was demolished in 1938 to make way for what is now the Benjamin Phelps Elementary School. (Author's collection.)

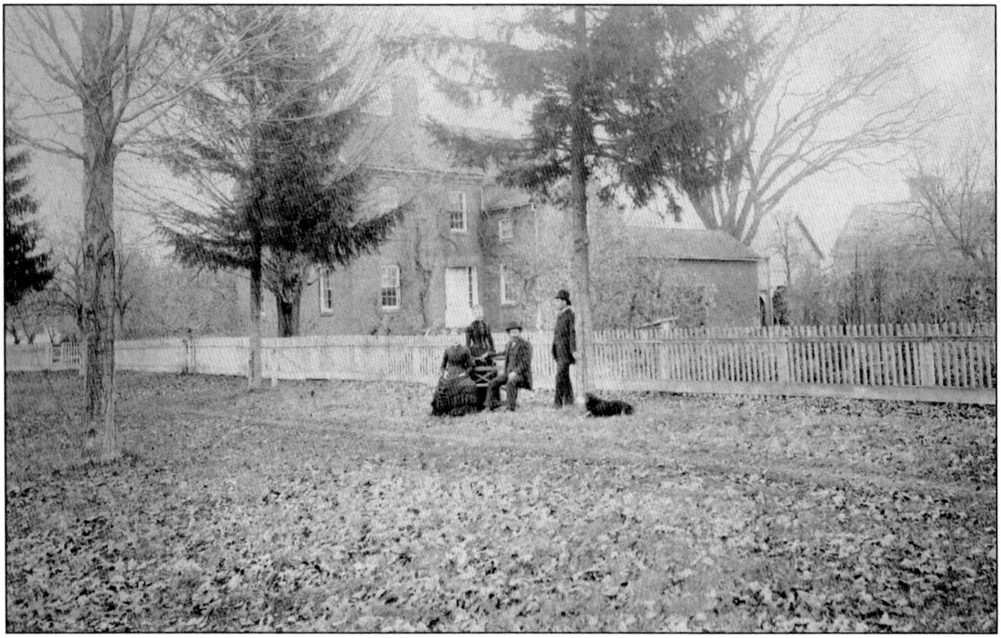

On December 19, 1834, Charles Campbell, a blacksmith from Killingworth, Connecticut, purchased 30 acres, a "dwelling house," and a barn from J. Howard Fosket for $1,700. Upon his move to Agawam, he took up farming and built this house with bricks made on the property. Elbert Road was originally part of this property. This home, which still stands at 769 Main Street, is pictured *c.* 1870 (see page 18). (Agawam Historical Association collection.)

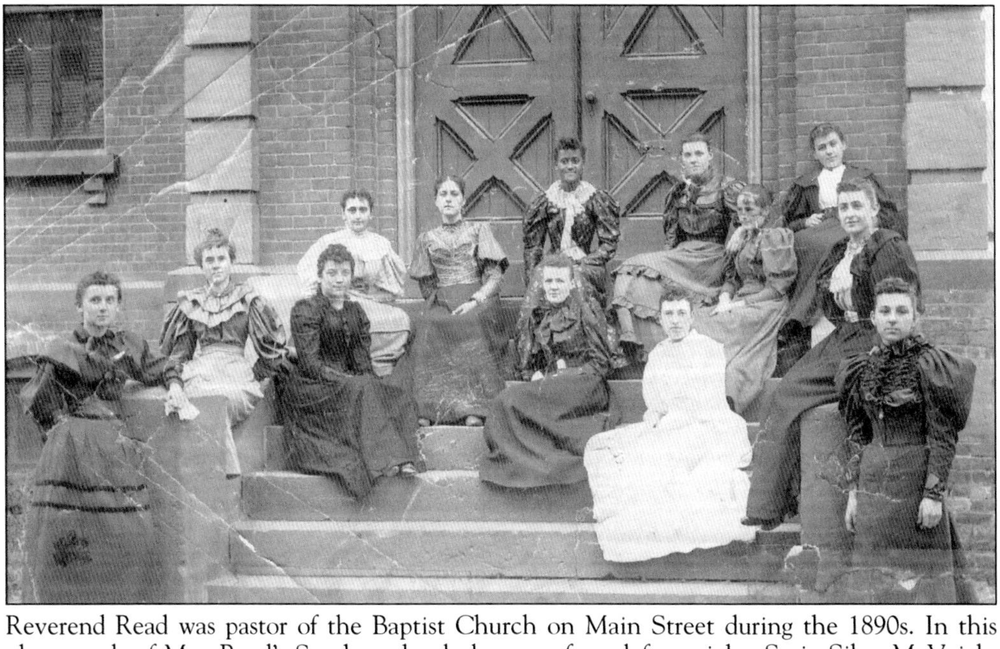

Reverend Read was pastor of the Baptist Church on Main Street during the 1890s. In this photograph of Mrs. Read's Sunday school class are, from left to right, Susie Sikes McVeigh, Anna Crouss, Louise Ahl, Belle Cook, Della Covill, Mrs. Addie Read, Edna Jones, Emily Talmadge, unidentified, Rose Worthington, Freda Schultz, Fannie Crouss, and Ellen Trull. (Agawam Historical Association collection.)

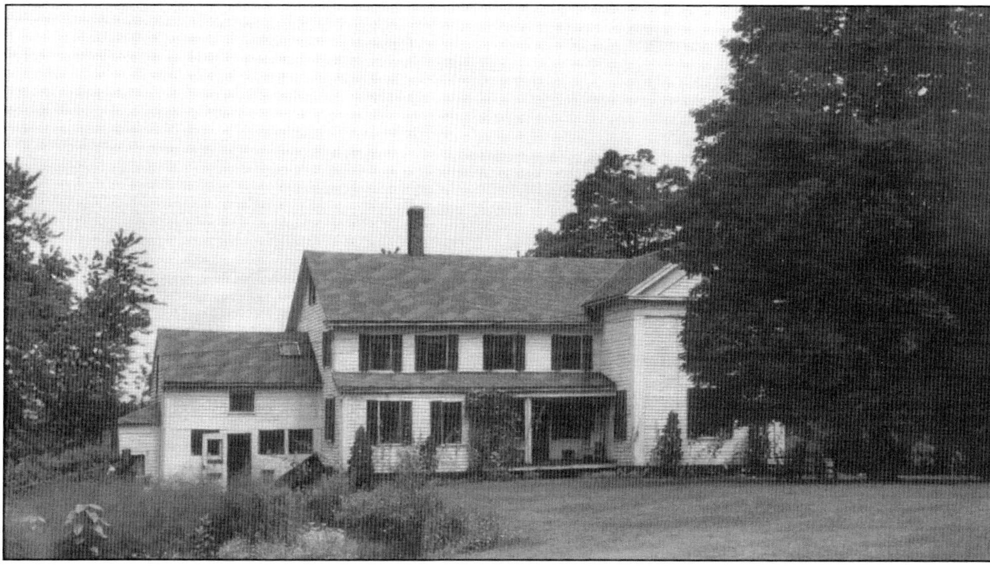

Built *c.* 1831 at the corner of Springfield and Suffield Streets (see page 102), this Federal and Greek Revival house was the home of Pliny Leonard from 1831 to 1857. Other owners included Frederick Leonard (owner from 1857 to 1896), Horace Worden (1896 to 1918), Sue Belle Worden (1918 to 1936), and H. Preston Worden (1936 to 1955). (Courtesy of Dennis Librera.)

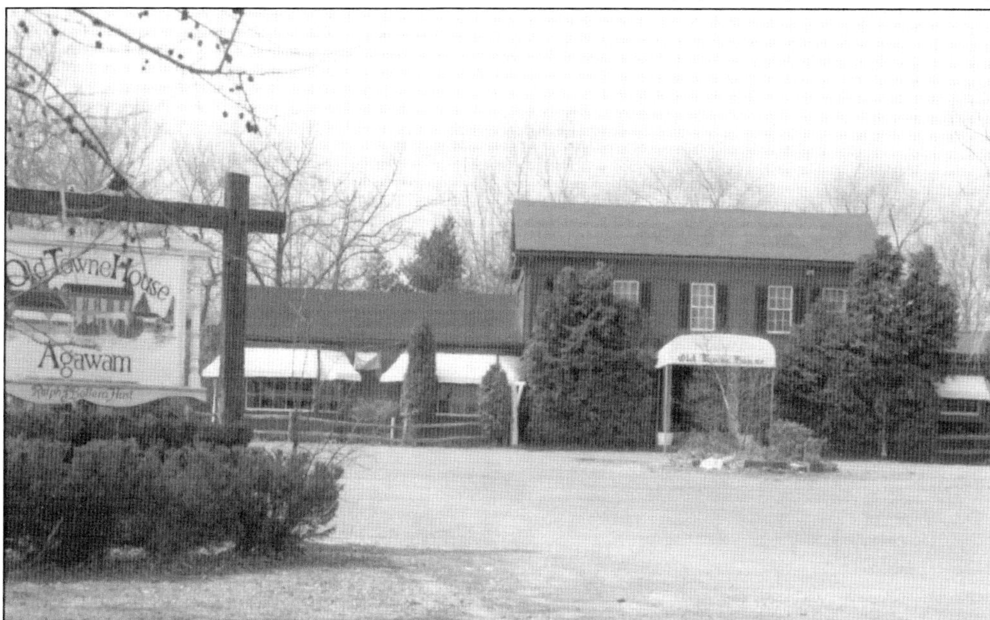

In 1955, the Bottaro family moved the Pliny Leonard House (shown) to the corner of Springfield and Walnut Streets for use as a banquet hall. Betty's Towne House was a popular setting for showers and receptions until 1999, when it was demolished to make way for a Walgreen's pharmacy. After the demolition, the Agawam Historical Commission had little opposition in its efforts to enact a demolition delay ordinance, which can delay the demolition of a historic structure up to six months while alternatives are explored. This photograph was taken *c.* 1970. (Courtesy of Jean Welt Taylor.)

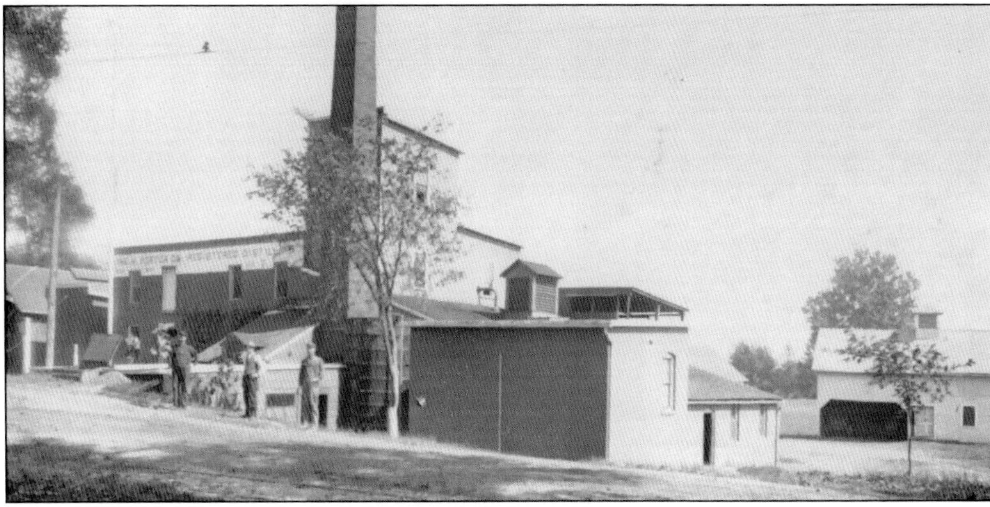

John Porter moved to Agawam in 1771 and built the house that still stands at 1410 Main Street. In 1780, he founded a distillery that made gin from Connecticut Valley rye. His grandson Harvey carried on the business as the H. Porter Distilling Company. The plant was sold in 1917 and during Prohibition produced cider and potato chips. Upon repeal of the Volsted Act, the mill again began producing gin, but closed again for good in 1938. The old gin mill on South Main Street currently serves as Agawam's department of public works garage. (Agawam Historical Association collection.)

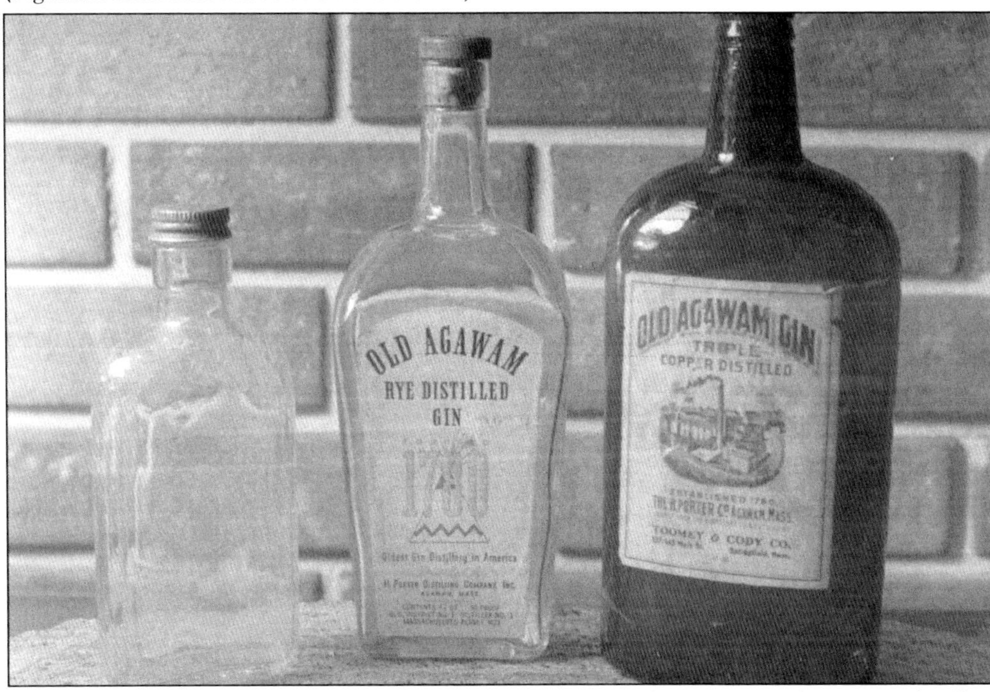

Agawam gin was very high quality and well known across the country. The Porter distillery had the best record of any in the country with an evaporation of only 20 gallons out of an allowance of 100. Although the distillery closed many years ago, several "Old Agawam Gin" bottles survive. Shown are three different bottle shapes produced over the years. (Courtesy of Leslie and Dale Melanson.)

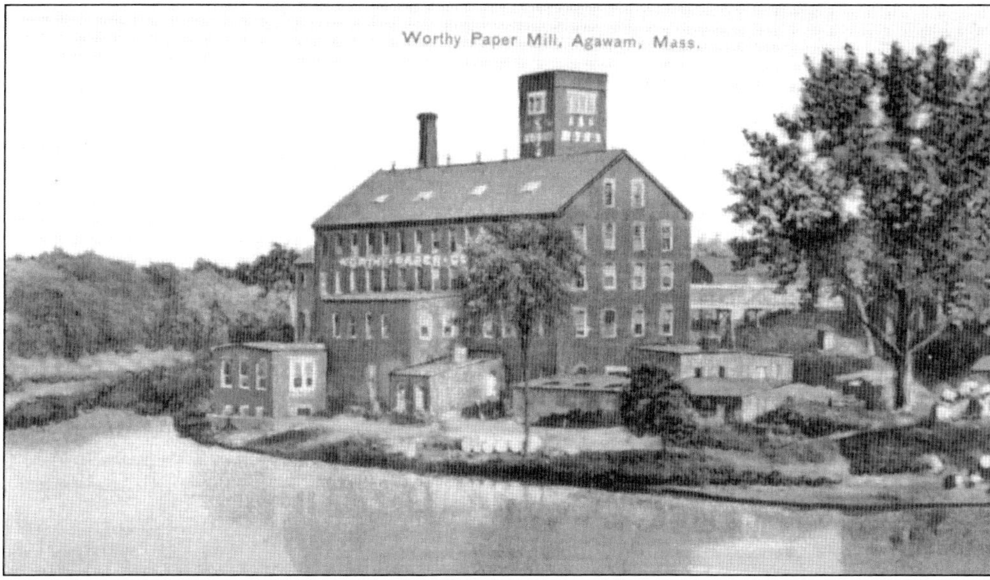

Gristmills were located at "Agawam Falls" on the Agawam River near the end of Walnut Street from 1649 until 1899. The Worthy Paper Mill was built there by Justin Worthy and George Wright in 1871 to produce their line of sterling linen, bond, and ledger papers. Paper for the town's 75th anniversary booklet was donated by the Worthy Paper Company. The company did not survive the Great Depression, however, and after a succession of owners and longtime vacancy, the mill was destroyed by fire on April 24, 1975. (Author's collection.)

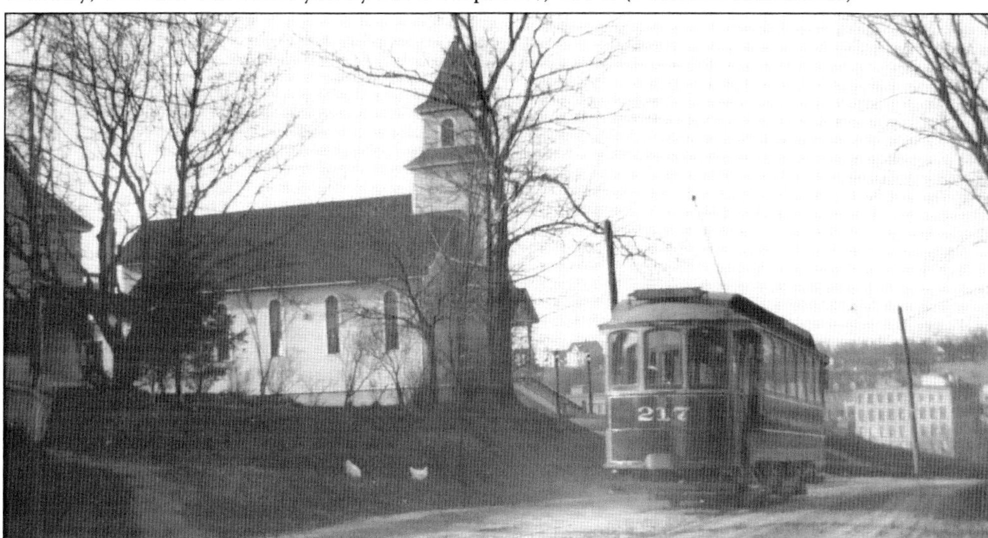

Shown in 1903, Agawam's first Catholic church, St. William's, stood at the corner of Bridge and Church Streets in North Agawam from 1878 until it was destroyed by fire in 1925. At that time, the foundation was roofed over for use as a social hall. In 1927, a new church was built on Bridge Street and the parish name changed to Sainte Therese De L'Enfant Jesus. The Strathmore Paper Mill, where many North Agawam families were employed, is at the right. The trolley crossed the Mittineague Bridge into Agawam and followed Bridge Street to Maple Street and then to Springfield Street at O'Brien's Corner and on to Feeding Hills Center. (Courtesy of Donald Goss.)

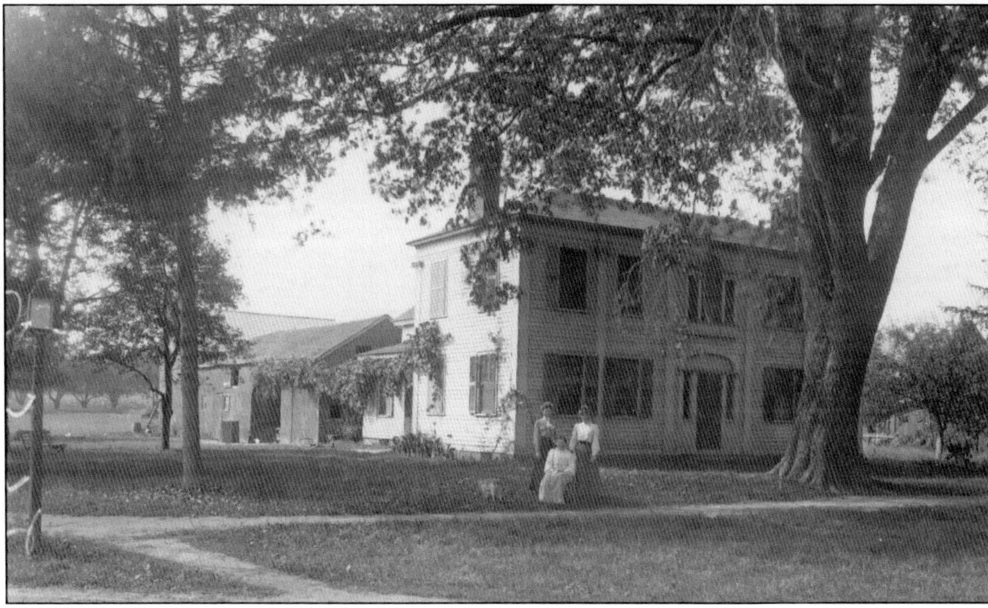

Located on the corner of Main and Elm Streets, the Rufus Colton House was built in 1806 (see page 11) and remains a Main Street landmark. Note the closed shutters on the south side of the house. At one time, shutters were a functional piece of architecture, helping to block out the sun's heat and keeping the house cool before there were electric fans and air conditioners. It is also known as the Colton-Gooch House. This photograph was taken c. 1903. (Agawam Historical Association collection.)

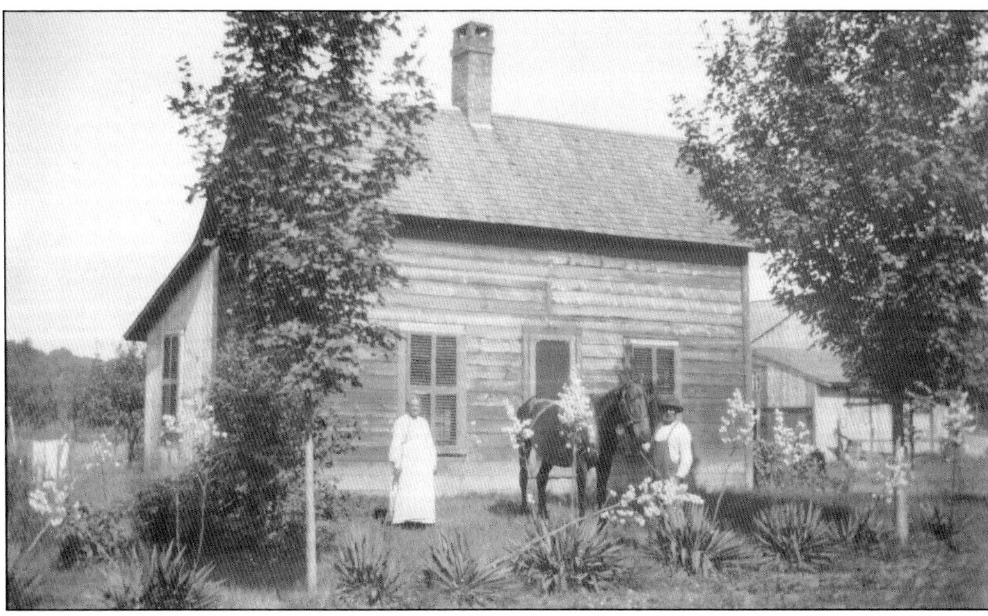

The handwritten caption on the back of this photograph reads, "Uncle Tom's Cabin, Tom Ray and wife. Silver Street-Airport Location. 1905." Perhaps this is the "Negro Town" lot in the southwest part of town mentioned in old assessors lists. Hinsdale Smith, who was listed as owning the lot, owned land from west of Silver Street (the former airport location, now the industrial park) east to South Westfield Street. (Courtesy of Donald Goss.)

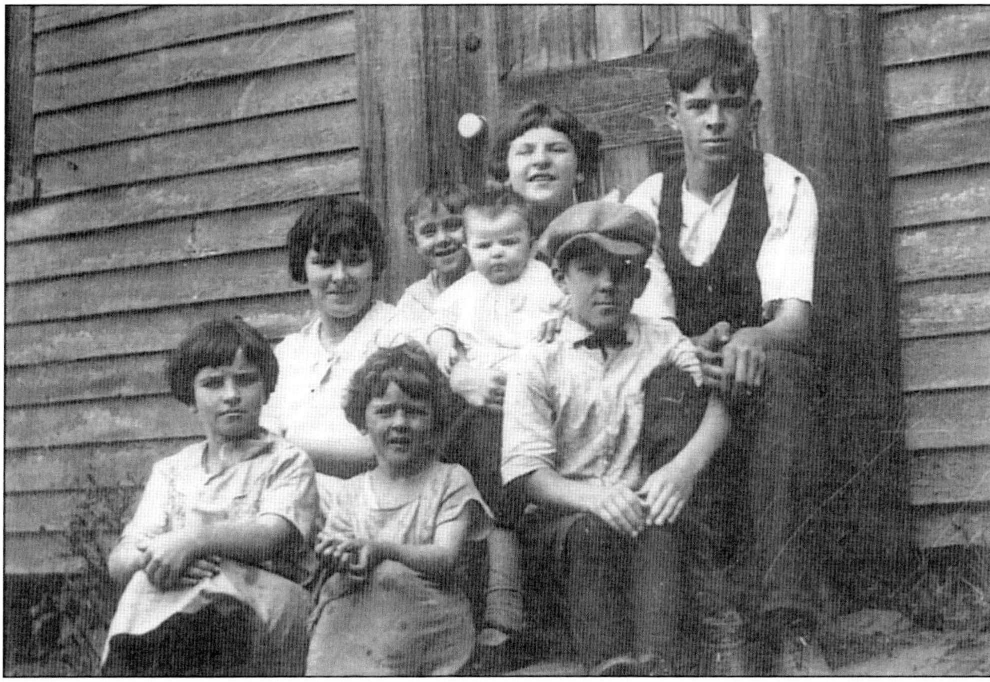

The Smith family is seen on the steps of their home on School Street in 1926. Shown, from left to right, are the following: (front row) Ruth and Jeanette; (middle row) Dorothy and Malcolm; (back row) Eugene, Thelma (holding baby Shirley), and Sterling. The Smith family rented the farm near the corner of School Street and River Road and had a vegetable stand on River Road. The farm later became known as the "jail farm" when Hampden County bought it as a farm for the inmates of the York Street Jail in Springfield to raise their own vegetables. The home fell into disrepair after the county stopped farming the land and was demolished in 2000. (Courtesy of Malcolm Smith.)

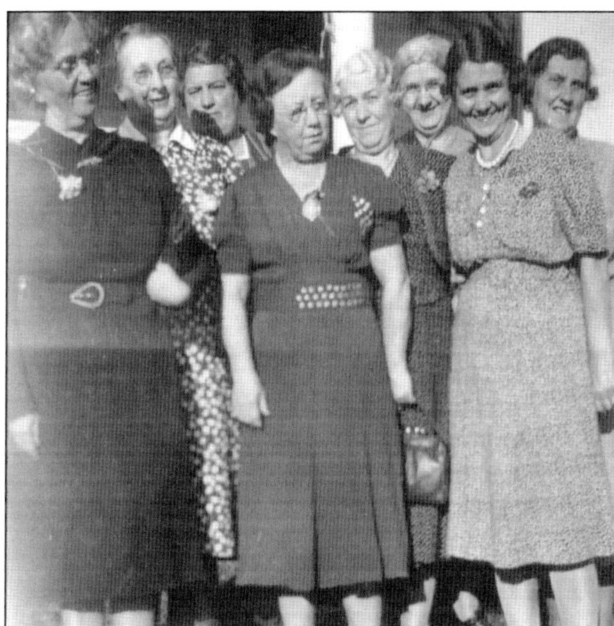

The East Agawam Current Events Club gathered regularly during the 1930s to discuss topics of the day. Pictured c. 1934 from left to right are Verna Allen, Mrs. Peterson, Ella Mae Morrison, Mrs. Saint Onge, Lilly Schwartz, Dora Wilson, and two unidentified members. (Courtesy of Leslie and Dale Melanson.)

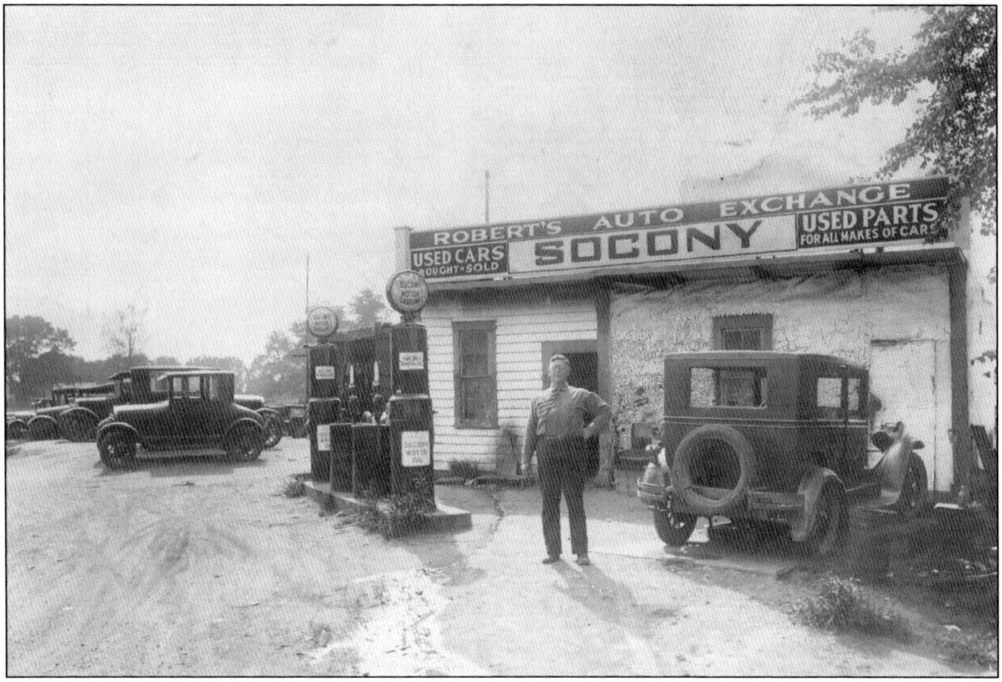

Frederick L. Roberts (no relation to the F.L. Roberts who owned gas stations in Springfield) opened the first gas station on the West side of the Connecticut River between Hartford and Springfield near the corner of River Road and Main Street during the 1910s. He later operated this used car business near the South End Bridge. This photograph was taken in 1926. (Courtesy of Mr. and Mrs. Norman Roberts.)

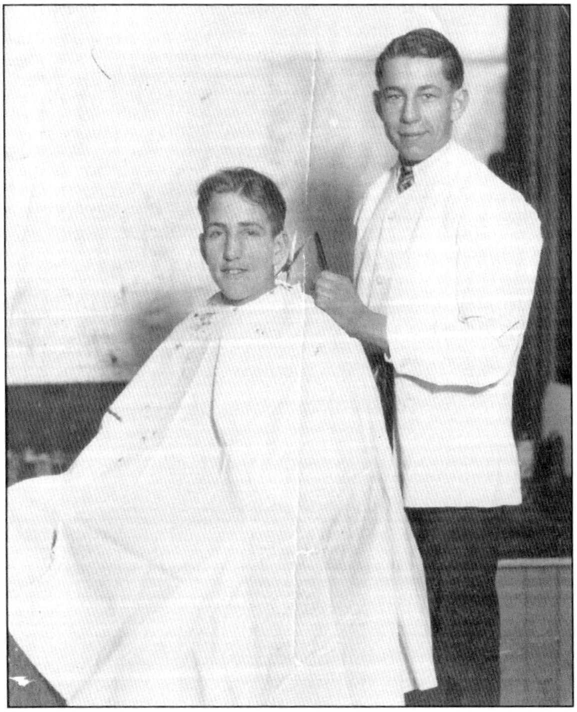

George Reynolds (right) worked his way through Amherst College by operating a barbershop in the ell of C.W. Hastings's store on Main Street during the 1920s. Here he gives Jackie Daly a trim. George Reynolds was a teacher at Agawam High School for many years, and later served on the planning board and as selectman. (Courtesy of Esther Reynolds.)

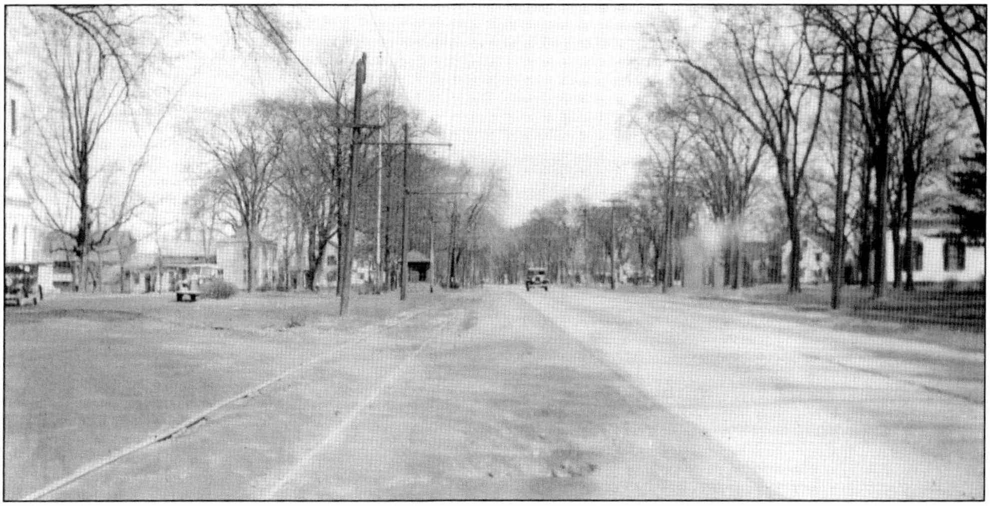

From Main Street looking north from just past Elm Street, the old Baptist church, the Rufus Colton House, and the Lyman Allen house are all visible on the left. The old Congregational Church is on the right. Note the trolley tracks and station near the center of this mid-1930s photograph. (Courtesy of Leslie and Dale Melanson.)

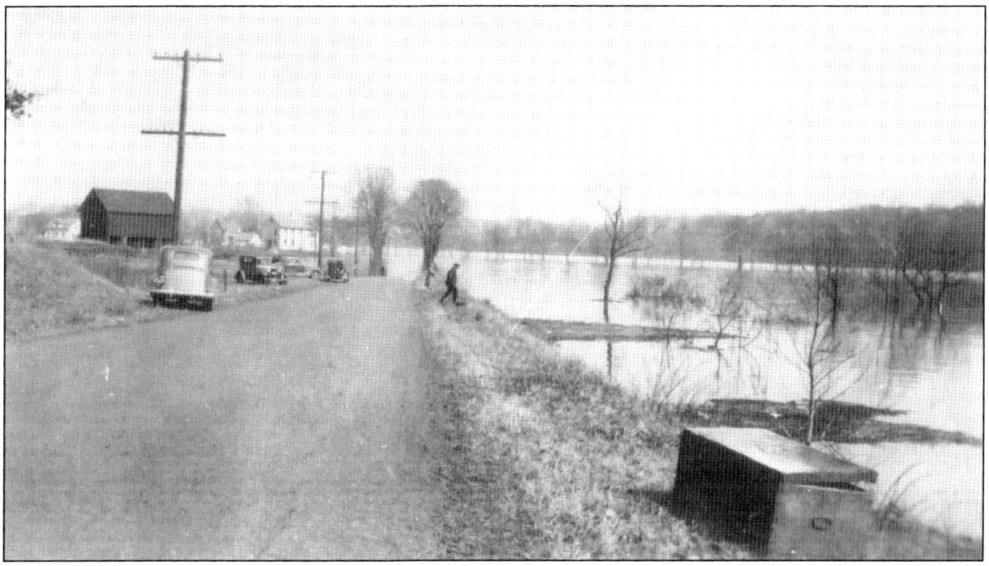

This view looks down School Street toward River Road during the 1936 flood. Smith Farm (later County Jail Farm) is at the left. The barn is still standing, although the house has been demolished. The Town currently owns the property and plans to develop the land into an athletic–recreation complex are under consideration. (Courtesy of Leslie and Dale Melanson.)

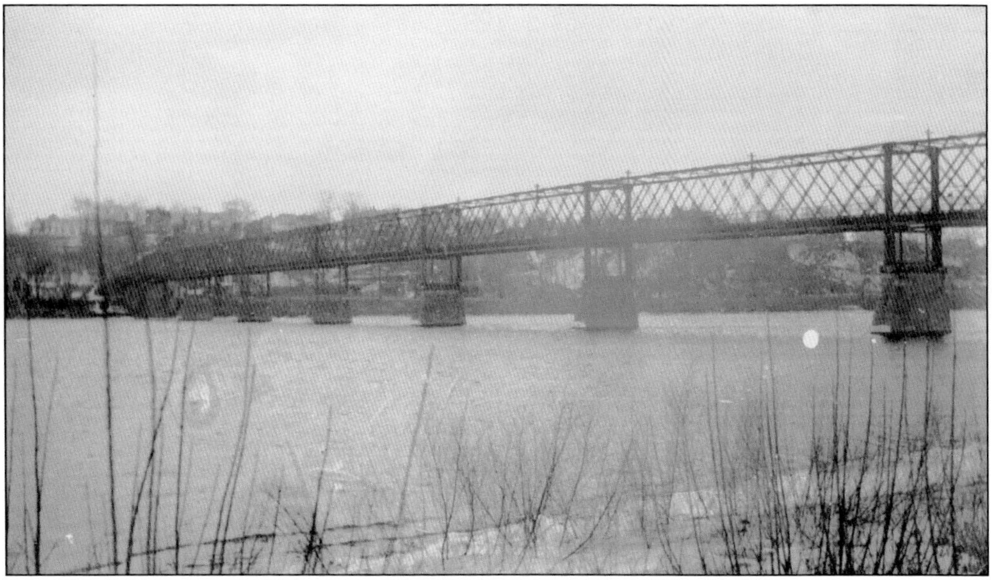

This image of the South End Bridge from the Agawam Side near the Agawam River was captured in February 1932. The photograph clearly shows the bridge after it had been raised in 1903 (see page 26). In 1974, the Agawam Lions Club and the Agawam Historical Association placed the original Anne Sullivan Memorial in Feeding Hills Center, using a granite block from one of this bridge's piers to hold the plaque. (Courtesy of John Bitgood.)

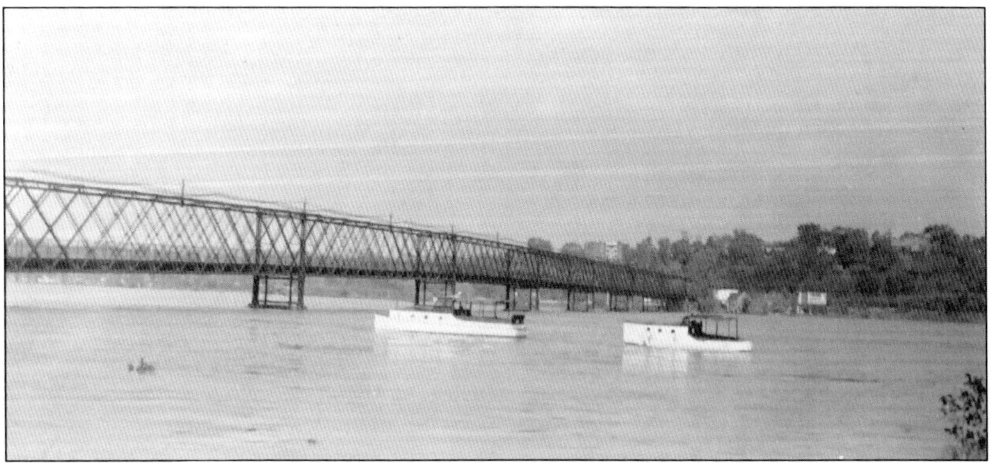

A good view of the South End Bridge in 1938 looking east to Springfield shows how high the waters rose after the hurricane of 1938 passed through the area. (Courtesy of Mr. and Mrs. Alvord Hutchinson.)

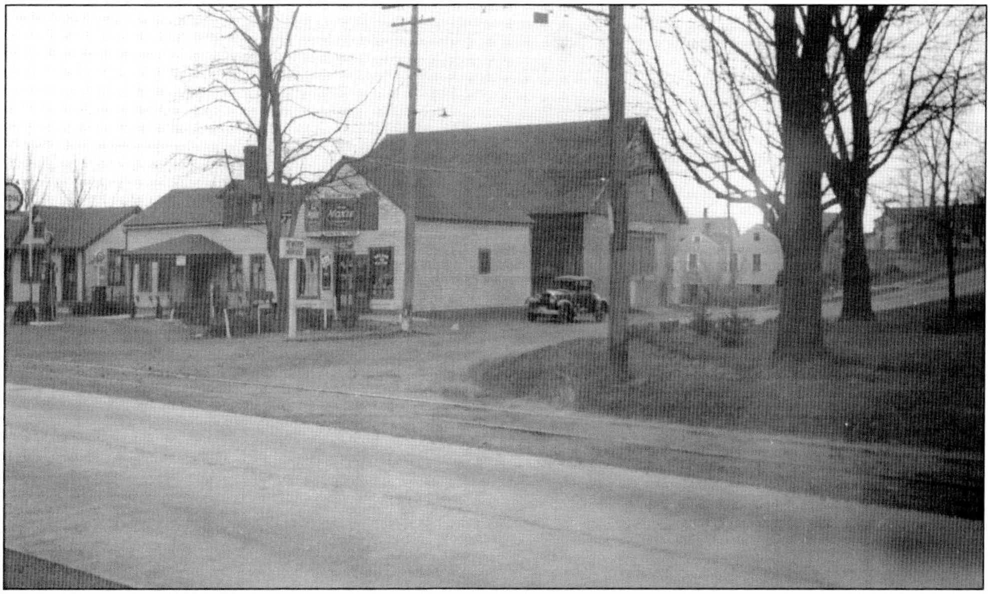

The Brookside grocery and general store, shown in 1936, later became Robinson's store. This business stood at the corner of Main and South Streets for many years. At one time, it was the oldest continuously operated store in town. It was also the sight of Agawam Parish's first post office in 1858. The buildings are now used as apartments. (Courtesy of Mr. and Mrs. Everett Hodge.)

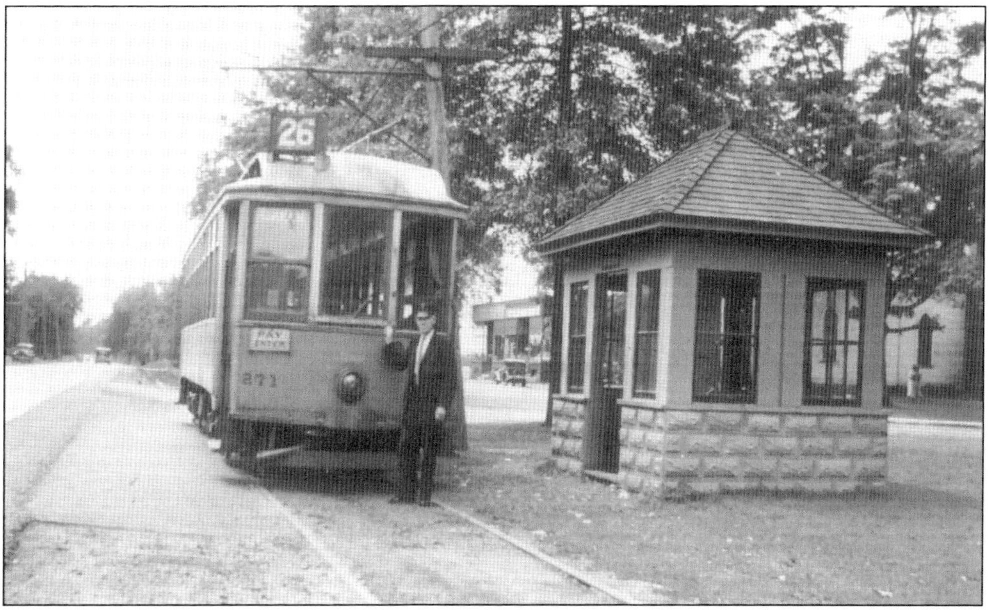

Smith's store (formerly C.W. Hastings's store) can be seen in the background of this 1936 photograph of the trolley station in Agawam Center. The Springfield Street Railway operated a trolley that ran from Springfield to the Connecticut line, where it connected with the Suffield Street Railway. Buses replaced the trolley in 1936. (Courtesy of Zophia Dempko.)

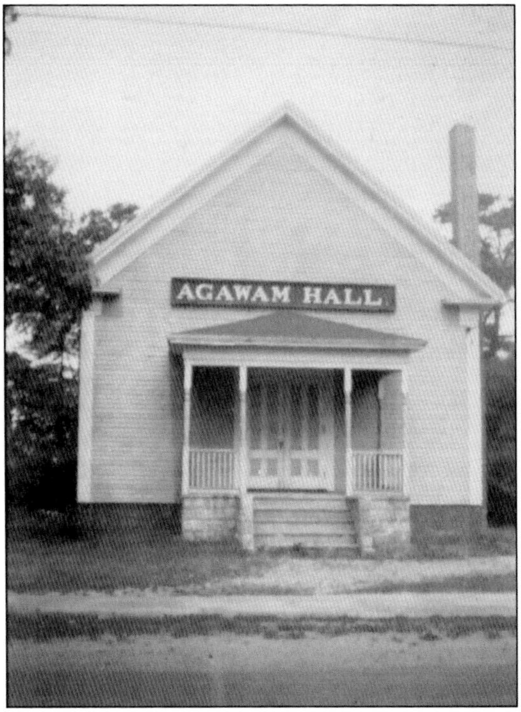

The Agawam Reform Club was formed in the late 1800s. It was renamed the Village Improvement Society in 1900, when they purchased the old Methodist Episcopal Church at 1477 Main Street. Remembered by many as the "V.I. Hall," this building stood at the foot of South Street, and was later converted into a two family residence. It was demolished in 1971. (Courtesy of Clyde Pomeroy.)

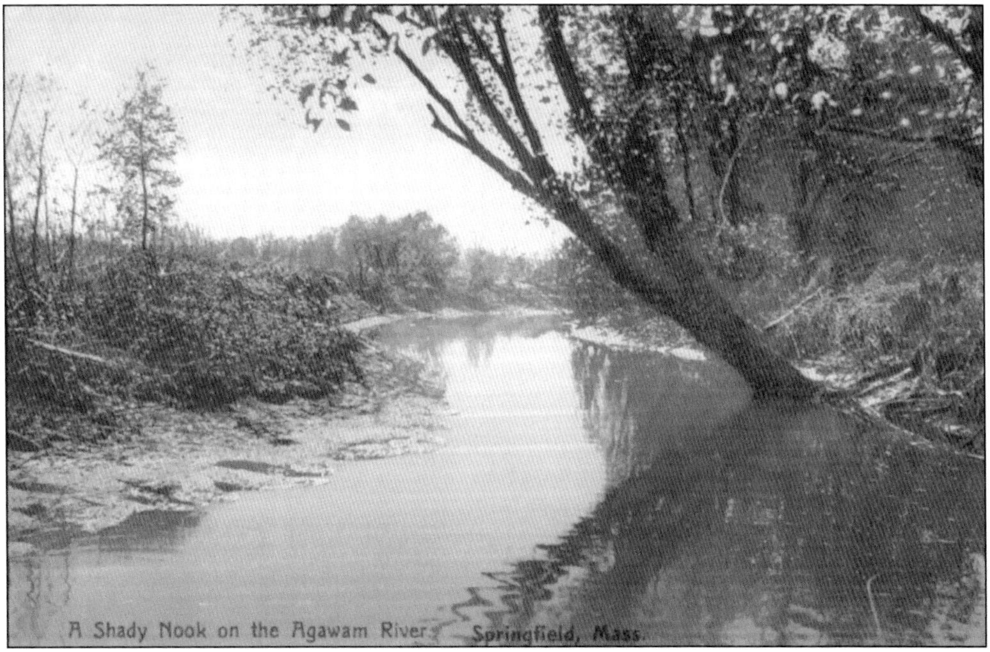

The river separating Agawam and Westfield has been called both the Agawam and the Westfield River at various times. In the 1930s, a committee was set up to decide what the name should be. The head of this committee was from Westfield and had some political pull. Hence the official name is Westfield River on maps today, even though it is customary to name rivers after the place of their mouth. Many in town still stubbornly refer to it as the Agawam River. (Author's collection.)

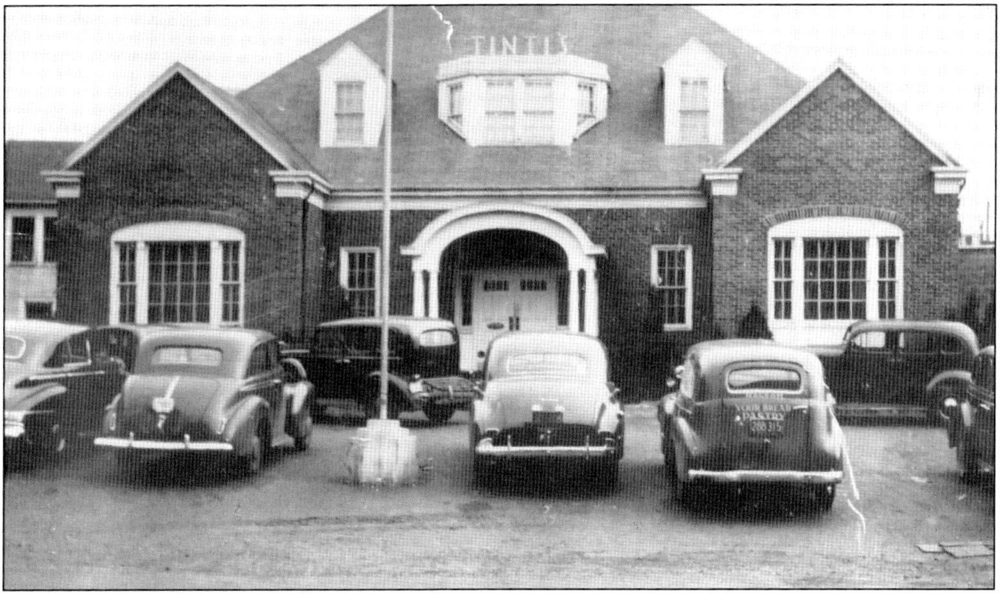

Tinti's Restaurant, located at 22 King Street in North Agawam, was founded in 1924 by Celso and Erminia Tinti. The restaurant was a popular dining place for many decades before closing in 1970. The building currently serves as a Masonic hall. (Courtesy of Anna Tinti Casali.)

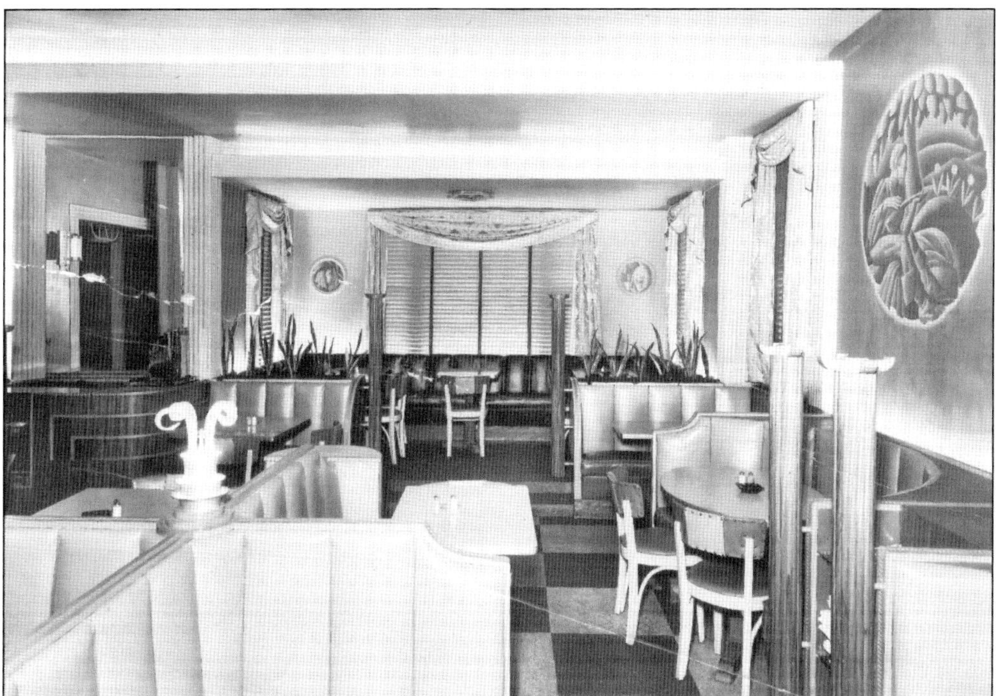

Since the 1930s, Tinti's expanded many times. Area artist and decorator Thurston Munson designed the interior and decorative murals. During Tinti's heyday, customers traveled from across New England to eat the authentic Italian cuisine. (Courtesy of Anna Tinti Casali.)

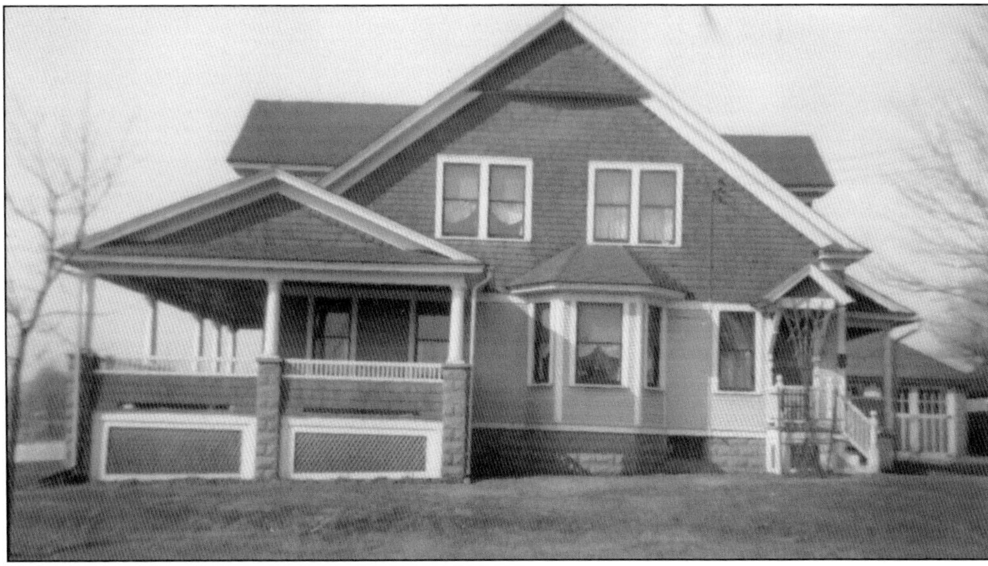

Development in Agawam in the early 1920s saw this home built at 468 Springfield Street on the corner of Wilson Street. It was part of the "Presidential Heights" neighborhood of Harding, Wilson, Taft, McKinley, and Clevelend Streets between Springfield and North Streets. It was home to Perley Hewey, Agawam chief of police for many years. Before the police department had its own quarters, he had a small office there, accessible through the side door at the right. In 1950, Ted Dynia (the author's grandfather) moved his family here from Enfield, Connecticut. Chief Hewey's office became Helen Dynia's sewing room. Ted Dynia served the town for many years as a member of the planning board, the housing authority, the Lions Club, and the Polish American Club. (Courtesy of Helen Dynia.)

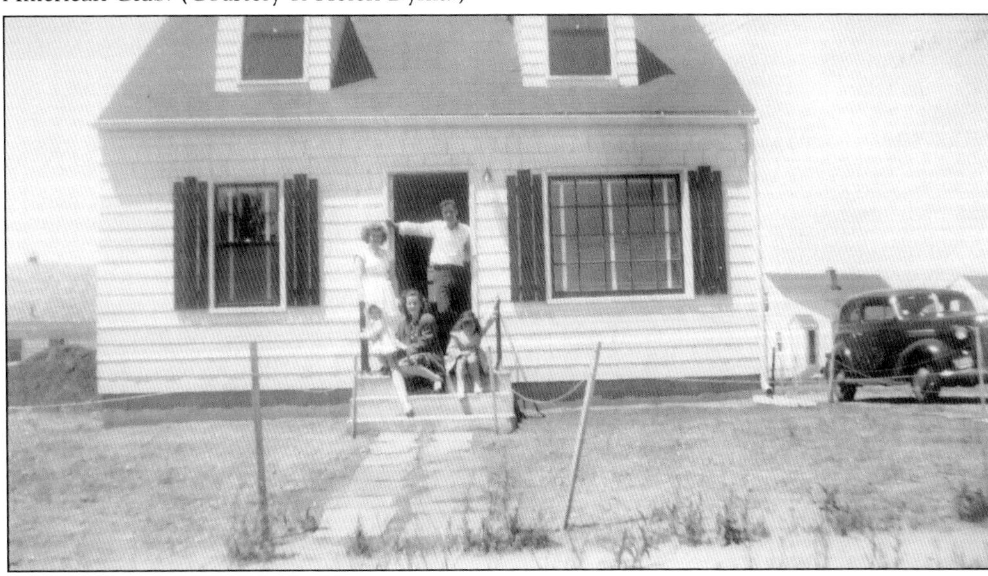

The Peckham family is shown on the porch of their new home at 30 Randall Street in 1947. In the doorway, Albert Peckham poses with his sister Marge. His wife, Sue Peckham, sits on the steps with their children—Karen, on the left, and Dale, on the right. This small cape was typical of the many homes that sprung up in Agawam after World War II. (Courtesy of Leslie and Dale [Peckham] Melanson.)

Four

Feeding Hills

In 1800, Agawam (then a parish of West Springfield) was divided into two separate parishes. The dividing line, the former boundary between the Inner and Outer Commons, was roughly where Line Street is today. Agawam remained as Second Parish, while Feeding Hills became West Springfield's Fourth Parish. Feeding Hills's strong rural character remained intact until the 1970s, when many farms were lost to development. It is still evident somewhat in the farms that remain in that section of town, especially on North West Street.

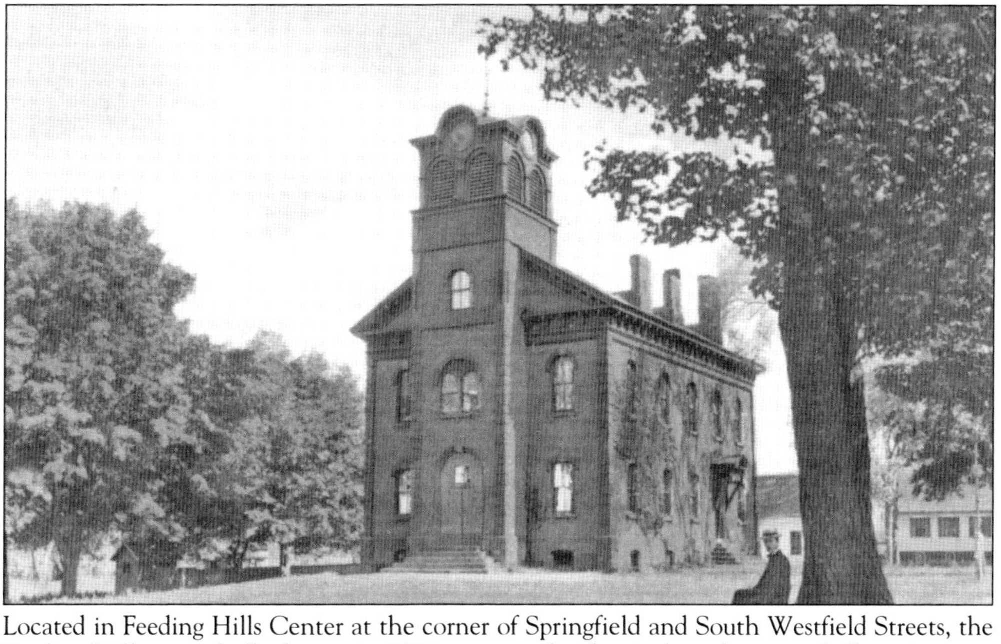

Located in Feeding Hills Center at the corner of Springfield and South Westfield Streets, the Feeding Hills town hall, shown in 1912, was nearly identical to the town hall in Agawam (see page 37). This building was demolished in 1950 to make way for the Clifford M. Granger Elementary School. The schoolhouse clock was saved during the demolition of the building by the late Walter T. Kerr, who later donated it to the Agawam Historical and Fire House Museum. (Author's collection.)

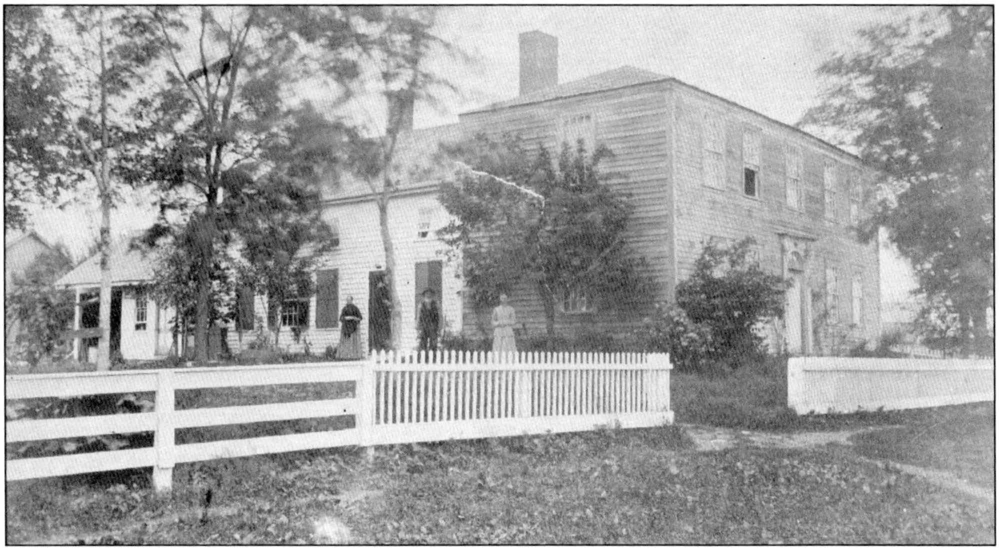

Shown at the Halladay House, from left to right, are Hannah (Flower) Halladay, James C. Hallady, and Mary R. Halladay. The house, which probably dates to the late 1700s or early 1800s, was substantially altered after the Civil War to bring it up to contemporary style. Later the residence of the Kellogg family (see page 61), this house is still standing at the corner of North Westfield Street and Blacksmith Road. (Courtesy of Patricia Noble.)

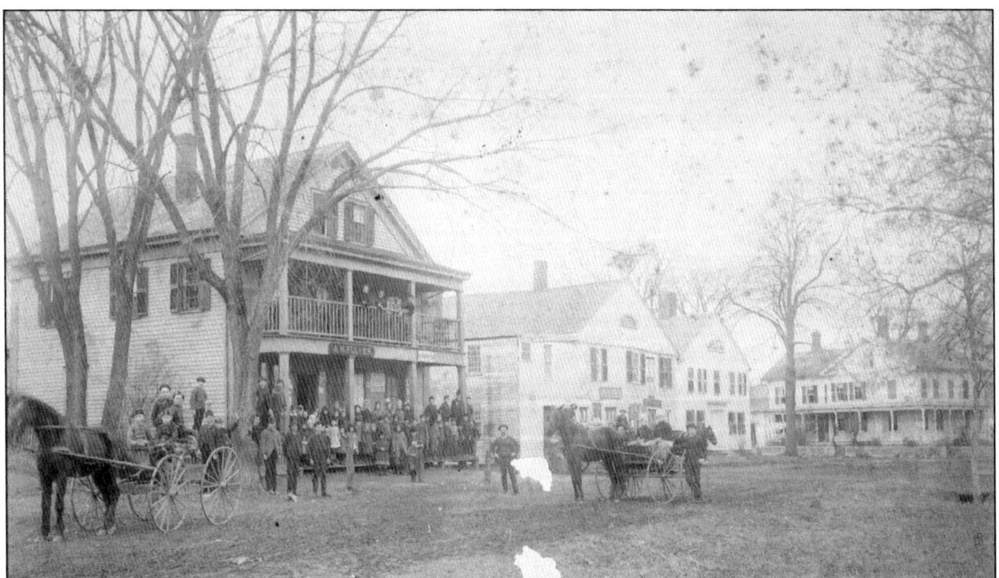

This photograph was taken a decade before A.K. Fuller's store in Feeding Hills Center burned in 1899 and was replaced by E.A. Kellogg's store. In this photograph, both the Charles Wright House (far right) and the Hamilton House (second from right) are clearly visible. The Hamilton House was demolished in the 1970s. The Charles Wright House, on the corner of Southwick and North Westfield Streets, has survived repeated threats of demolition and currently houses several small businesses (see page 56). Another view of Fuller's store and the old Methodist church is shown on the cover. (Agawam Historical Association collection.)

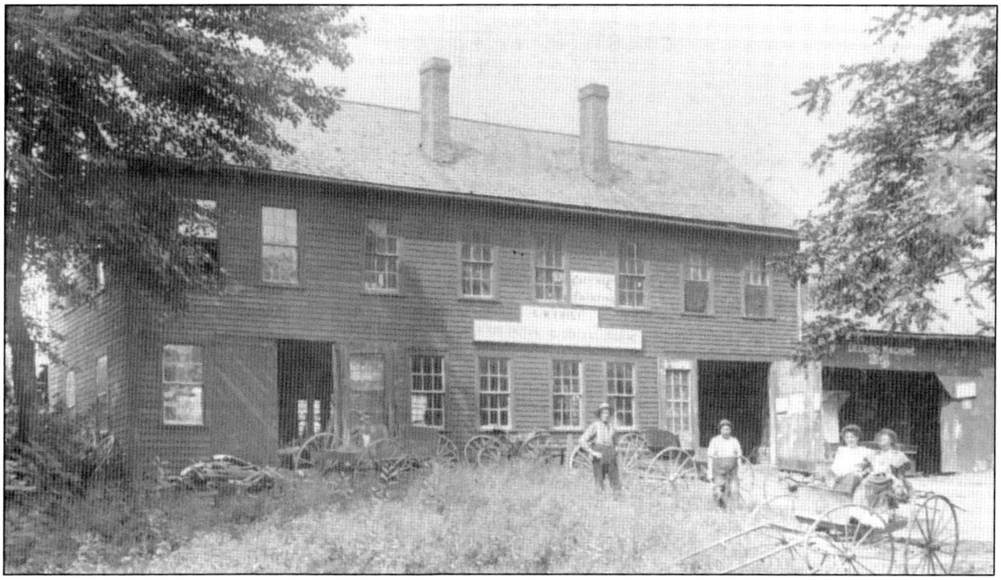

The C.W. Twist blacksmith shop was located near where Route 57 and South Westfield Street meet. This photograph was taken in 1901 by the Howes Brothers of Ashfield, Massachusetts. A sign on the building advertises, "Carriage Painting, Horse Shoeing, and General Jobbing" as well as "Deering Machine Agency." (Agawam Historical Association collection.)

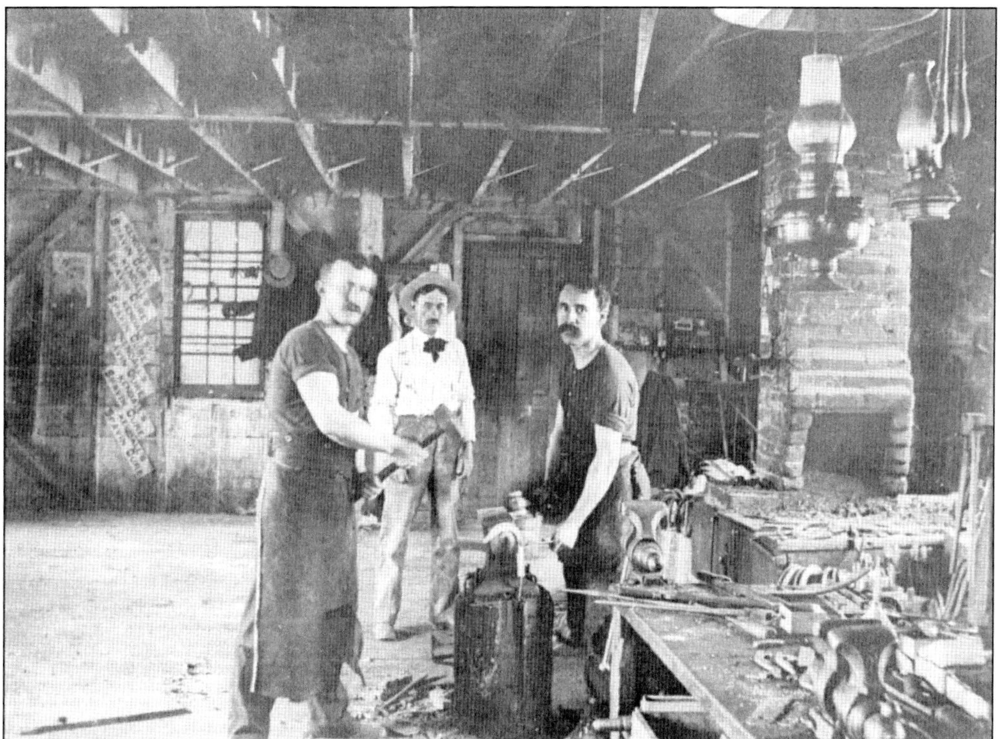

This photograph shows the inside the C.W. Twist blacksmith shop on South Westfield Street. At the turn of the century, Feeding Hills had many large farms using horses for the daily chores and the Twist shop was one of several blacksmiths in town. (Courtesy of Jean Welt Taylor.)

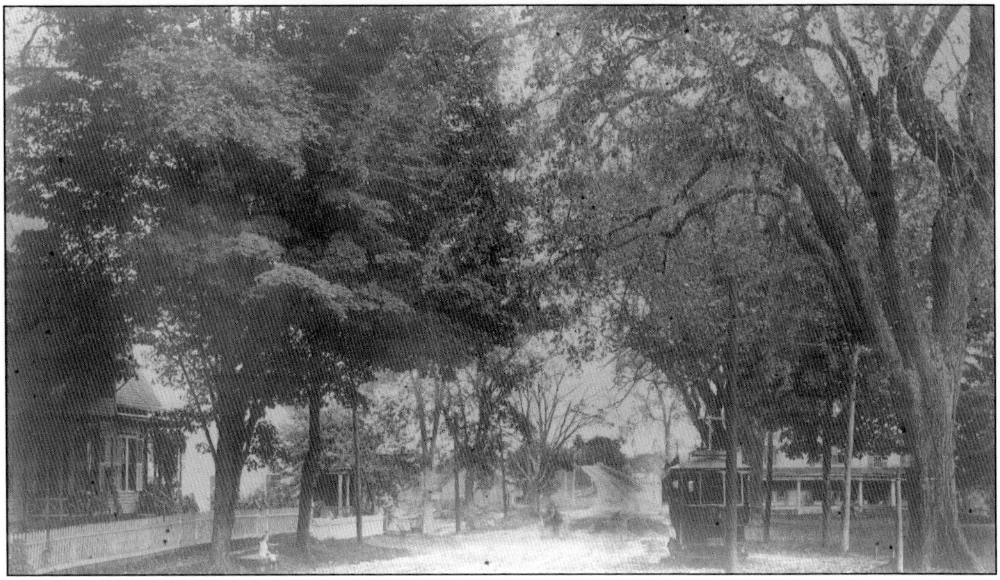

Springfield Street is shown, looking east from Feeding Hills Center, *c.* 1902. The trolley is about to head back toward Springfield—note the "Forest Park" sign on top. The embankment allowing the Central New England Railroad tracks to pass beneath is clearly visible in the center of the photograph. The current Stop & Shop would be on the left at the top of the rise. The Jimmie Moore house is on the left. The Burbank Hotel can be seen on the right. (Agawam Historical Association collection.)

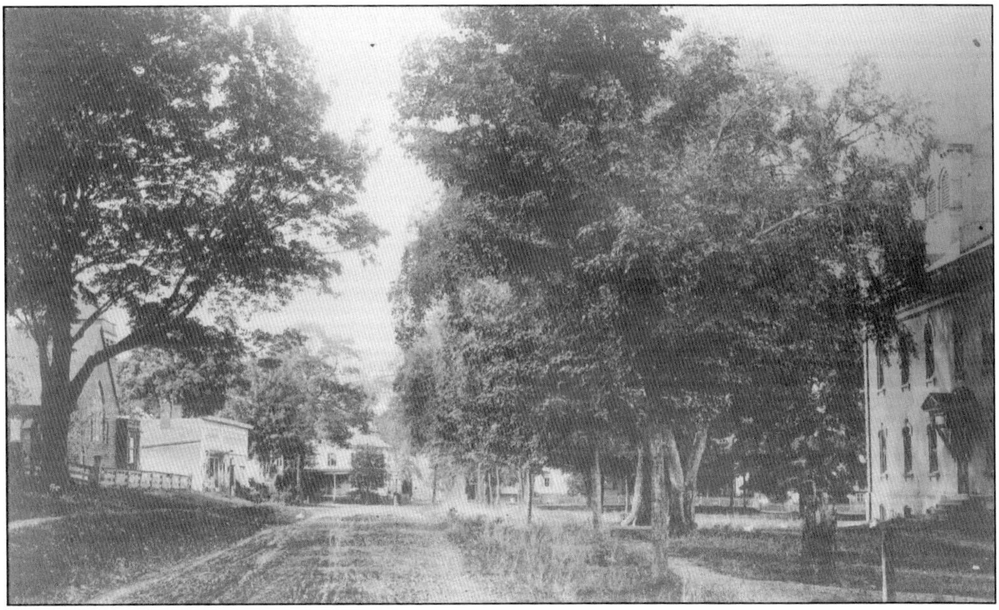

South Westfield Street is in this photograph, looking north toward Feeding Hills Center, *c.* 1902. The Charles Wright House is visible in the center of the photograph. The Feeding Hills Town Hall and school is at the right. E.A. Kellogg's store has replaced A.K. Fuller's store, which burned in 1899 (see page 52). The new Lay Memorial Methodist church is also visible at the left. This building replaced the old Methodist church that was destroyed by fire and can be seen on the back cover. (Agawam Historical Association collection.)

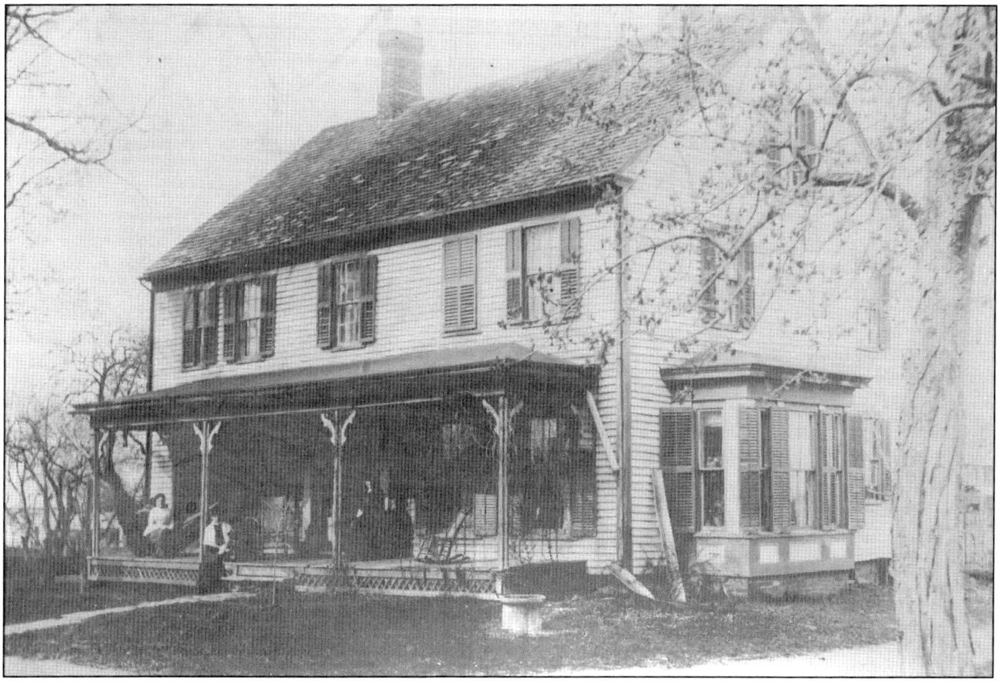

This home was built for minister Sylvanus Griswold in 1762. In 1841, it became home to Dr. Cyrus Bell, whose son Charles founded the Young People's Unique Society of Feeding Hills, a precursor to the Feeding Hills library. Later, Albert K. Fuller (see page 52) lived there. Upon his death, his daughter Genevieve (Fuller) Bamforth (see page 88) and her husband took up residence there, operating the Unique Poultry Farm on the property for many years. The old parsonage, located just south of the present Granger School, was demolished in 1965 in order to build the apartment complex now occupying the site. (Agawam Historical Association collection.)

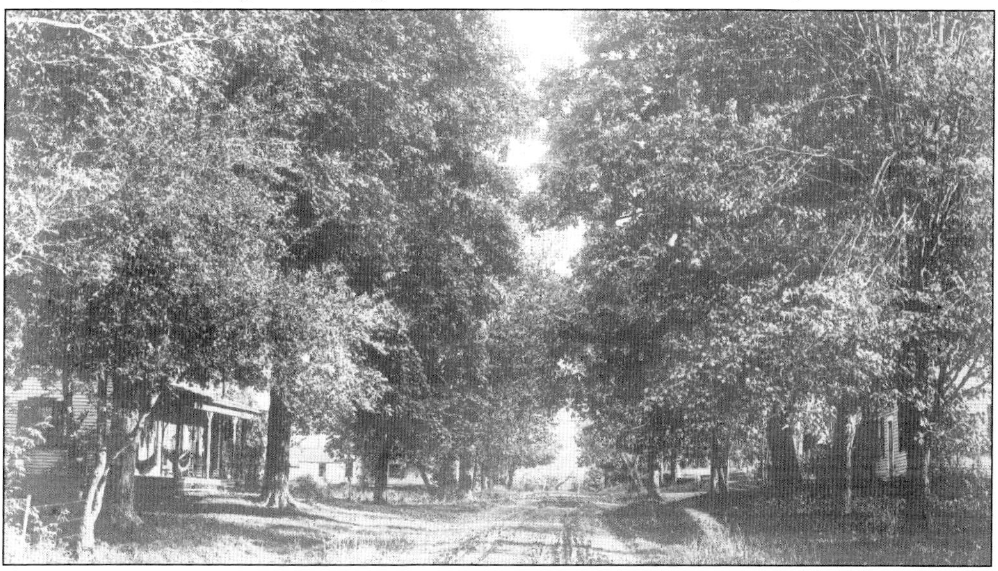

On South Westfield Street, looking south from Feeding Hills Center, c. 1902, the Sylvanus Griswold House can be seen on the left. What a difference 100 years makes! (Agawam Historical Association collection.)

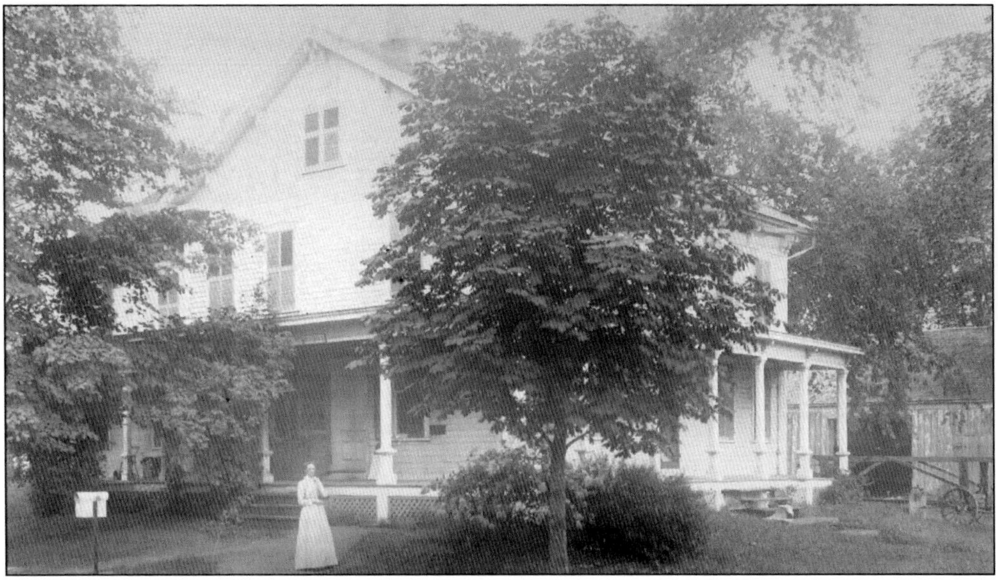

Built in 1863 on the site of the old Palmer Inn at the corner of Southwick and North Westfield Streets, the Charles Wright House is of traditional design with Italianate influences. Mr. Wright's daughter, Jennie, became postmaster of Feeding Hills on November 22, 1892, and kept the post office in the house for over 20 years. The post office sign can be seen hanging over the porch on the left in this photograph taken by the Howes Brothers in 1901. (Agawam Historical Association collection.)

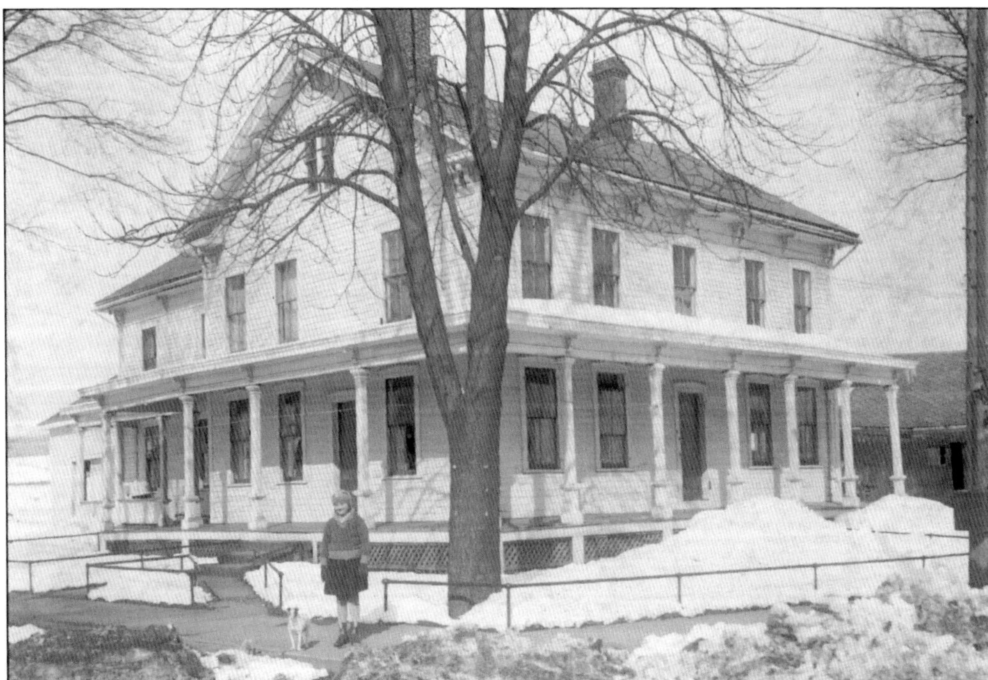

After Jennie Wright died in 1920, Harry and Louise Brown moved into the Charles Wright House. Their daughter, Esther, is shown here in the 1920s. The Italianate detail mentioned above is clearly visible in this photograph. (Agawam Historical Association collection.)

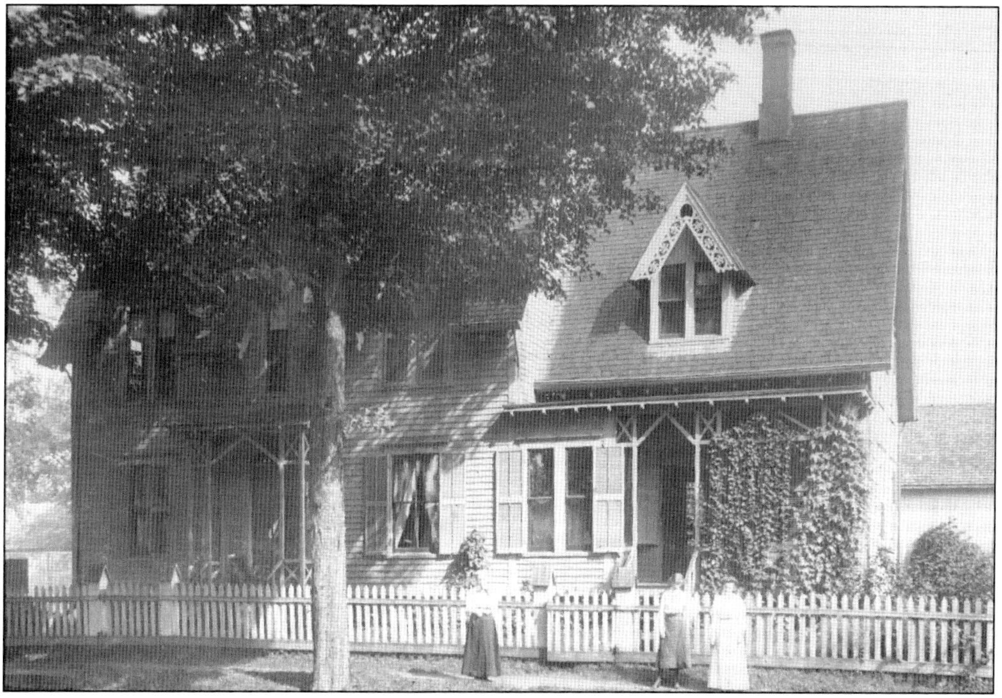

The charming Jimmie Moore House, 1901, stood on the corner of Springfield and North Westfield Streets for many years. It was demolished in the 1930s to build a gas station on that corner, where one has remained ever since. (Agawam Historical Association collection.)

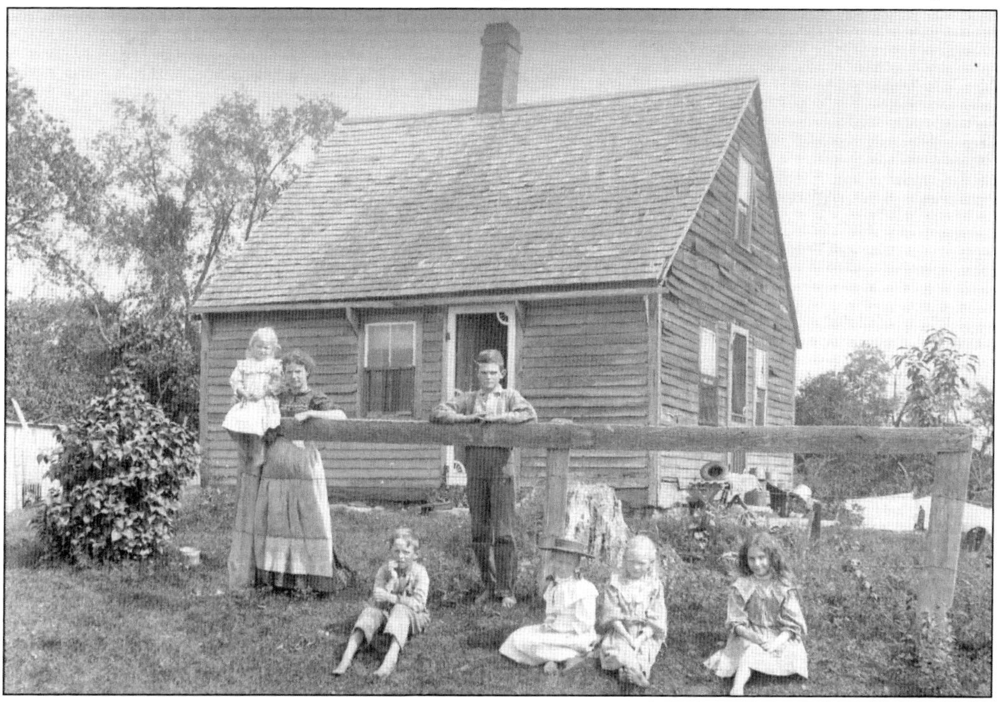

This home on South West Street was owned by George Spear. It is no longer standing. (Agawam Historical Association collection.)

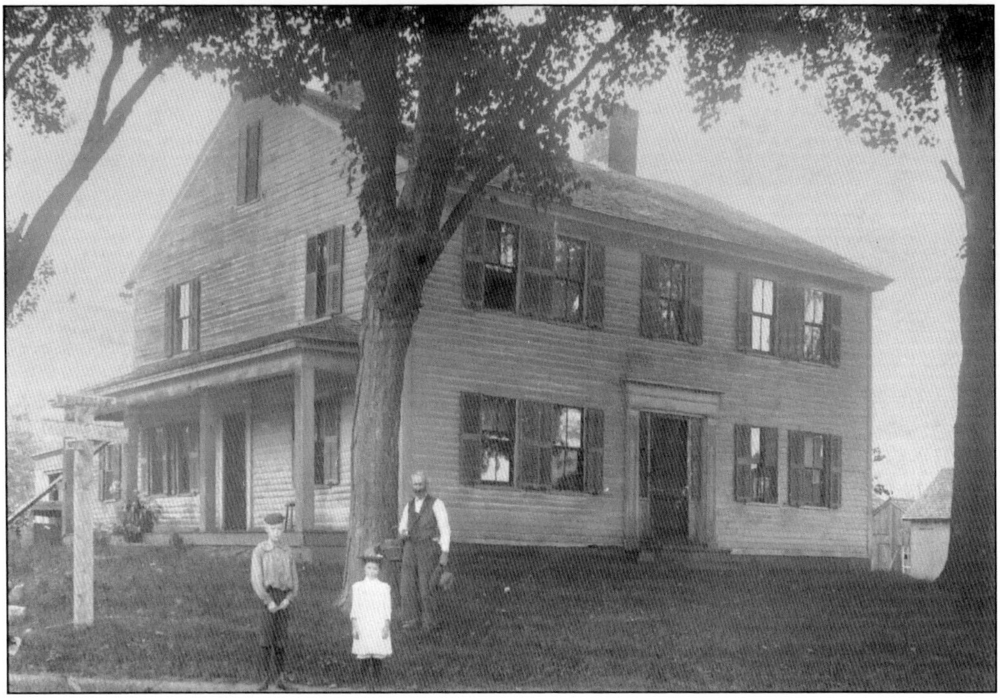

Still located at the corner of Southwick and North West Streets, this large Federal-style home, the King House, was built *c.* 1850 by the Smith family and descended through Herman Smith, Horace Smith, and Delia Smith. The Smith family is most likely pictured here. The house was sold to Nelson King in 1910 and remained in his family until 1964. The photograph dates to 1901. (Agawam Historical Association collection.)

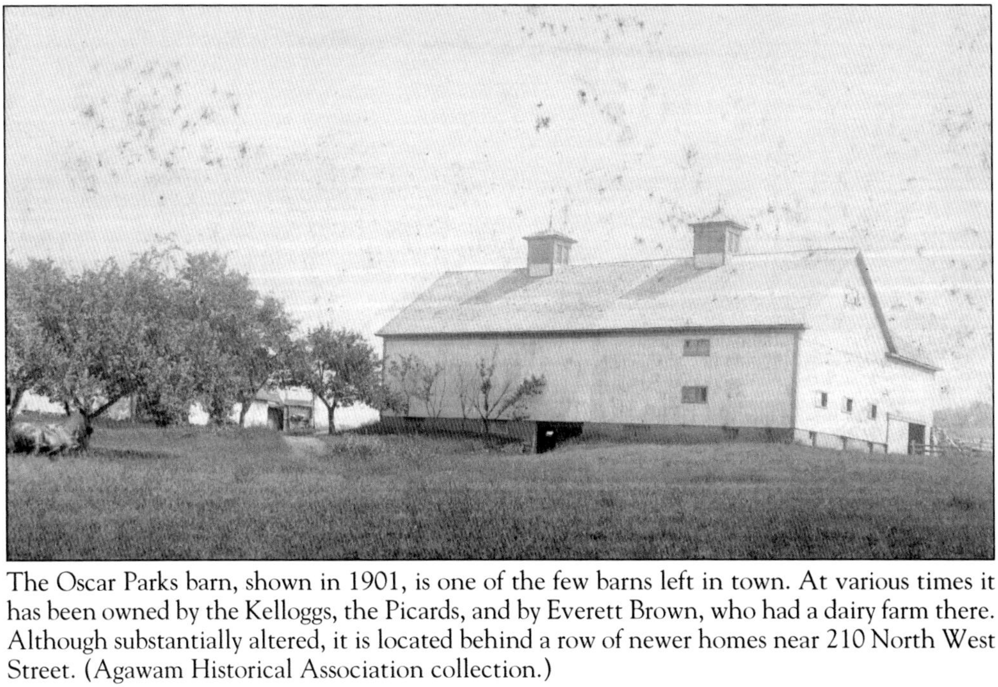

The Oscar Parks barn, shown in 1901, is one of the few barns left in town. At various times it has been owned by the Kelloggs, the Picards, and by Everett Brown, who had a dairy farm there. Although substantially altered, it is located behind a row of newer homes near 210 North West Street. (Agawam Historical Association collection.)

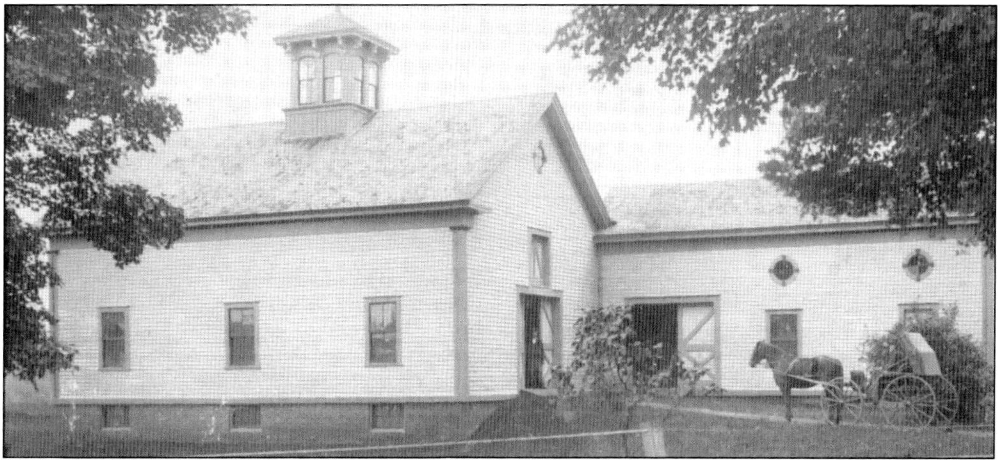

The intersection of Southwick, North West, and South West Streets came to be known as Johnson's Corner since the Johnson farm was located there for many years. In 1920, the property was bought by Charles Gustafson, the retired engineer at the Indian Motocycle Company who designed the Indian Twin motocycle and invented the motorcycle kick starter. He opened a garage in the small block building at 311 Southwick Street and had an experimental dirt track for motorcycles behind his home. The barn pictured here was later used as a doctor's office for many years. It still stands at 317 Southwick Street, minus the addition on the right and the cupola. (Agawam Historical Association collection.)

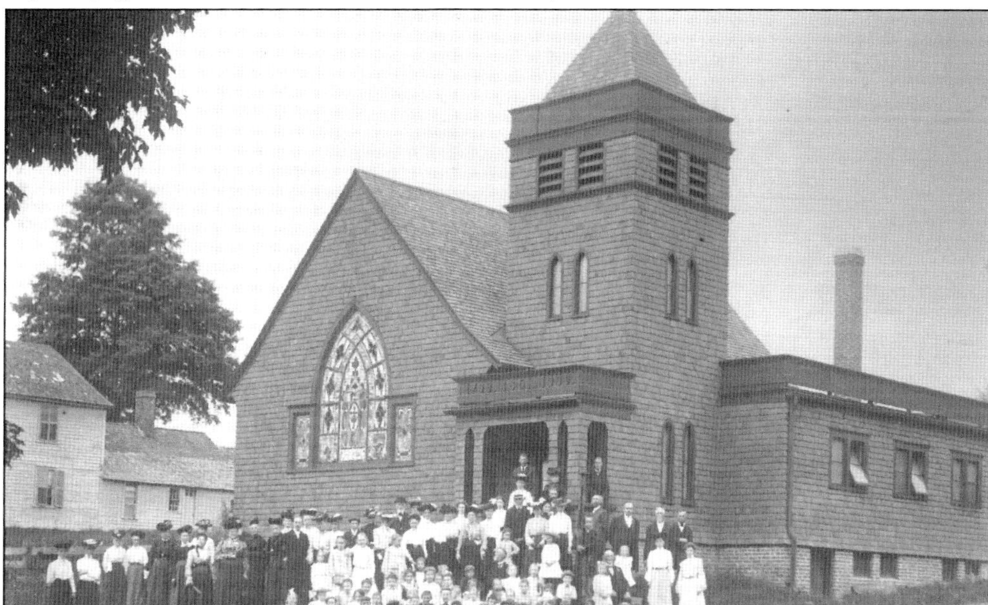

The first Methodist church in Feeding Hills was built in 1799 on the site of the current Calvary Assembly of God church at 18 South Westfield Street. It was replaced in 1851 with the church seen on the back cover, which was destroyed by fire on February 14, 1899. The building pictured, built in 1900, was moved back in 1906. That year, Edwin Lay (second from right) of Westfield paid for construction of a new, larger sanctuary in front of it in memory of his father, Gibbons Lay, who was an organizer of the first Methodist Society. The church then came to be known as the Lay Memorial Methodist Church. (Courtesy of Patricia Noble.)

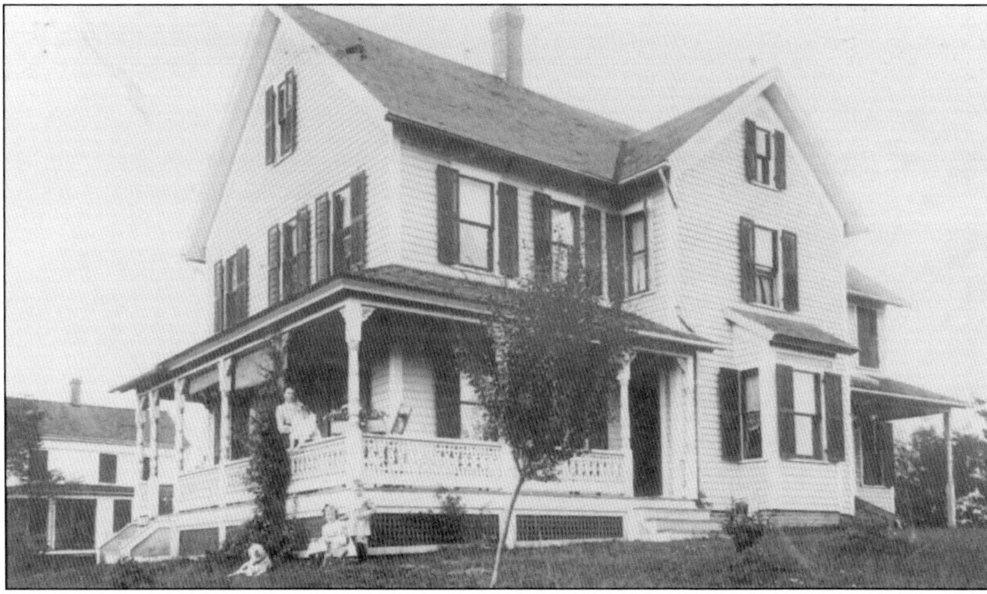

This home, on the former Phelon farm, still stands at 573 South West Street. It was built c. 1894 for the marriage of James and Margaret Barry (see page 87). James Barry operated a large farm there and later started the Barry Coal Company in Feeding Hills Center (see page 94). Pictured, from left to right, are Margaret, on the porch holding Ruth; Kathryn, sitting in front of the porch; and James, standing. The dog's name was Grover, after Pres. Grover Cleveland. This home and farm was later owned by the Labb family (see page 84). (Courtesy of Jay and Mary Barry.)

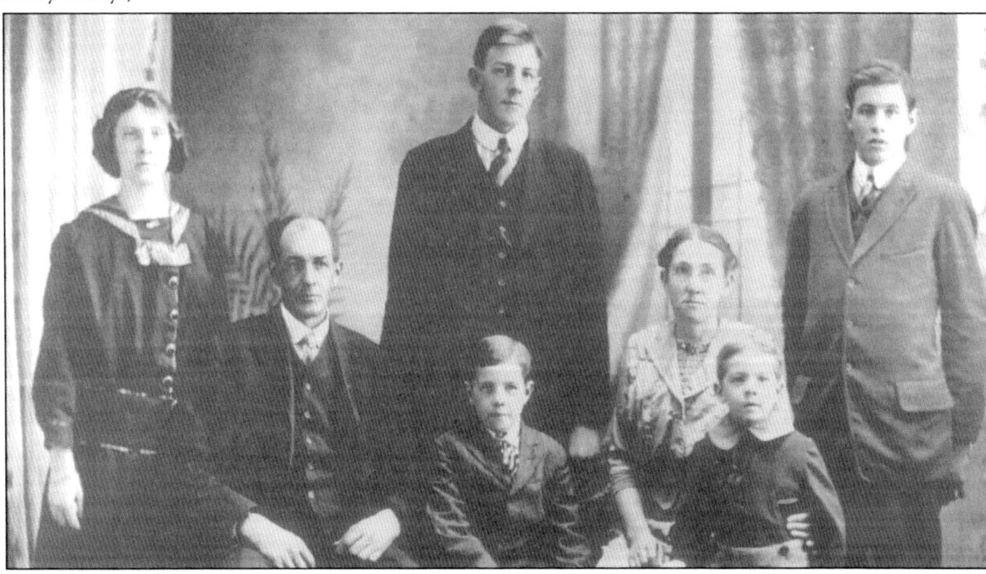

The family of LeGrand (Lee) and Delmar Jenks is pictured c. 1915. Shown, from left to right, are the following: (front row) LeGrand Jenks, Frank Jenks, Delmar Jenks, and Elbert Jenks; (back row) Cassie Jenks Davis, Bertley Jenks, and Prentiss R. Jenks. Prentiss Jenks was employed by the H.C. Puffer Grain Company in Feeding Hills Center (see page 94). His son, Russell "Rusty" Jenks, was a member of the Agawam Fire Department and later became chief. (Courtesy of Mr. and Mrs. Russell Jenks.)

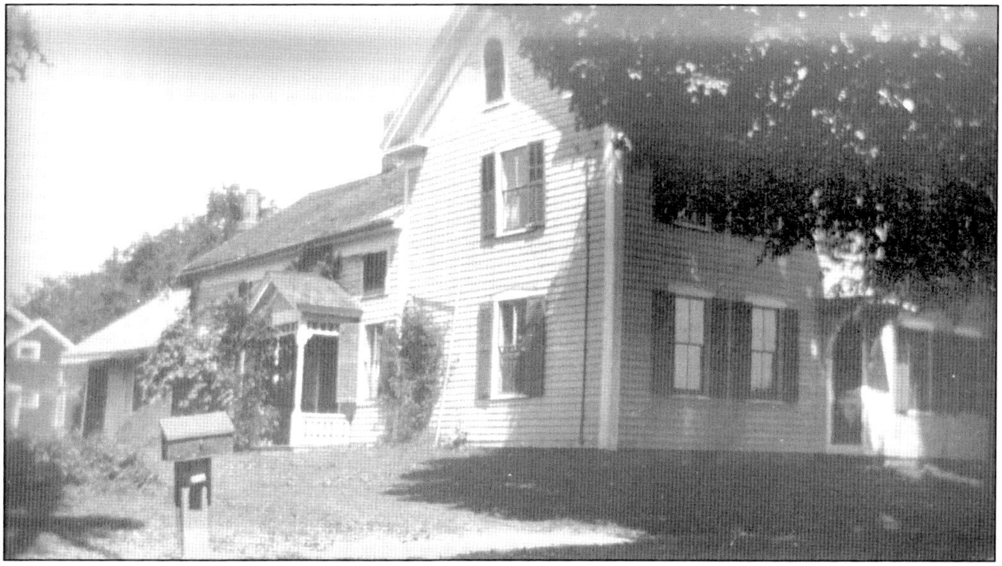

This photograph of the Halladay House clearly shows the changes made to the house to keep current with contemporary architectural styles (see page 52). The house was bought from Mary Halladay *c.* 1912 by Alvin Kellogg Sr., whose family lived there for many years. The house is still in use as a residence at the corner of North Westfield Street and Blacksmith Road. (Courtesy of Mr. and Mrs. Alvin Kellogg Jr.)

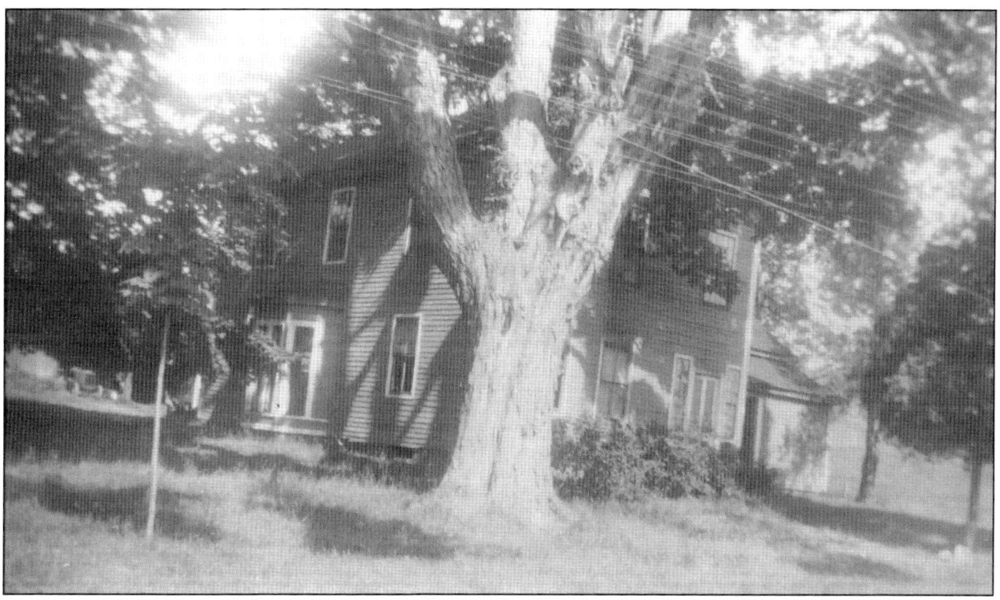

Richard and Electa Kellogg moved from Southampton, Massachusetts, to this house in Feeding Hills in 1843. It was built in the mid-1700s and remained the Kellogg Homestead for many years, later serving as living quarters for farm hands. It was demolished after 1940. The Kellogg farm included the area now known as Kellogg Drive and extended from behind the Feeding Hills Cemetery past North Westfield Street (then called Front Street) and west toward North West Street (then called Back Street or West Street). (Courtesy of Mr. and Mrs. Alvin Kellogg Jr.)

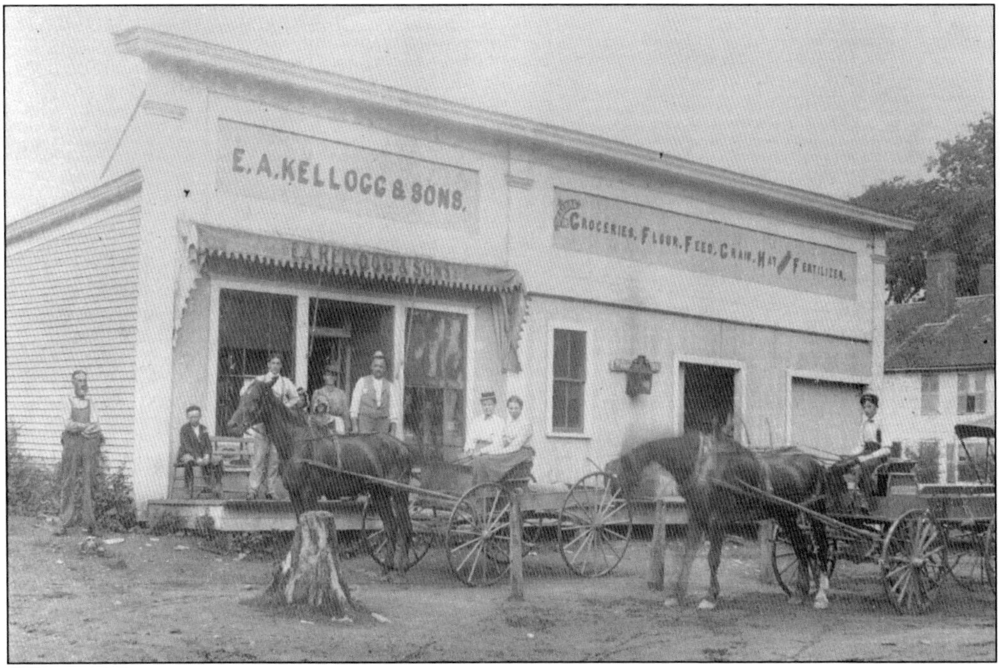

Edward A. Kellogg opened a general store and grain business on South Westfield Street in Feeding Hills Center in 1897, at first operating from the former A.K. Fuller store building (see page 52). When that building burned in 1899, he built the building shown here. Fred Halladay, who later built a library on this site and gave it to the Town (see page 65), is standing to the left of the building. E.A. Kellogg is standing in the doorway. To the left of him are Mrs. Albert Fisk, Lil Fisk, and Grace Fisk. The two women in the wagon are Mame Glenn and Alice Glenn. This building was moved to Springfield Street in 1903 (see page 63). (Courtesy of Mr. and Mrs. Alvin R. Kellogg Jr.)

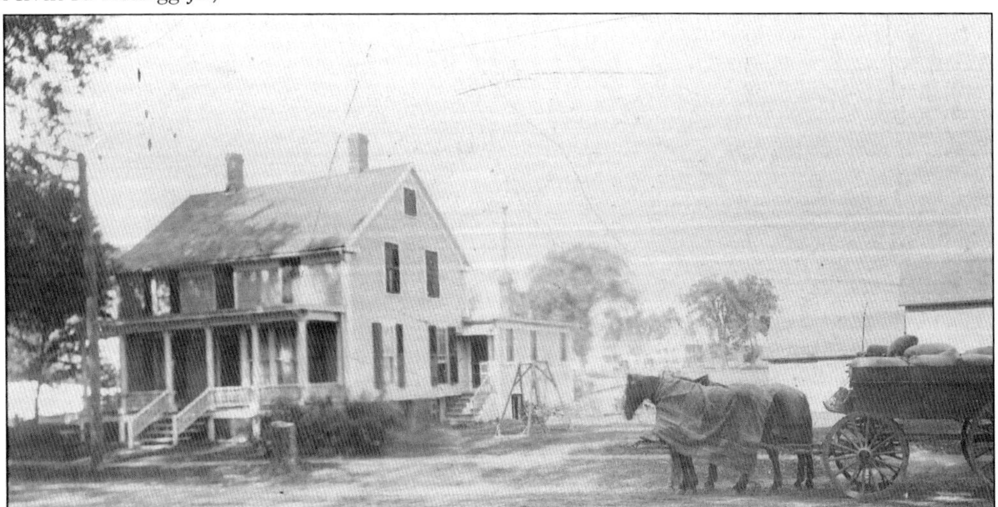

Edward A. Kellogg built this home at 1368 Springfield Street at the turn of the century. The Jimmie Moore house, pictured on page 57, would have been located to the left, just out of frame. The Kellogg store grain wagon is at the right. This home was demolished in 1994. (Courtesy of Mr. and Mrs. Alvin R. Kellogg Jr.)

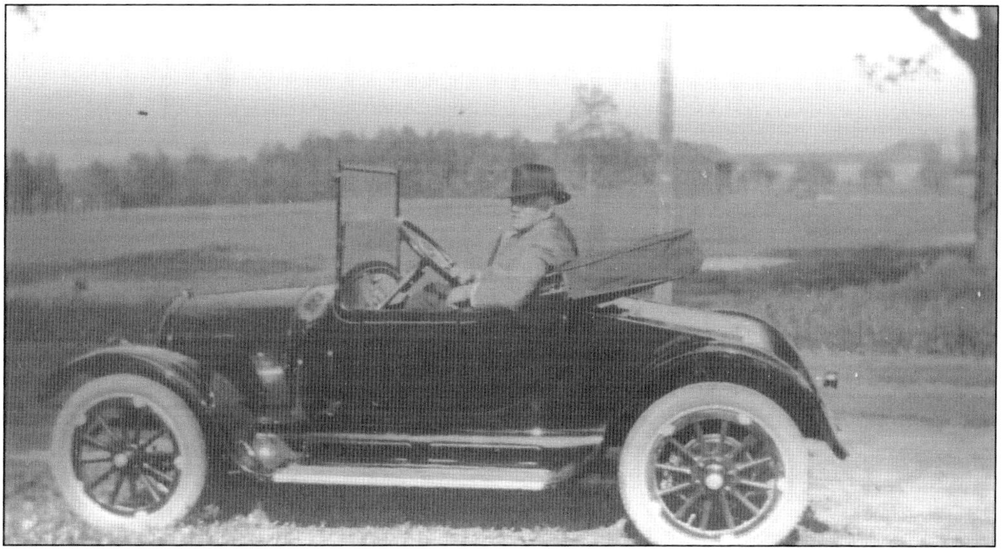

E.A. Kellogg & Sons flourished in the early 1900s, at one point employing six clerks and five automobile delivery wagons. Tobacco and other crops were raised on the Kellogg farm, and a large herd of fine Holstein cattle was kept in a modern barn, which was lit by electricity. Edward Kellogg, shown here in the 1920s, served for five years as street commissioner. He was chairman of the water commission for several years. During his term, 27 miles of water main was laid in town. (Courtesy of Mr. and Mrs. Alvin R. Kellogg Jr.)

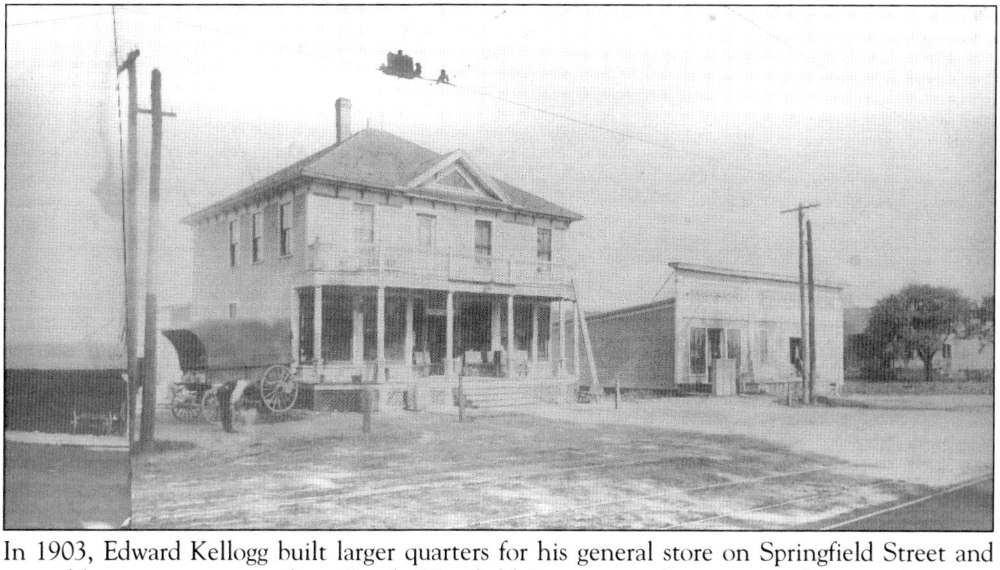

In 1903, Edward Kellogg built larger quarters for his general store on Springfield Street and moved his one-story store from South Westfield Street next-door to serve his grain business. Edward's wife, Alice, and their two sons, Richard and Alvin Sr., were all active in the business. In 1928, the general store was sold to Rufus Ferry and William Bardwell of Granby and operated as Ferry & Bardwell for many years. The grain business was sold to H.C. Puffer and was moved across Springfield Street to the train depot area (see page 94). (Courtesy of Mr. and Mrs. Alvin R. Kellogg Jr.)

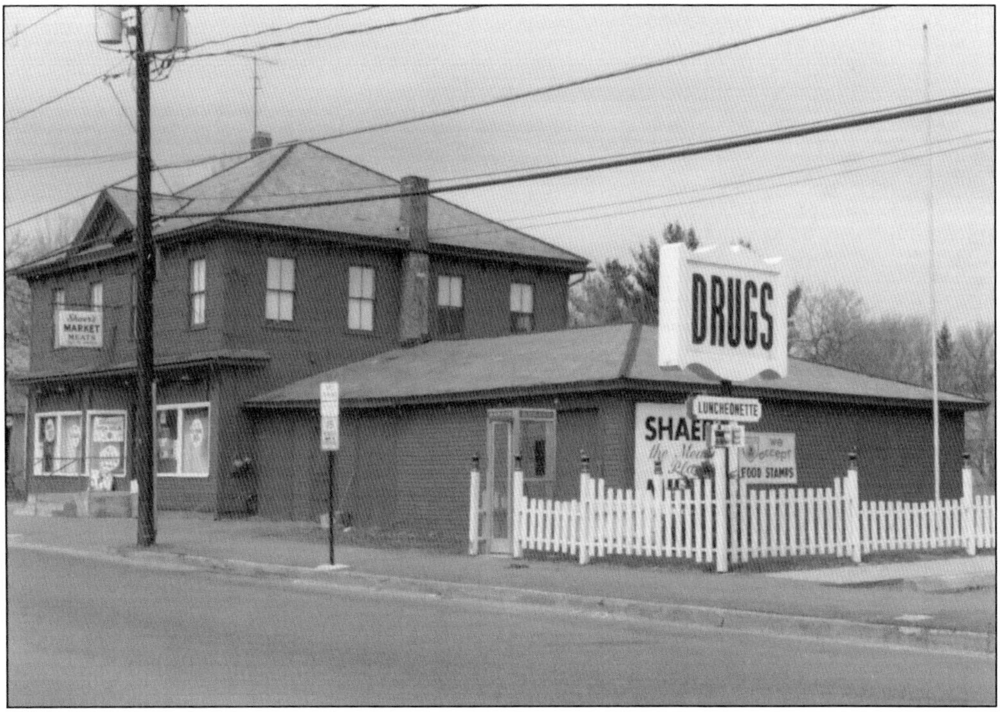

After Ferry & Bardwell, the grocery business was run by Walter Bodman and later by Domit "Dom" Shaer. The author remembers stopping at Shaer's Market, shown here *c.* 1970, on his way home from Granger School. The building was demolished in 1986. (Courtesy of Jean Welt Taylor.)

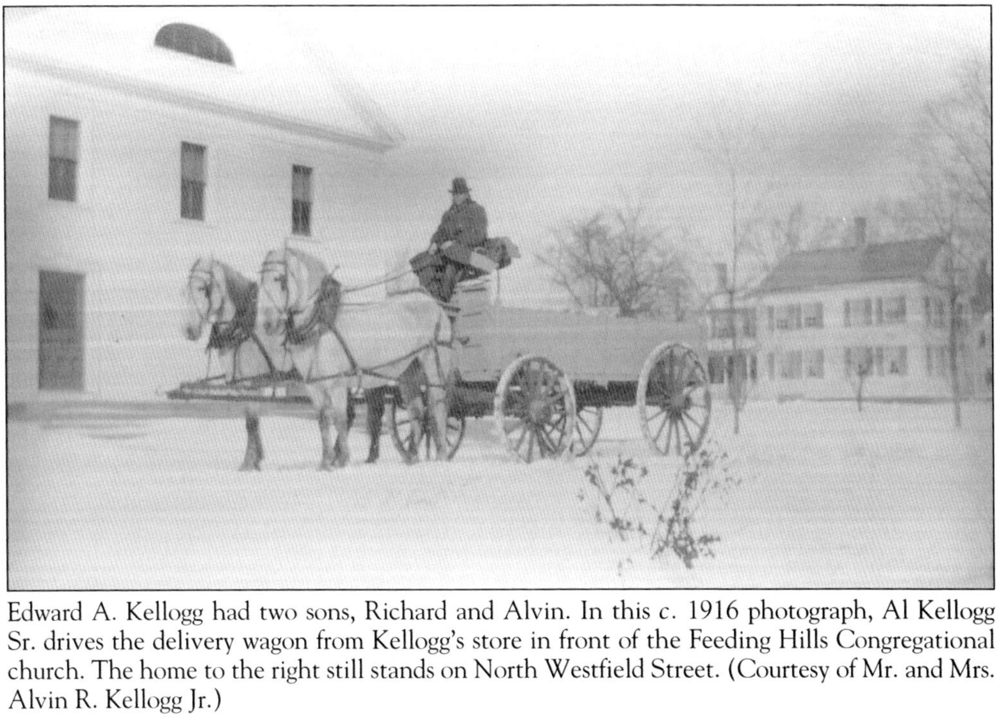

Edward A. Kellogg had two sons, Richard and Alvin. In this *c.* 1916 photograph, Al Kellogg Sr. drives the delivery wagon from Kellogg's store in front of the Feeding Hills Congregational church. The home to the right still stands on North Westfield Street. (Courtesy of Mr. and Mrs. Alvin R. Kellogg Jr.)

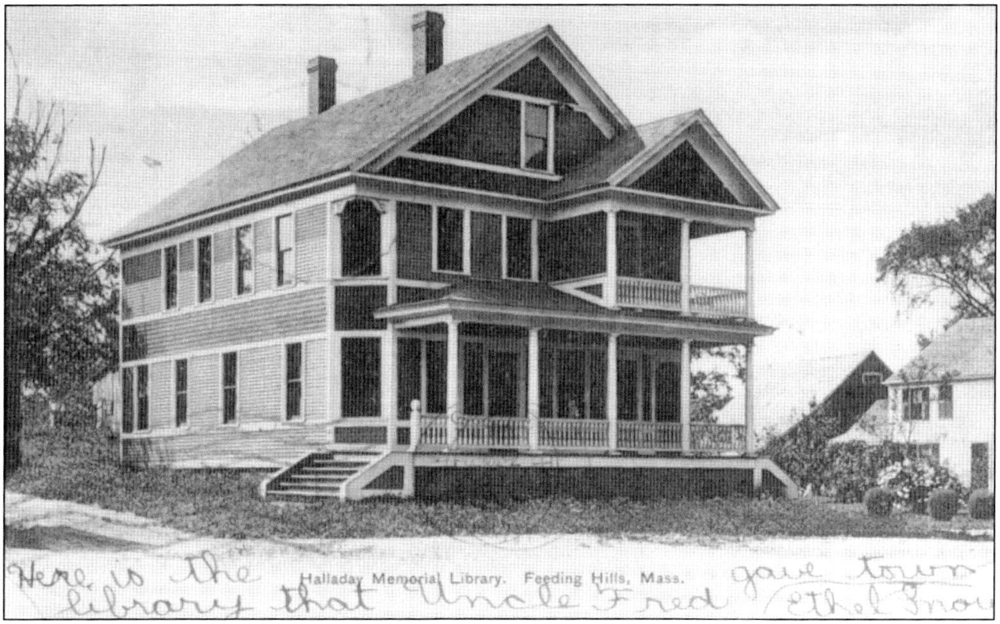

In 1905, Fred Halladay offered the Town "a piece of real estate with buildings thereon in Feeding Hills for the benefit of the inhabitants of the Feeding Hills part of the town of Agawam." Over time, the entire building came to be used as a library. In 1974, the Halladay Library was declared unsafe, and the books were removed. After remaining vacant for many years, the building at 14 South Westfield Street was recently renovated as office space. (Author's collection.)

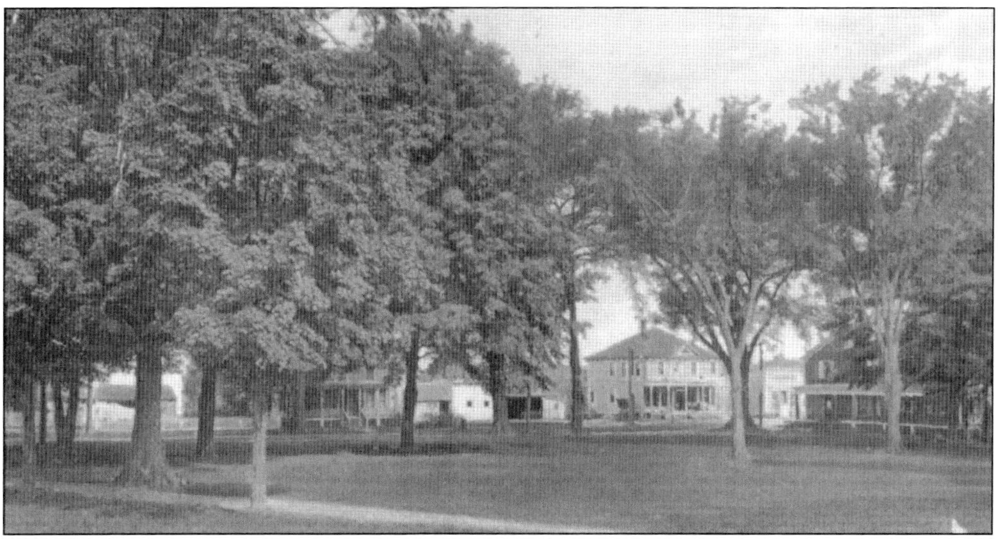

There has been a green at the corner of Springfield and South Westfield Streets since the earliest days of Feeding Hills. It was used as a place of parade for troops in both the Revolutionary War and the War of 1812. This 1907 postcard shows, from left to right, the Jimmie Moore House (see page 57), the Edward A. Kellogg residence (see page 62), Kellogg's store (see page 63), and the Burbank Hotel on the right. The green is now home to the Anne Sullivan Memorial (see page 46) and the Anne Sullivan sculpture *Water* by Mico Kaufman that was dedicated in June 1992. (Author's collection.)

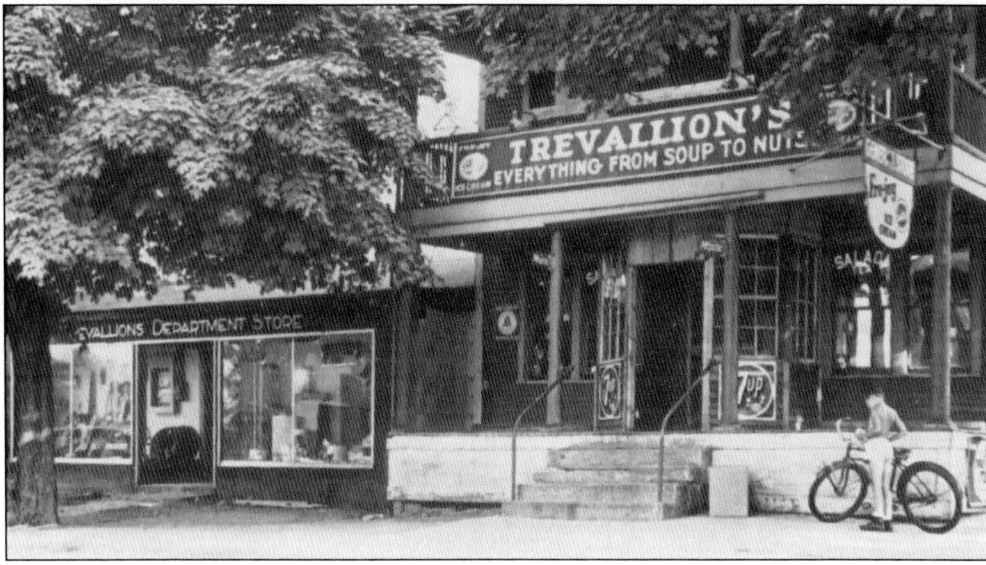

Located in Feeding Hills Center just east of the green on the south side of Springfield Street, Trevallion's, shown *c.* 1946, was truly a general store that sold just about everything. A department store was added to the main store just before World War II. Trevallion's closed by the mid-1950s. (Courtesy of Jean Welt Taylor.)

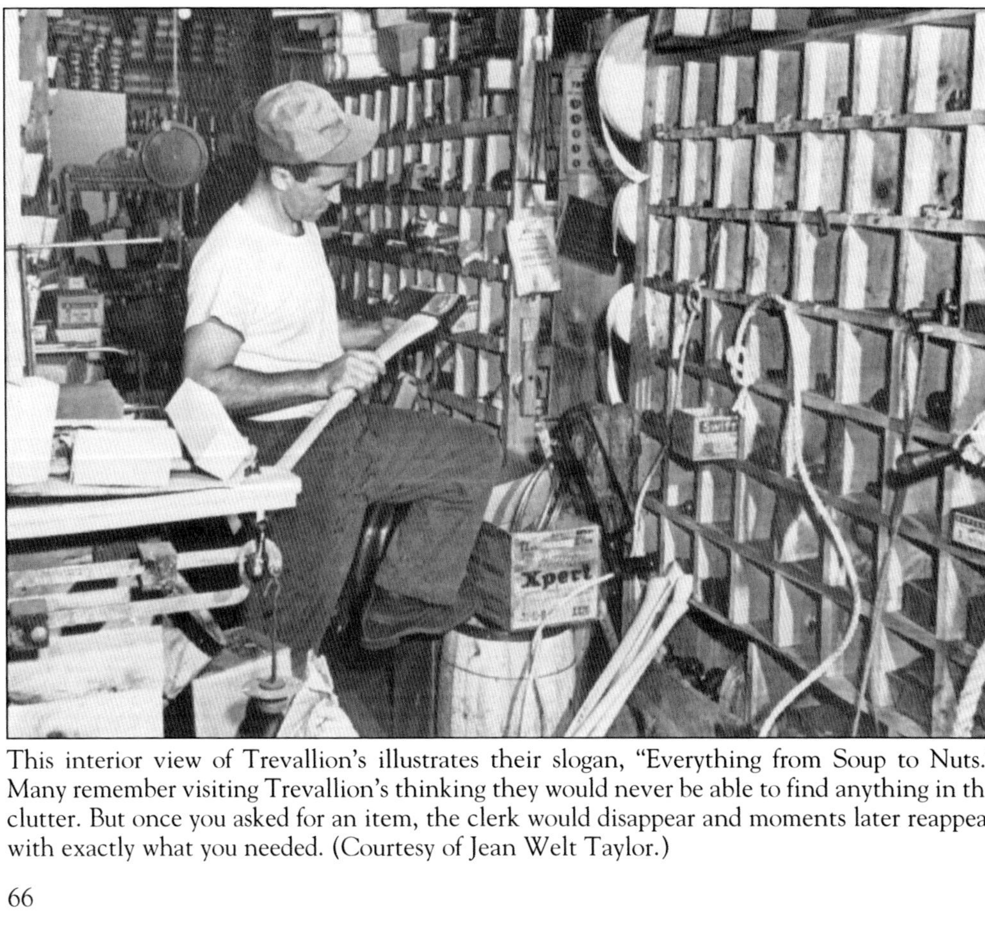

This interior view of Trevallion's illustrates their slogan, "Everything from Soup to Nuts." Many remember visiting Trevallion's thinking they would never be able to find anything in the clutter. But once you asked for an item, the clerk would disappear and moments later reappear with exactly what you needed. (Courtesy of Jean Welt Taylor.)

Five

AGRICULTURE

With the exception of the woolen mill on Elm Street, the distillery on Main Street, and a few other small industries, Agawam was primarily a farming community well into the 20th century. There were many dairy farms, tobacco farms, and later market gardens, as well as several greenhouse ranges that raised everything from asparagus to potted plants. The 1960s and 1970s saw massive tracts of farmland in Feeding Hills become subdivisions, a trend that continues today. The 1999 street list contains just 23 names listed as "farmer, farm worker, or farm manager," or just .07 percent of the current estimated population of over 32,000.

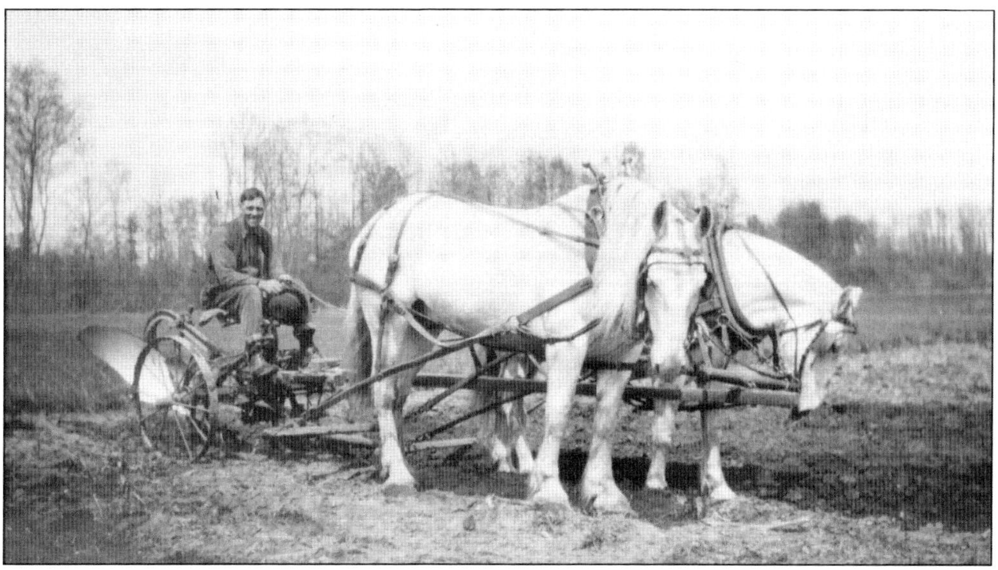

Before the use of tractors became widespread, a team of good horses was indispensable. Here, Al Kellogg Sr. is seen *c.* 1917 on his North Westfield Street farm ready for some spring plowing. (Courtesy of Mr. and Mrs. Alvin R. Kellogg Jr.)

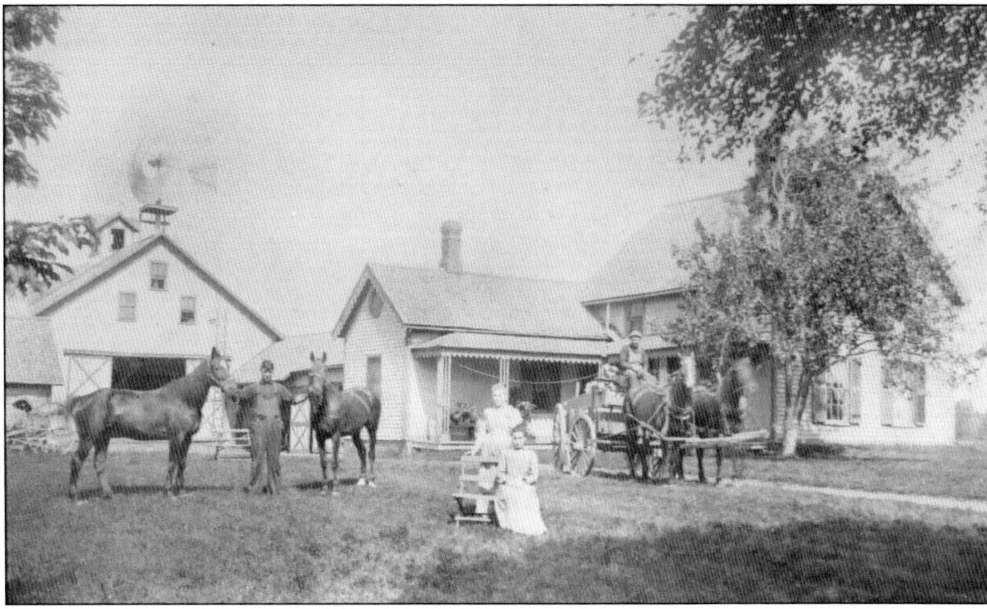

The Clark Jones Farm was located at 589 River Road and is shown *c*. 1900. This later became the home of Mr. and Mrs. George Reynolds (see page 44). The home is nearly identical today; the front porch has been enclosed, but the wonderful "cake icing" trim remains. The barns were demolished many years ago. (Courtesy of Esther Reynolds.)

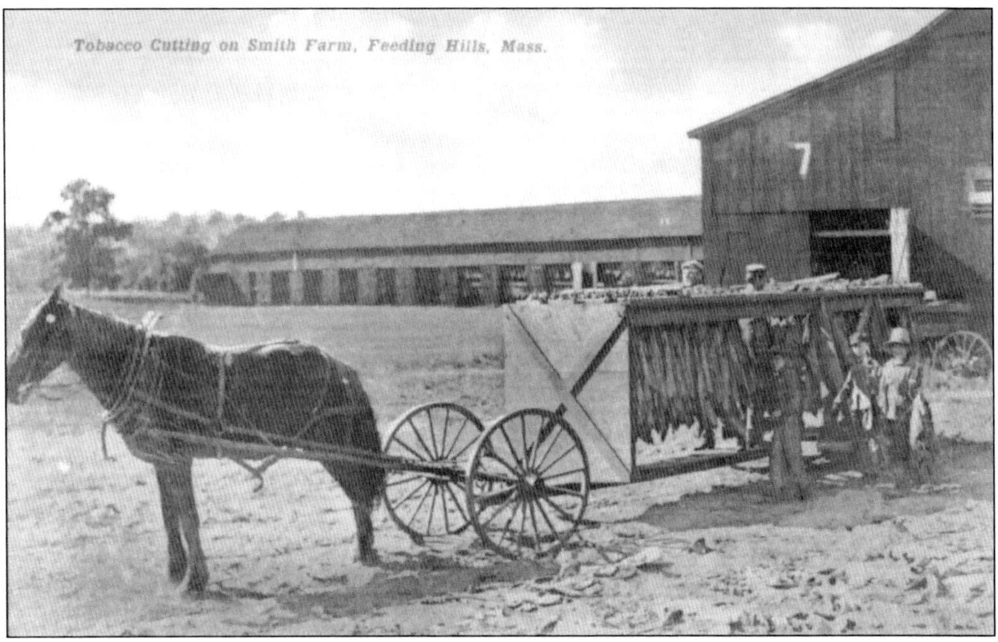

In 1858, Hinsdale Smith, treasurer of the Hampden Cigar Company, owned 20 acres tillage, 2 horses, 4 oxen, 3 cows, 3 two-year-olds, and 4 swine. By 1915, as the Cuba Connecticut Tobacco Company, the farm had over 400 acres of tobacco under cultivation, extending west from Silver Street past South Westfield Street. Bowles Airport was built on the east farm in 1928 (see page 96). (Courtesy of Rick Bellico.)

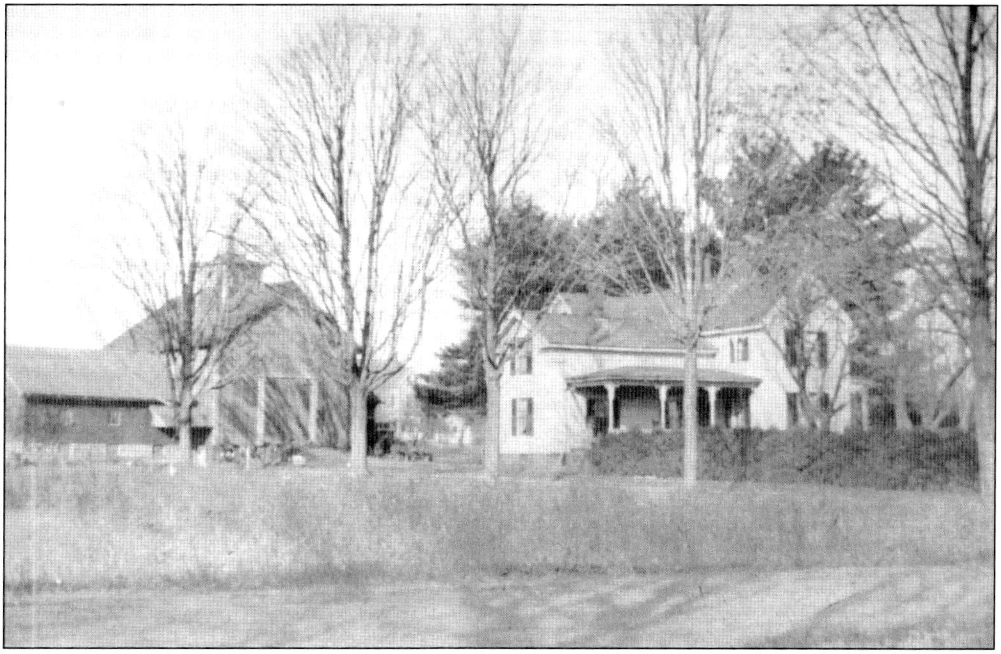

The Charles T. Crouss dairy farm was located on the corner of Suffield and Silver Streets. The home and barns were demolished when the Southgate Plaza was built there in the 1970s. (Courtesy of David Cesan.)

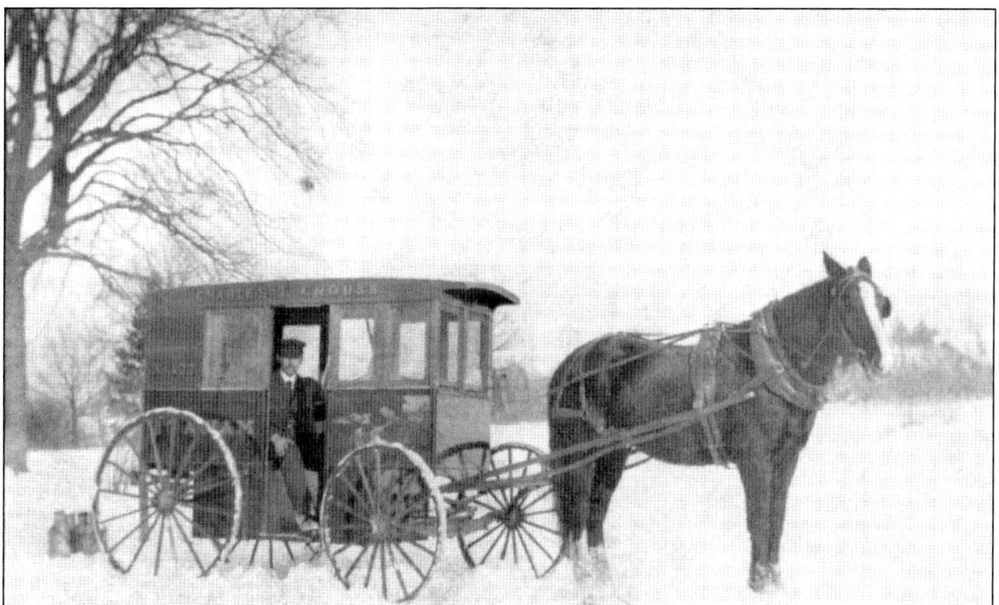

Charles Crouss was a well-known dairyman and milk dealer with routes in West Springfield and Agawam for more than 60 years. He and his brothers, Willard and Herman, were also partners in a grocery business. Charles died at age 93. (Courtesy of David Cesan.)

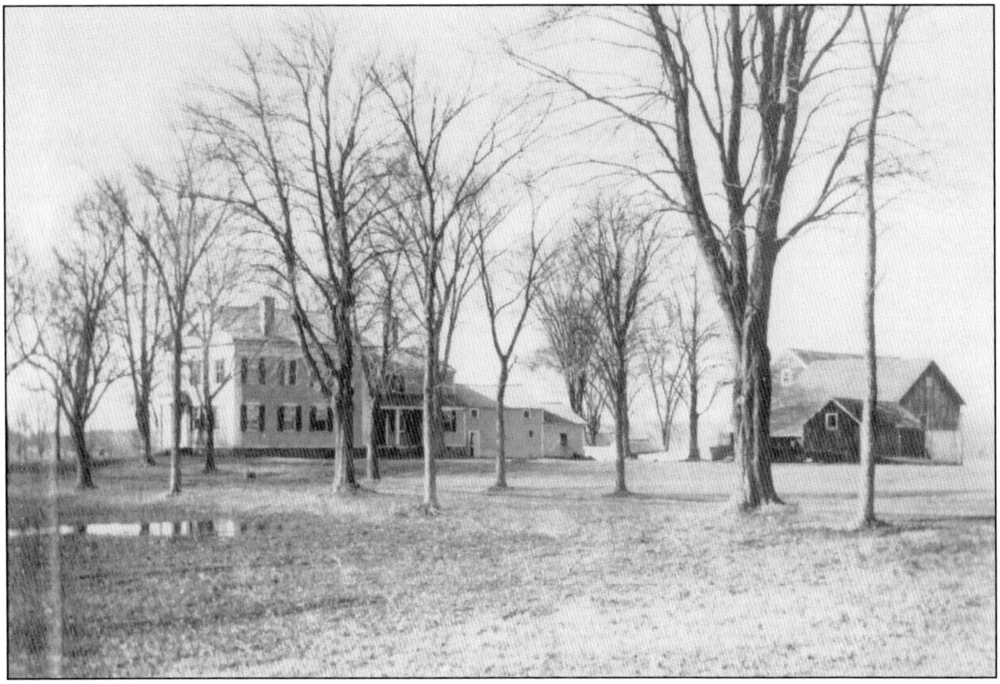

This photograph, taken on April 1, 1905, by Elmer Bodurtha, shows the farm purchased from Fremont King by Dwight E. Bailey in 1903. This homestead was located approximately where Crestview County Club is located on Shoemaker Lane. The home and barns have since been demolished. (Courtesy of Mr. and Mrs. Howard Bailey.)

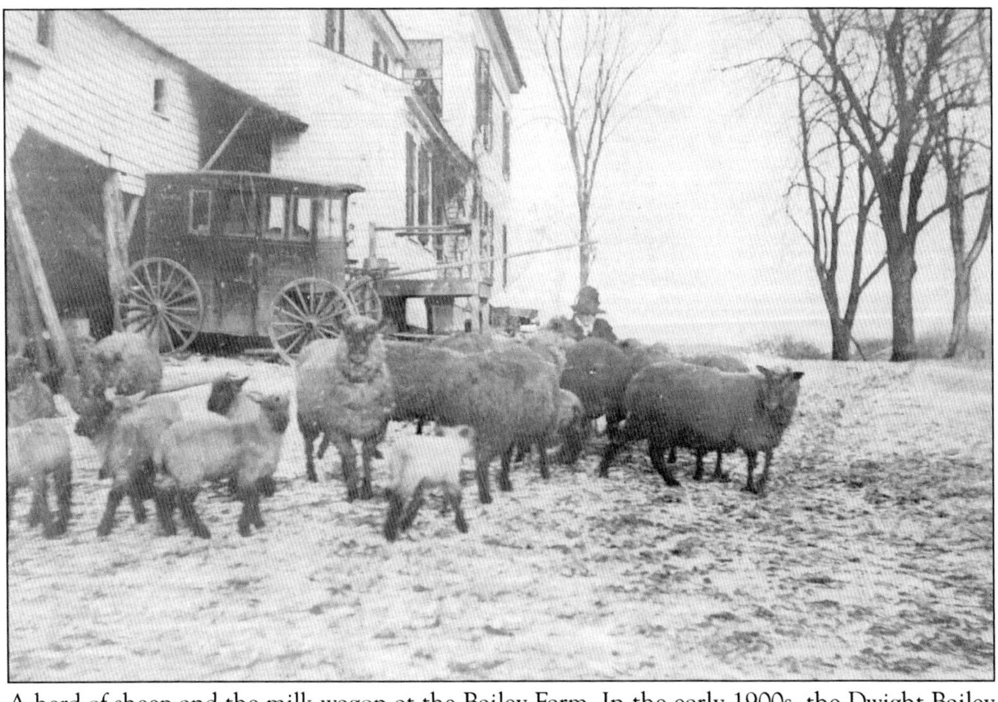

A herd of sheep and the milk wagon at the Bailey Farm. In the early 1900s, the Dwight Bailey farm was one of several in town of over 100 acres. (Courtesy of Dorothy Dickinson.)

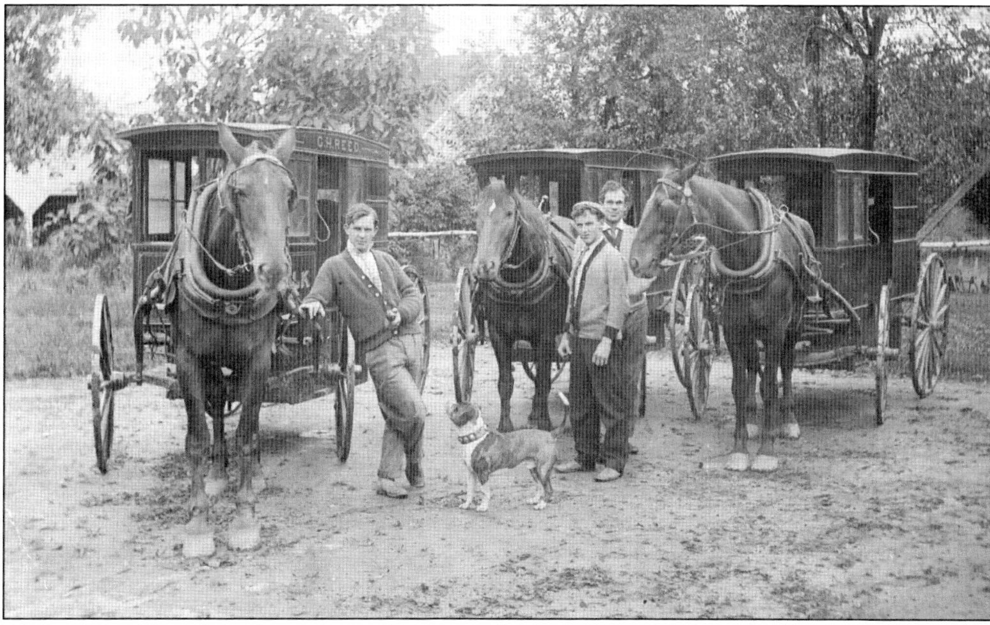

George Reed lived at the corner of Main and Central Streets. Shown are his fleet of milk wagons and their drivers. (Courtesy of Donald Goss.)

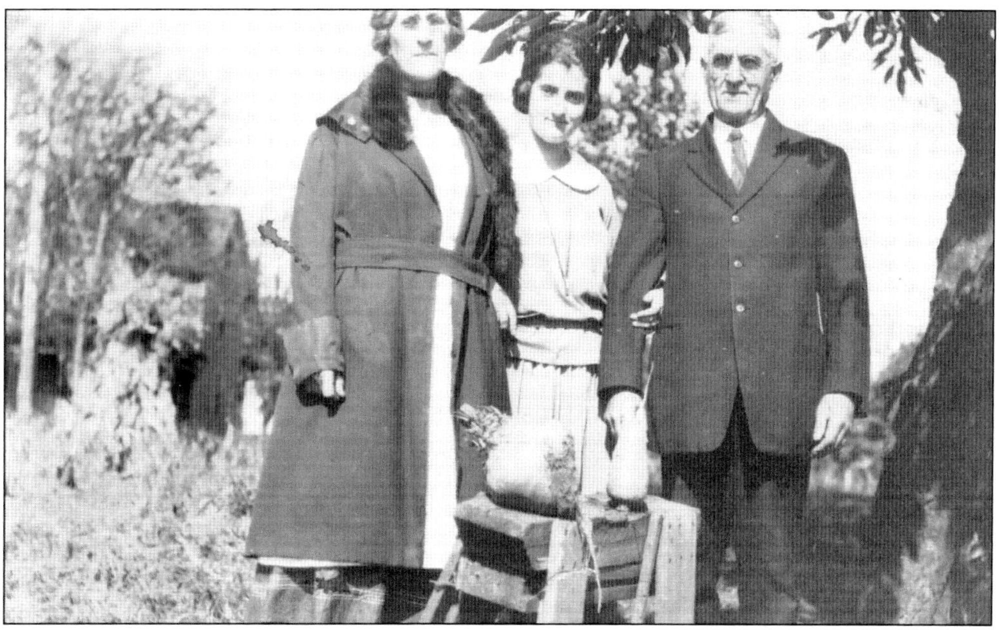

Daucette, Euphemie, and Yvonne LeBlanc display their prize-winning beet and carrot, September 1919. (Courtesy of Mr. and Mrs. Robert Keefe.)

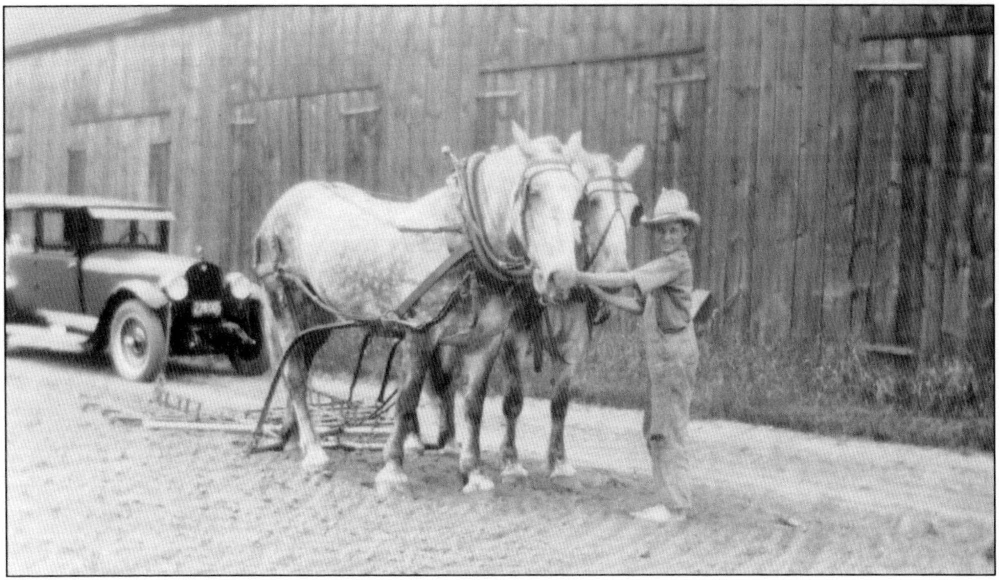

Al Kellogg Jr. is in front of the Kellogg Farm tobacco barns with his team and harrow, c. 1917. Al Kellogg Jr. is a graduate of the Stockbridge School of Agriculture and worked on his family's farm for many years. (Courtesy of Mr. and Mrs. Alvin R. Kellogg Jr.)

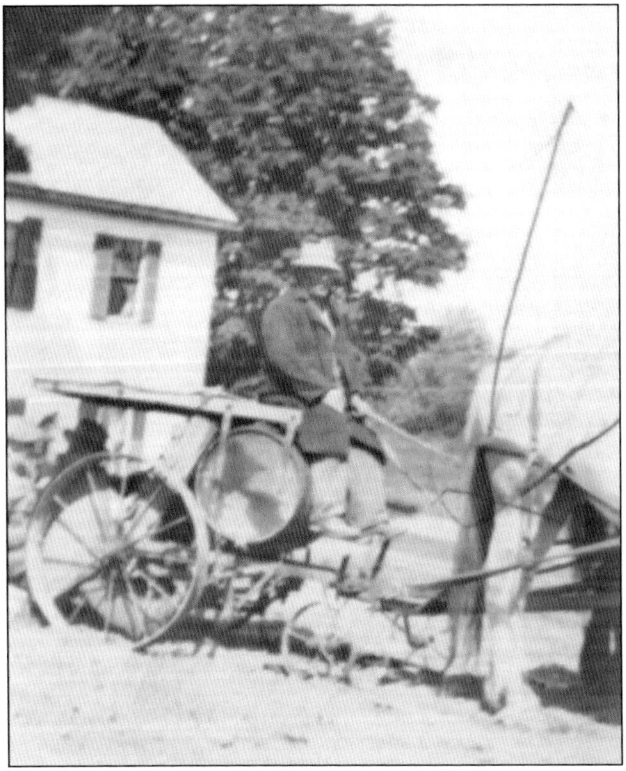

Tobacco was an important crop in Agawam for hundreds of years. In 1915, there were more than 200 tobacco barns located in Agawam and Feeding Hills. The world's largest grower and packer of broadleaf tobacco, the J.E. Shephard Company was established in 1888 and grew tobacco in Feeding Hills. This c. 1915 photograph shows an early horse-drawn tobacco transplanting machine. (Courtesy of the Walter T. Kerr family.)

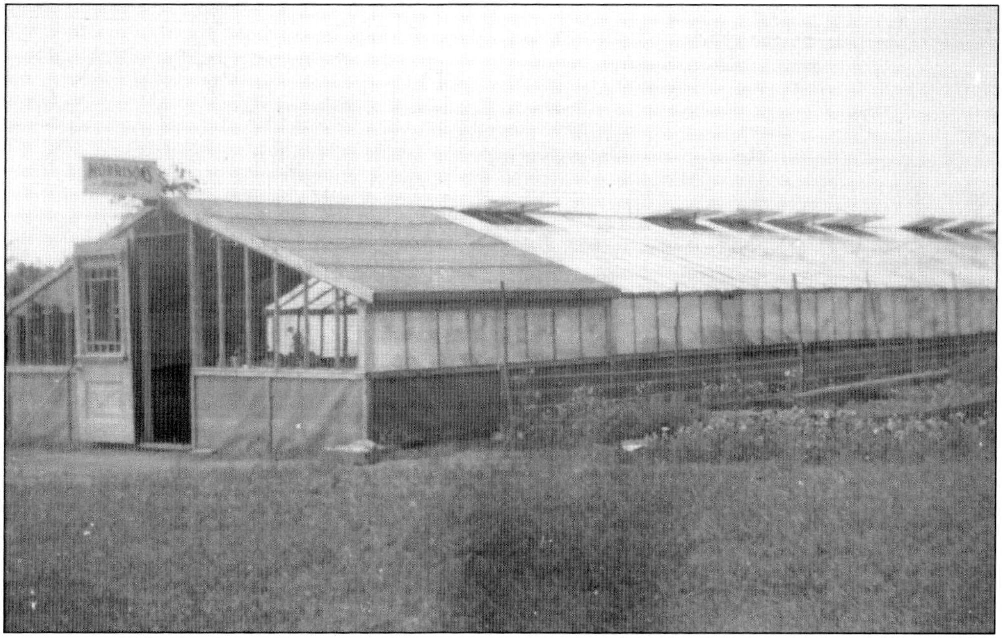

Located on River Road, Morrison's Greenhouse grew a variety of flowers. They were especially well known for their violets. (Courtesy of Leslie and Dale Melanson.)

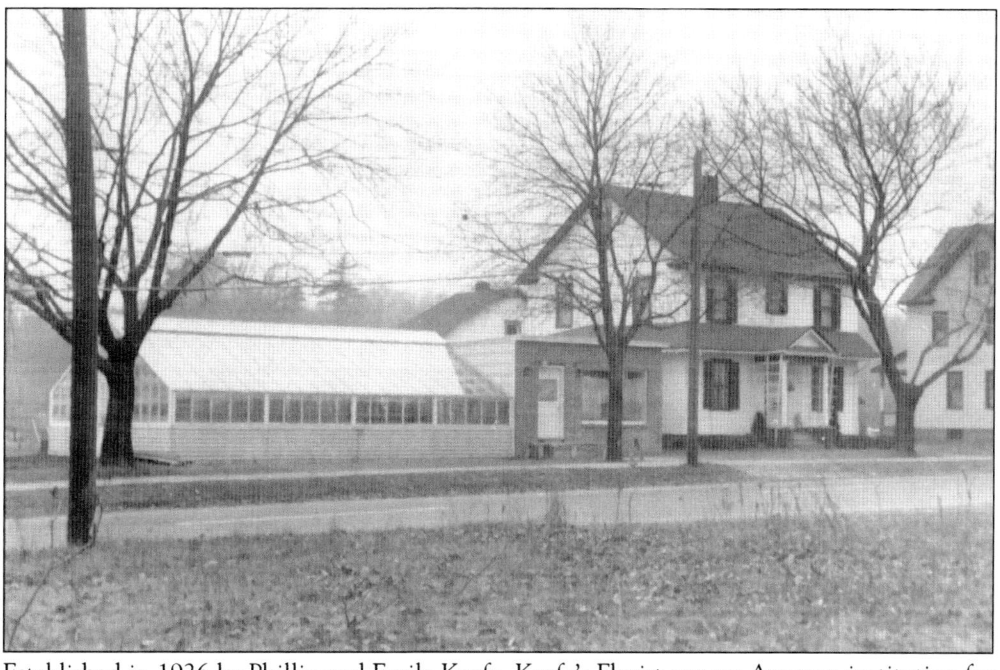

Established in 1926 by Phillip and Emily Keefe, Keefe's Florist was an Agawam institution for almost 70 years. Several greenhouses were added over the years to the Keefe residence and flower shop. When the Keefes retired in 1993, the business was bought by Dennis Librera and Tom Fredette, who operate it as Floral Concepts by Tom. This photograph was taken in the 1940s. (Courtesy of Mr. and Mrs. Robert Keefe.)

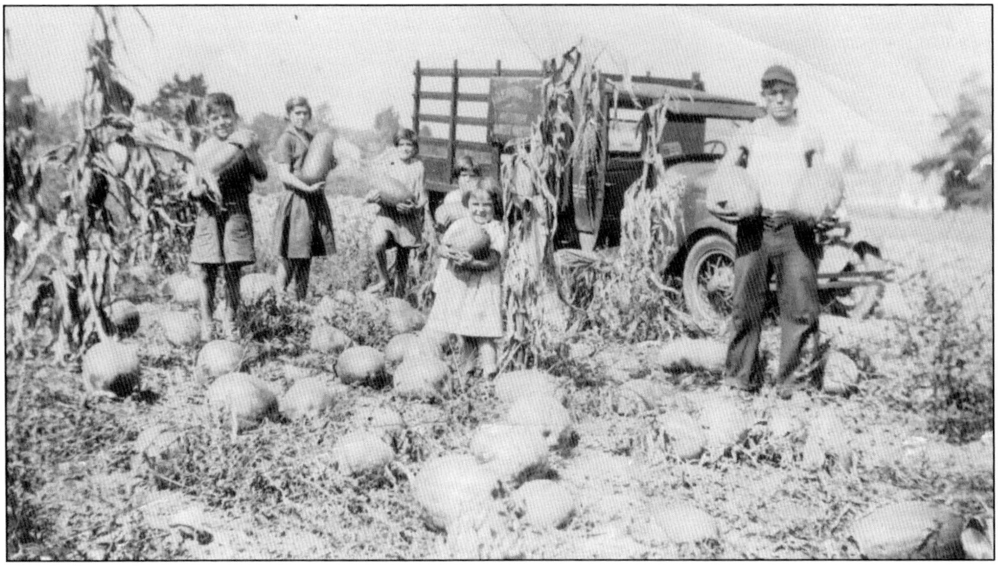

At the Joseph Morris Farm c. 1933 those shown picking watermelons are, from left to right, Herb, Betty, Rose, Dorothy, Ann, and Frank Morris. Herb Morris was later president of the Springfield Cooperative Farmer's Market for many years. (Courtesy of Dorothy Morris.)

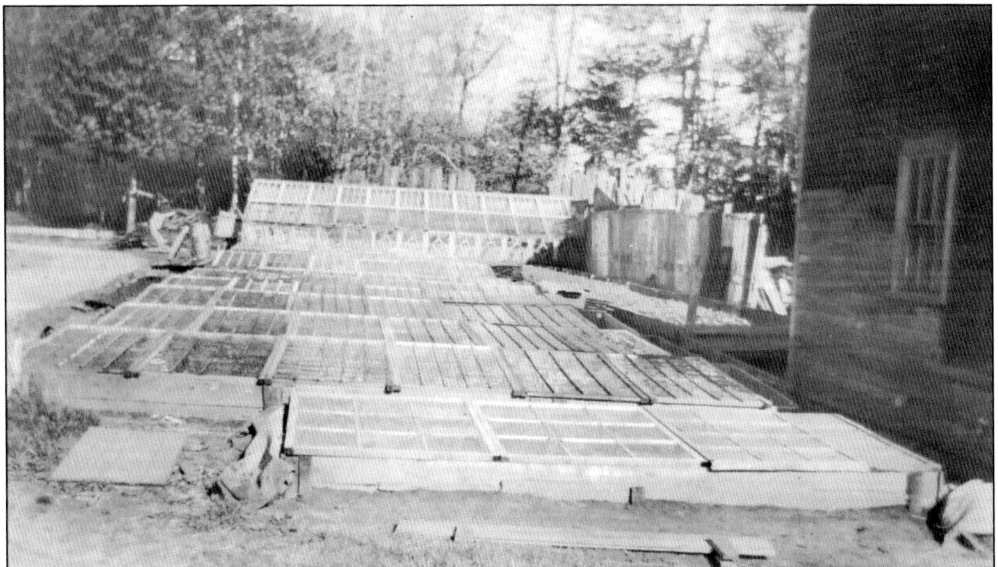

The Morris family has operated a market garden on Rowley Street since 1906, when Frank and Maria Morris purchased the property. Plants to be grown in the field were given a head start in these hotbeds. Beans were a specialty; the author remembers Herb Morris bringing truckloads of beans to the farmer's market on Avocado Street in Springfield. (Courtesy of Dorothy Morris.)

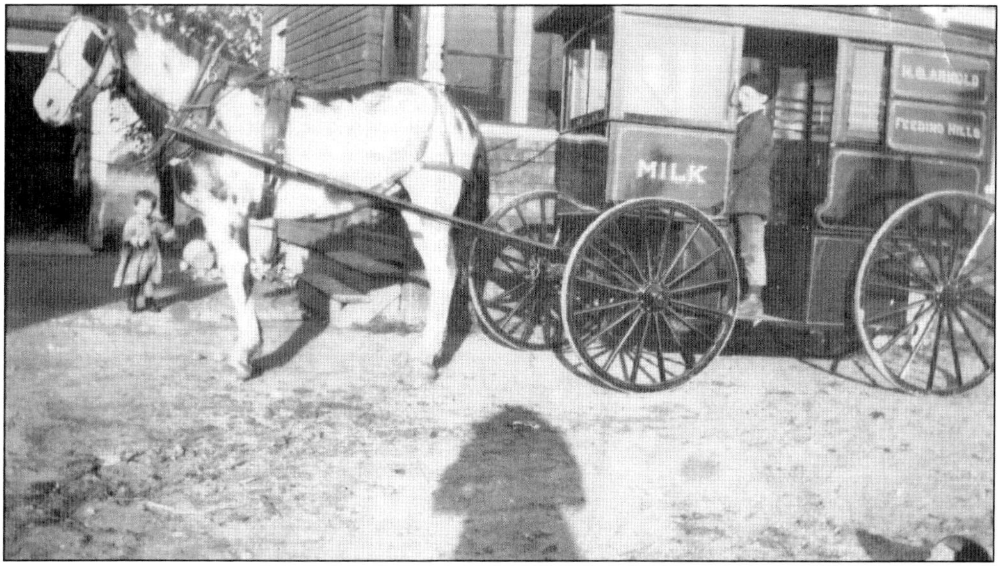

The Arnold brothers were well-known milk dealers. The H.G. (Henry) Arnold Dairy was located at 850 Springfield Street. A 1928 directory also lists "Philip Arnold, milk dealer" at 556 Springfield Street. A third brother, Andrew, had a farm at 1131 Springfield Street, which was later bought by Erminio Cecchi (see page 82). Barbara Arnold lived at 1103 Springfield Street, the current Sacred Heart Church rectory. (Courtesy of Rick Miller.)

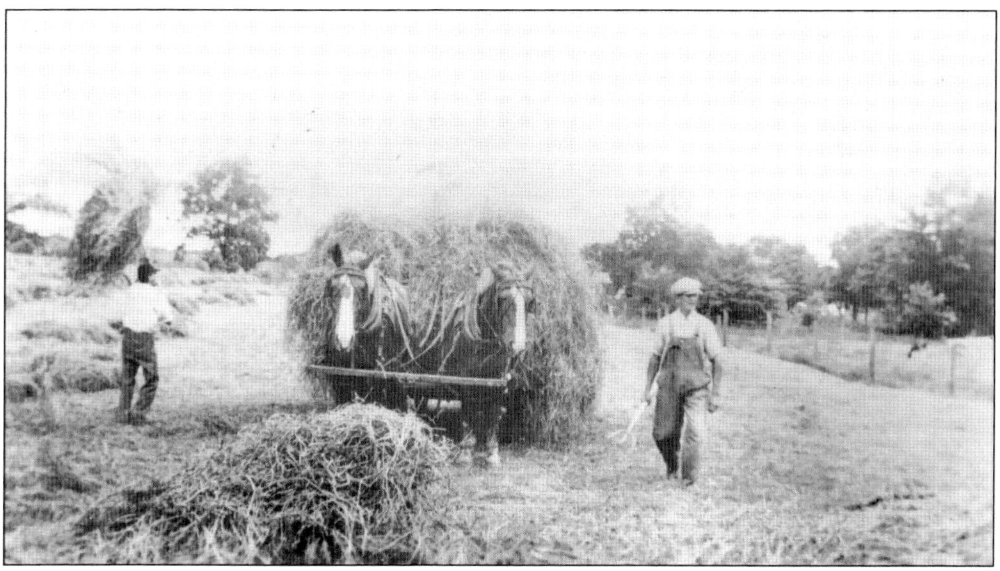

Giles Halladay operated a farm at the corner of North Westfield and North Street Extension and raised turkeys across North Westfield Street. He was a selectman in town for 27 years. Halladay is shown haying at the farm in this c. 1932 photograph. (Courtesy of Bernice [Halladay] Burton.)

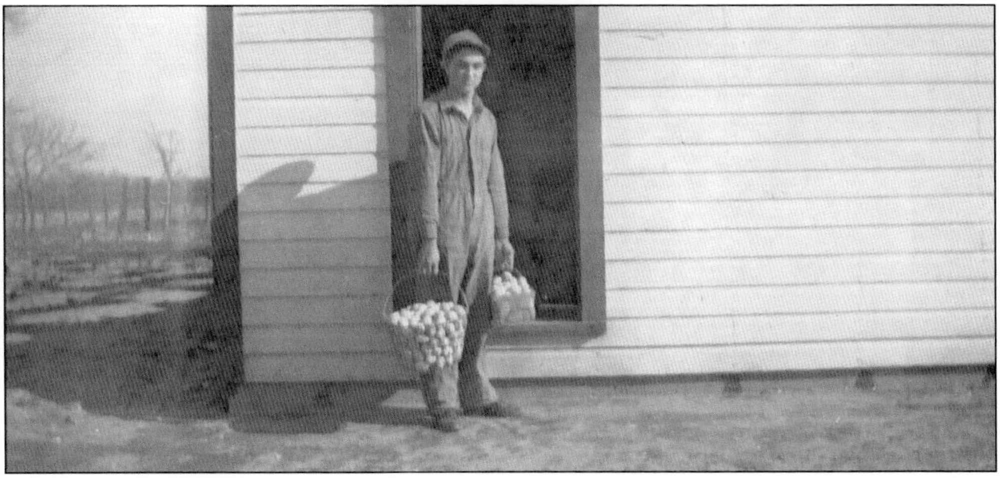

Before Albert Christopher became known as the "Corn King," he was known for his chickens. In August 1936, he built this two-story chicken coop, which still stands at the intersection of Garden and Poplar Streets. In 1938, he was national 4-H club poultry judging champion, the first in the East. He and his brother Michael sold eggs, broilers, and vegetables from their truck. (Courtesy of Jenny Christopher.)

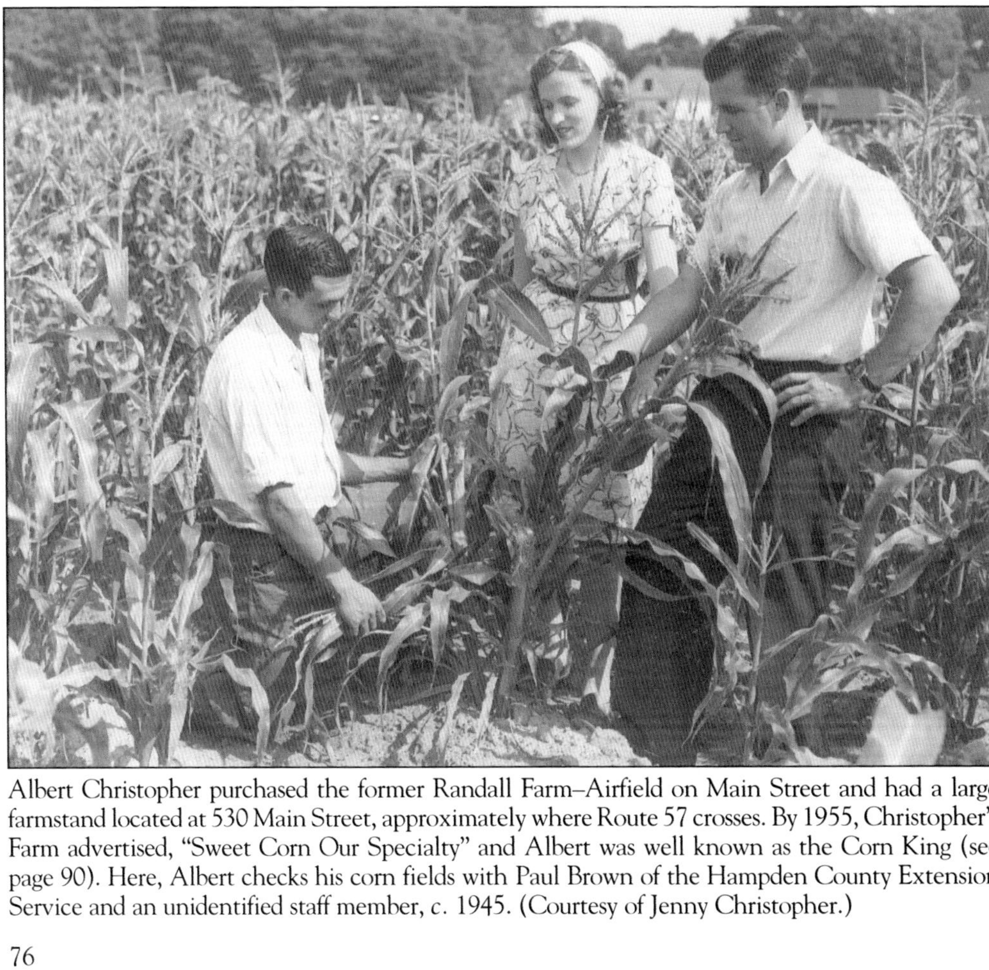

Albert Christopher purchased the former Randall Farm–Airfield on Main Street and had a large farmstand located at 530 Main Street, approximately where Route 57 crosses. By 1955, Christopher's Farm advertised, "Sweet Corn Our Specialty" and Albert was well known as the Corn King (see page 90). Here, Albert checks his corn fields with Paul Brown of the Hampden County Extension Service and an unidentified staff member, c. 1945. (Courtesy of Jenny Christopher.)

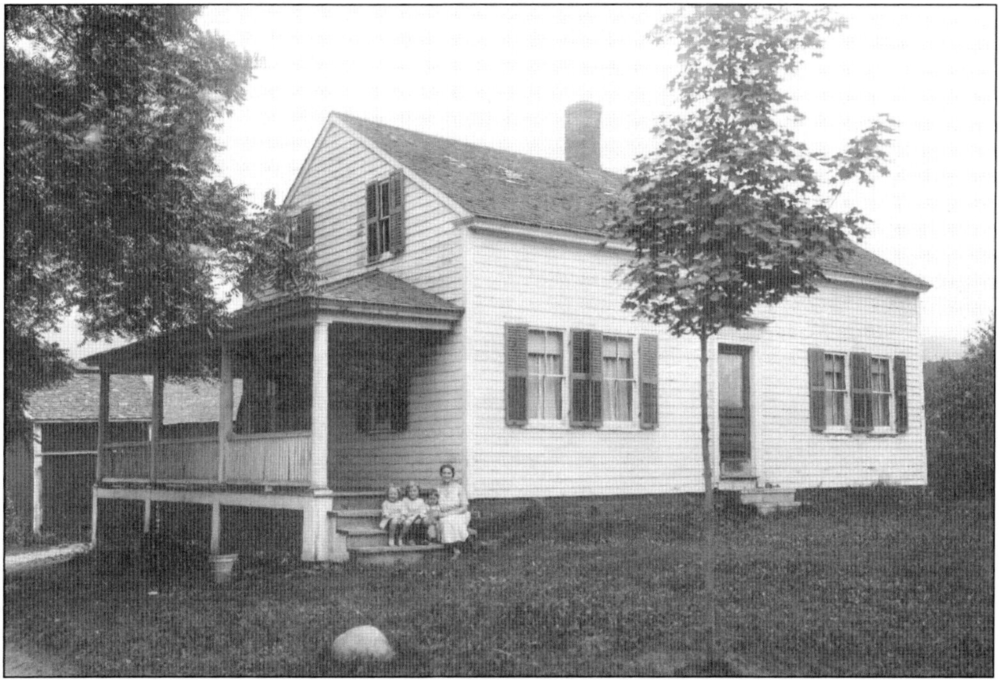

The Cesan family operated a large farm on North West Street for many years. They were known for their tomatoes and strawberries, among other crops. Pictured *c.* 1933 in front of the Cesan homestead, which still stands at 407 North West Street, are, from left to right, Edith, Bertha, Harry, and Olga Cesan. Noel Brown now farms most of the former Cesan property. (Courtesy of Marilyn [Cesan] Campagnari.)

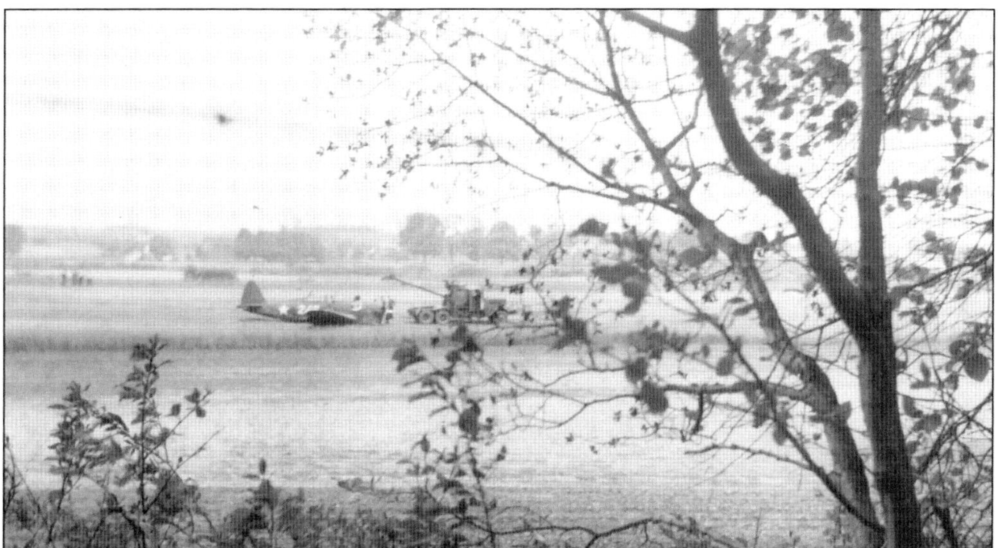

During World War II, a military plane crash-landed on the Cesan farm. Marilyn (Cesan) Campagnari remembers that once the authorities arrived on the scene they cordoned off the area and would not let anyone near it. The plane was dismantled, put on a large trailer by crane, covered with a tarp, and hauled away. (Courtesy of Marilyn [Cesan] Campagnari.)

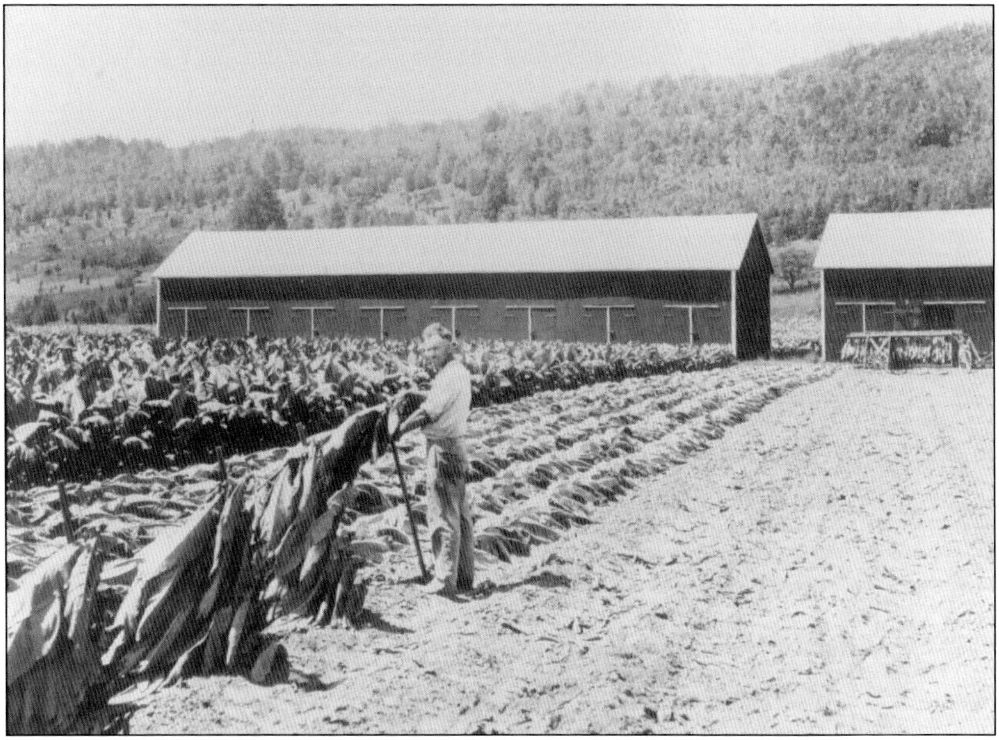

The Kerr family operated a large farm on the north end of North West Street for many years. This 1927 photograph shows James Kerr in the tobacco field. In the distance, a load of tobacco heads for the barn to be hung in the rafters to dry. (Courtesy of the Walter T. Kerr family.)

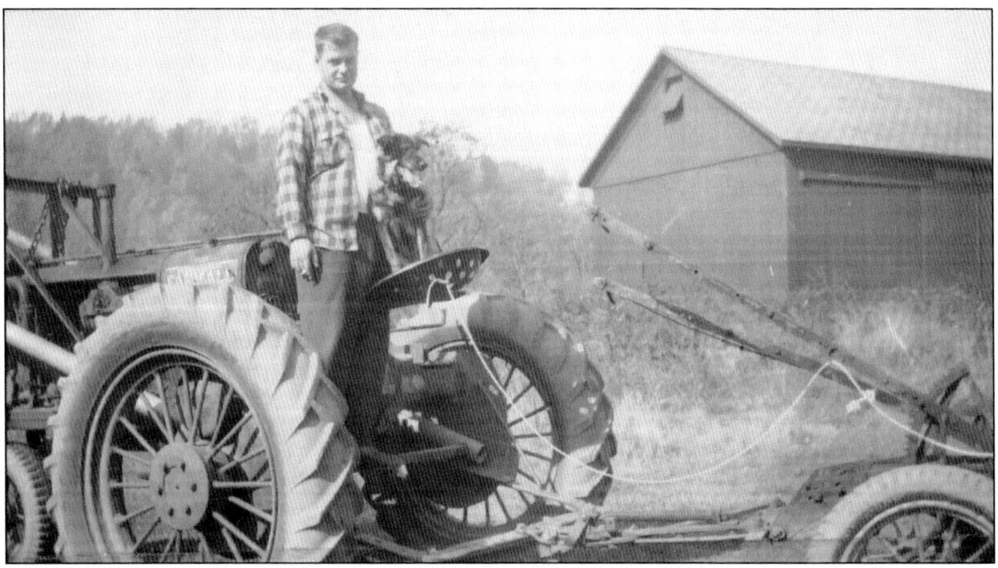

Walter T. Kerr is shown on the Kerr family Farmall tractor in 1946. After serving in the army during World War II, he returned to Agawam and ran for public office, serving on the board of selectmen for many years and then as Massachusetts state representative from 1966 to 1970. (Courtesy of the Walter T. Kerr family.)

The Taylor Farm was located on South Westfield Street. Together, the Taylor brothers farmed more than 100 acres. Shown here in 1949 is Jean Welt backing a tobacco rack into the barn using an old Fordson tractor. (Courtesy Jean Welt Taylor.)

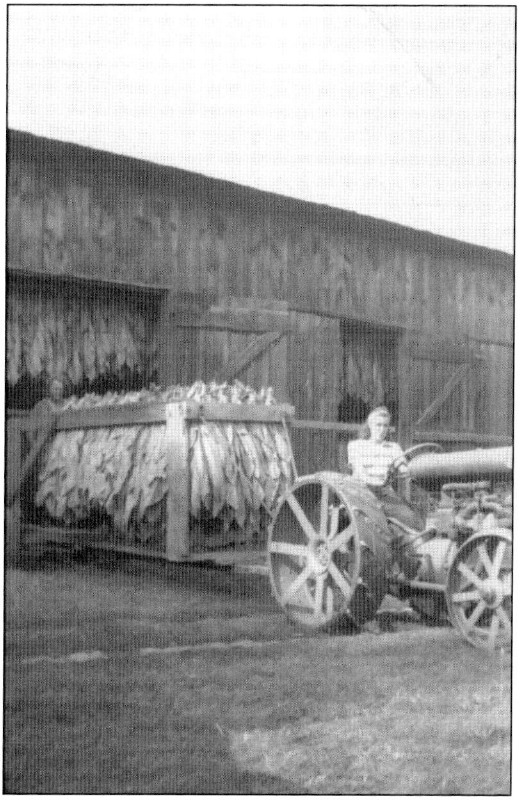

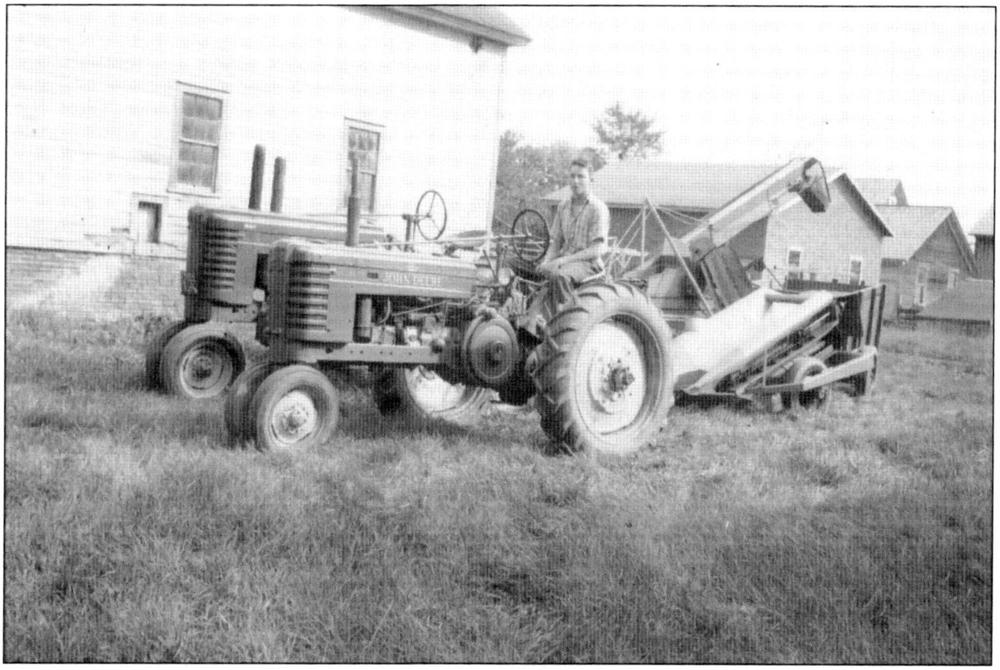

Don Taylor sits on his cousin's John Deere tractor, with a corn picker behind, South Westfield Street, *c.* 1948 (Courtesy Jean Welt Taylor.)

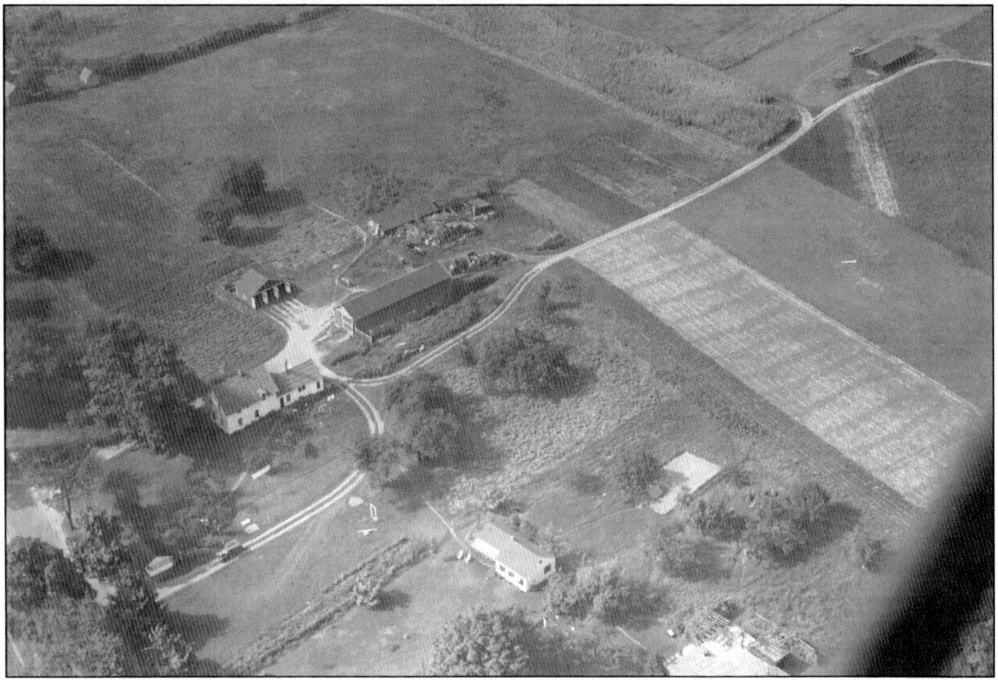

Sumner and Lillie Schwartz operated a farm for many years at 639 River Road. The Schwartz family grew a variety of crops, including strawberries and tobacco. The Schwartz homestead, lower left, was demolished in 1971. The homes on Glendale Street now occupy the former Schwartz farm. (Courtesy of Esther [Schwartz] Reynolds.)

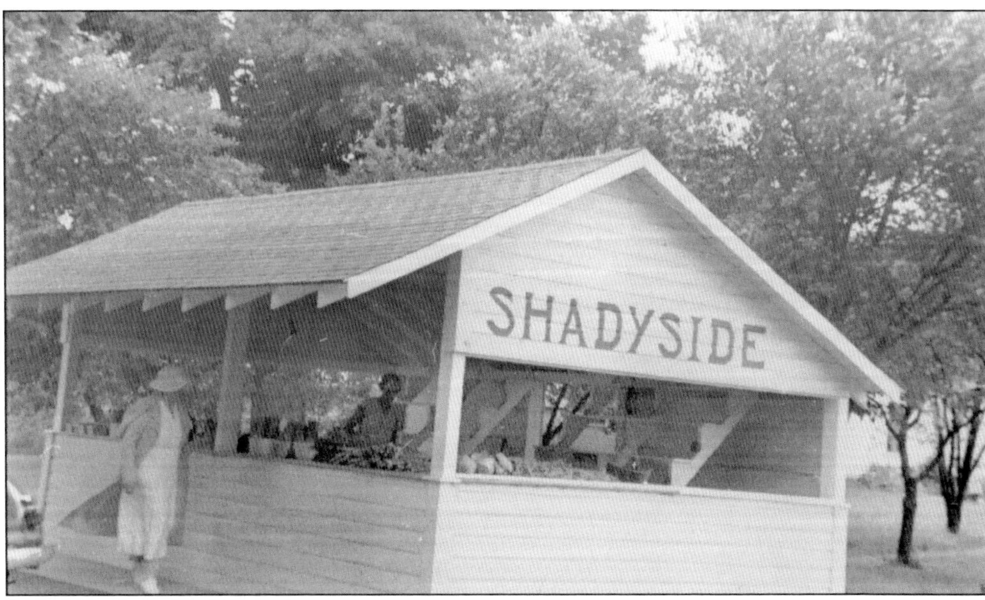

The Schwartz family also operated a roadside stand on River Road called Shadyside, where they sold the fresh vegetables grown on their farm. (Courtesy of Esther [Schwartz] Reynolds.)

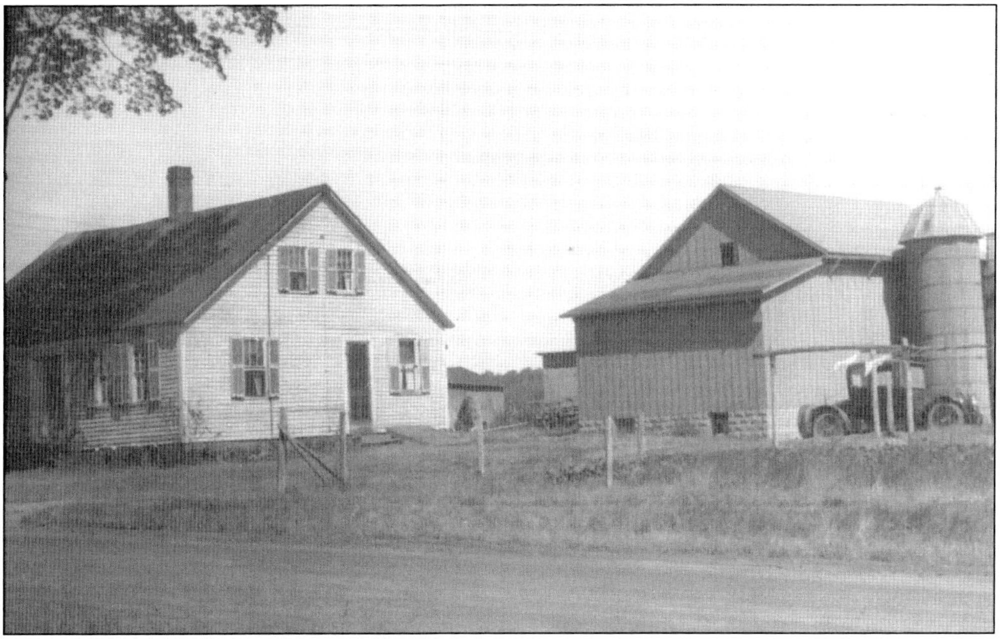

The Leon Hale farm, shown *c.* 1924, was at 39 South Street (now 164 South Street). The original owner named the farm Glendale. (Courtesy of June Cook.)

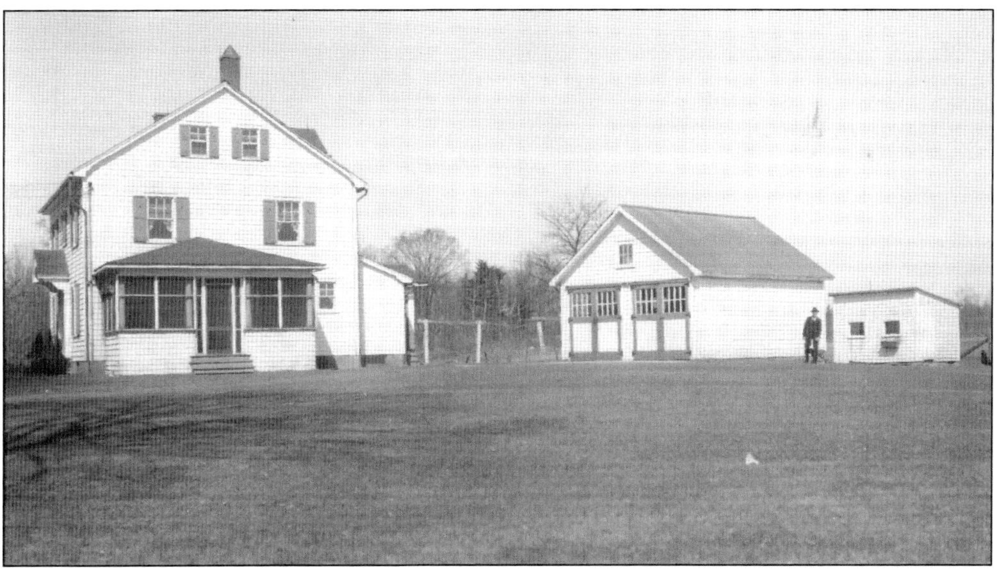

The new Leon Hale house at 164 South Street was built *c.* 1930 across the driveway from the house shown above. The older home was then demolished. A barn and chicken coop were also built on the property and stood until 1976, when they were destroyed by fire. The farm is currently owned by Leon Hale's grandson, Donald Hale Cook. (Courtesy of June Cook.)

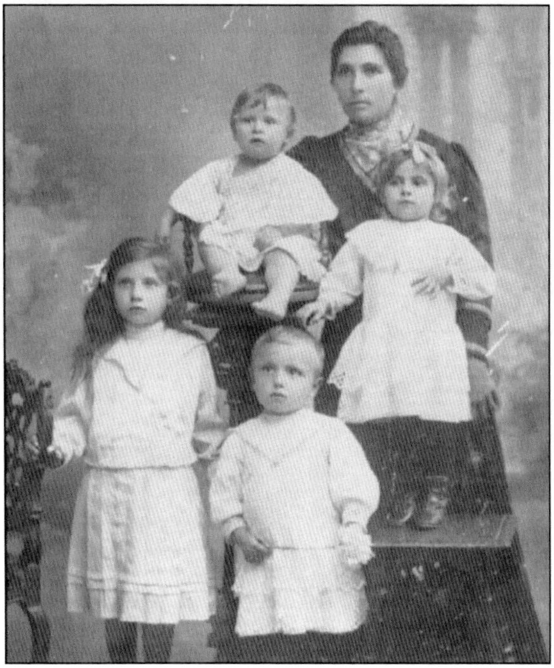

Shown, from left to right, are Henrietta, Erminio, Serafina, and twins Josephine and Peter Cecchi, c. 1913. Guiseppe Cecco (later Cecchi) moved here in 1924, buying 60 acres of the John Hubbard farm located at Hubbard Corners at Shoemaker Lane and Suffield Street. Henrietta married Carl Lanati and moved to Windsor Locks. Josephine married Frank Chriscola Jr. (see page 83) in 1936. Peter married the former Stella Morelli in 1937. Erminio married the former Anna Ferrero in 1939. In the early years, the Cecchis grew mostly peaches, plums, and apples. (Courtesy of Anna Cecchi.)

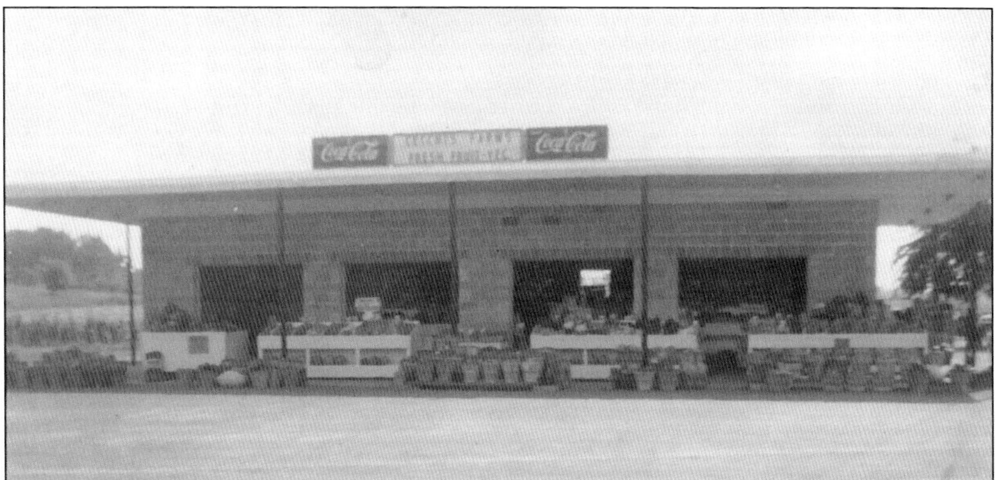

In 1946, the author's grandparents, Erminio and Anna Cecchi, purchased "a certain plot of land of or about thirty acres known as the Bailey Homestead" at 1131 Springfield Street in Feeding Hills for $12,000 and moved there with their two young children, Carol and Robert. Later, the Cooley property on the opposite side of Springfield Street was added. They sold vegetables from tables under the trees in the front yard. In 1947 the first greenhouse was built, and in 1953 a permanent farmstand was added. It is now the largest farmstand in town and a Feeding Hills landmark. Erminio's son, Robert, and grandsons, Robert Jr. and Michael (the author's father and brothers), continue the family business. (Courtesy of Anna Cecchi.)

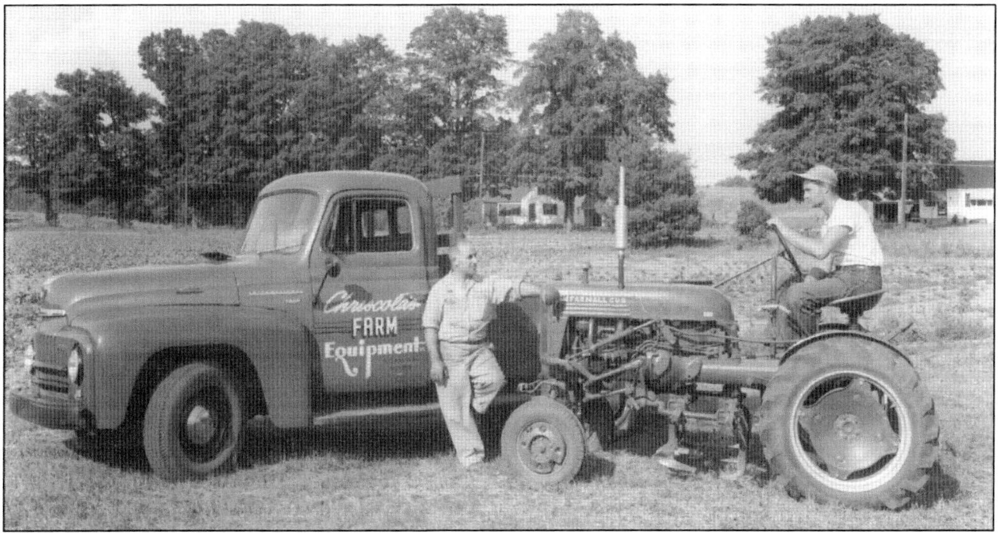

In 1928, Andrew and Frank Chriscola Jr. (see page 88) began selling McCormick-Deering equipment, selling one horse-drawn mower and one horse-drawn hay rake that first year. Later, their brother John joined them. The Chriscolas also farmed about 100 acres on Suffield Street and Shoemaker Lane until 1950. In this photograph, Frank Chriscola Jr. (left) talks with Sonny Kent of Suffield. The Chriscola brothers have served (and still serve) on many town boards and committees. Andrew died in the 1970s. (Courtesy of Frank Chriscola Jr.)

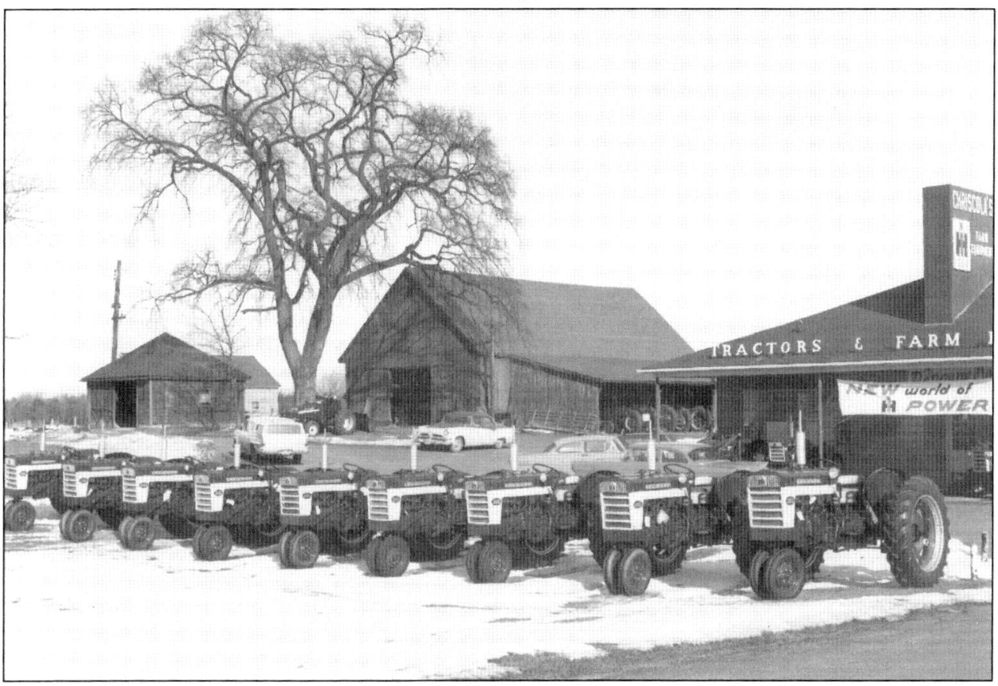

By the late 1950s, Chriscola's Farm Equipment was one of the largest International Harvester dealerships in the area and was the largest in New England for several years. Here, a fresh shipment of International 340s is on display in front of the dealership. Tractors were delivered by train, nine to a car. The property, located at 1123 Suffield Street, is now a used car dealership and machine shop. (Courtesy of Frank Chriscola Jr.)

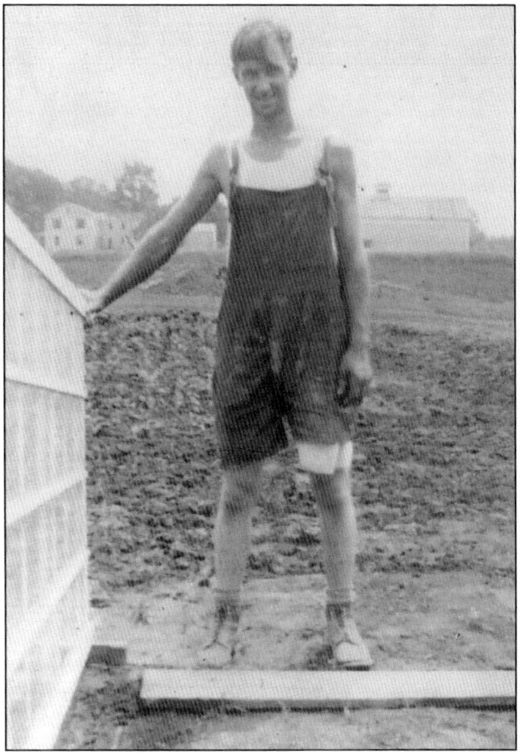

Frank W. Hess, who worked with Sam Woodbury at the Woodbury Nursery, is shown here in the late 1930s. The nursery was located on Main Street across from Meadow Street and later became the Lauriente Nursery. A nursing home now occupies the site. Sam's father was a partner in the Rood and Woodbury grocery stores in Springfield. In the background is the Randall Horse Farm, which had an airfield. The Randall farm was later bought by Albert Christopher (see page 76). (Courtesy of John Y. Hess.)

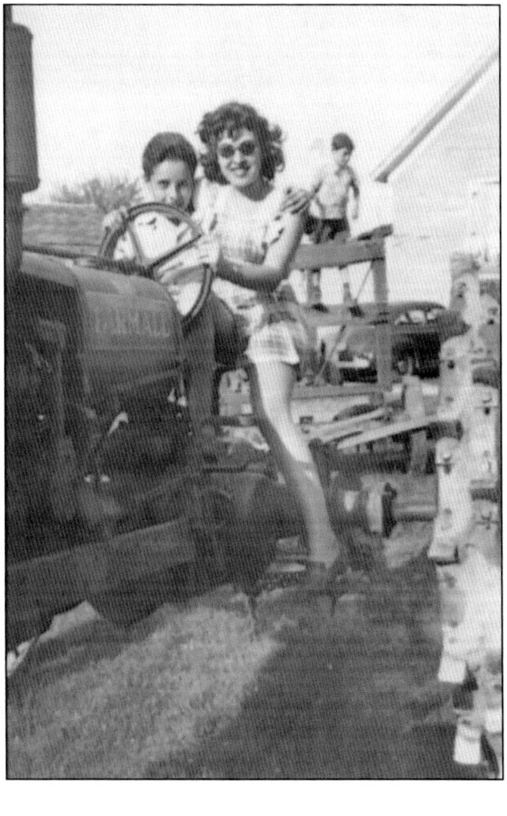

The former Barry farm (see page 60) at 573 South West Street was purchased by Abraham and Anna Labovitz (later Labb) around 1915. They had six sons and two daughters. Louis and Jacob Labb ran the farm with their father, growing tobacco, keeping dairy cows and chickens, and tending a large vegetable garden. In 1963, the farm was sold and later became Red Fox and White Fox Drives. Here, Labb grandchildren Bill Labb and Edie Labb Bobier drive a tractor on the farm in 1946 (see page 89). (Courtesy of Bill Labb.)

Six

CELEBRATIONS

The Town of Agawam, although first settled in 1635, did not become an independent town for over 200 years, finally incorporating on May 17, 1855. Maybe due to that fact, citizens took every chance they could to celebrate in the ensuing years, holding a 50th anniversary celebration in 1905, a 75th anniversary celebration in 1930, and a four-day centennial celebration in 1955. In the years between and since, there have been many other celebrations, both public and private.

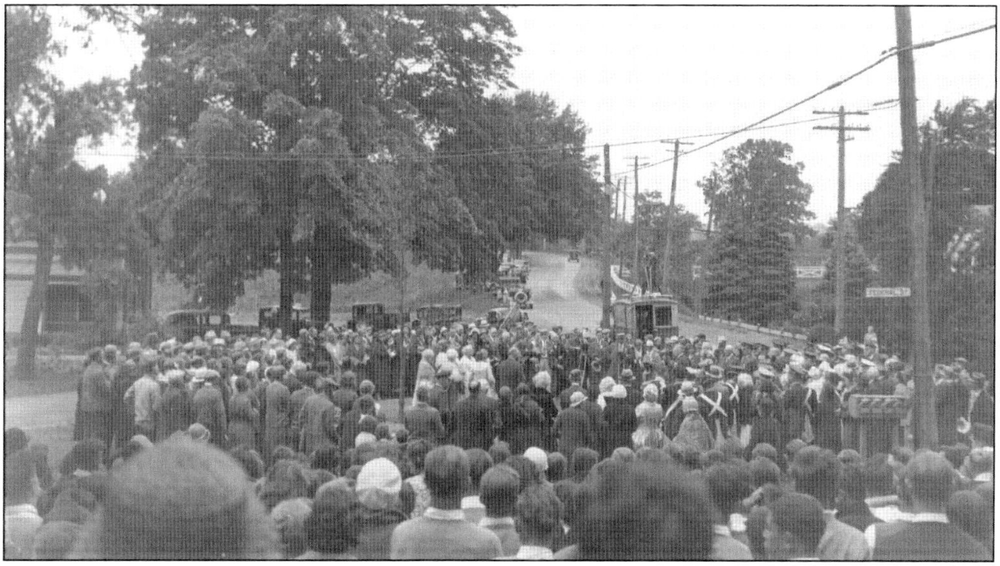

Shown is the dedication of the George Washington Highway tablet, at the corner of Main and Federal Streets, June 8, 1932. To commemorate the 200th birthday of our first president, the Massachusetts George Washington Bicentennial Commission sponsored the dedication of the "Massachusetts George Washington Memorial Highway," which followed the route traveled by Washington through Agawam to Boston during the Revolution. The tablet was stolen several years ago, but the stone remains. (Agawam Historical Association collection.)

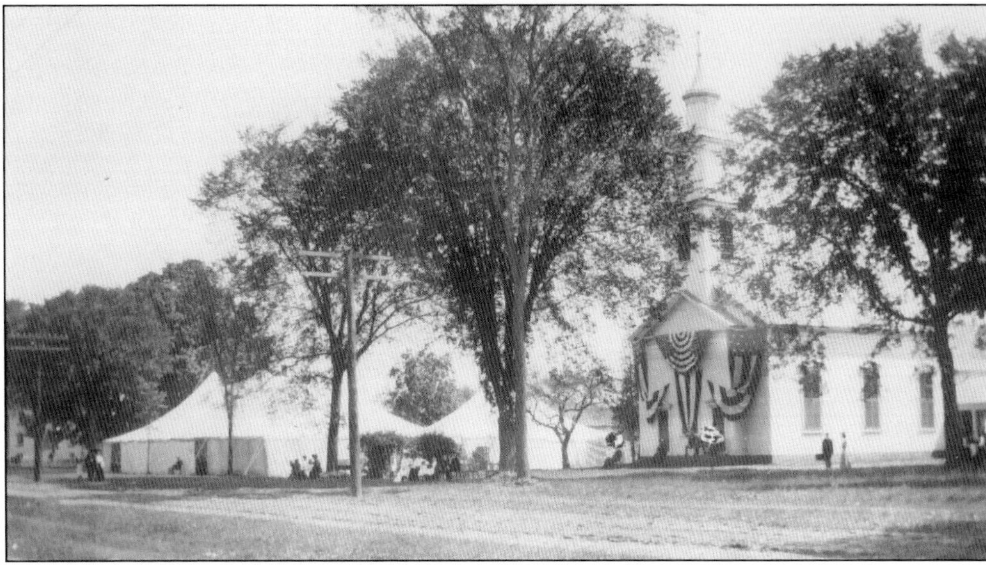

In 1905, $600 was appropriated for the celebration of the 50th anniversary of the town's incorporation. Shown is the tent that was set up next to the old Congregational church on Main Street. A partial list of expenditures follows: "E.C. Barr, catering, $31; the F.A. Bassette Company, badges and programs, $30.75; Burgin Brothers, rent of tents, $80; Charles E. Burt, tickets and handbills, $4.50; the Loring & Axtell Company, invitations, $5.25; Twelfth Regiment Band, music, $96." The total came in more than $200 under budget. (Courtesy of Donald Goss.)

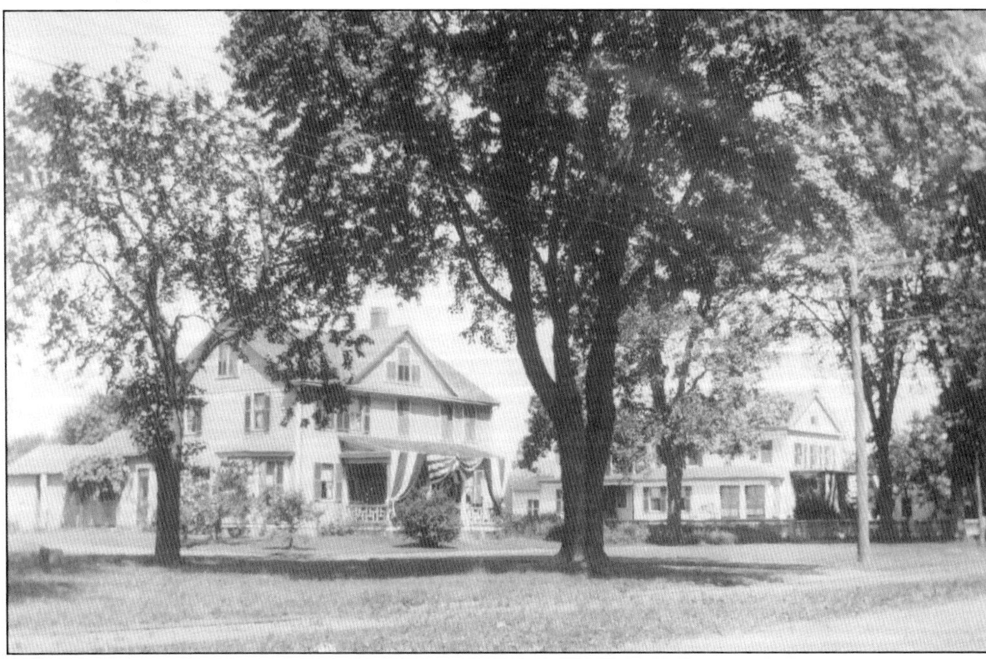

Many homes along Main Street were decorated for the 1905 celebration. Shown at left is the *c.* 1795 Allen-Hastings House, and the *c.* 1855 Baptist Society House, both of which still stand at 692 and 684 Main Street, respectively. The triangular dormer and front porch of the Allen-Hastings House have since been removed. (Courtesy of Donald Goss.)

James Barry dressed as "Mr. Liberty" for the 1905 celebration. James Barry was born in Feeding Hills on December 6, 1857, and was very active in town politics in the early 1900s, serving ten years on the Democratic town committee, 16 years as selectman, and 16 years on the board of health. He also represented Agawam in the state legislature for four years. In addition to his civic duties, he ran his 125-acre farm on South West Street (see page 60) and the Barry Coal Company (see page 87) in Feeding Hills Center for many years. (Courtesy of Jay and Mary Barry.)

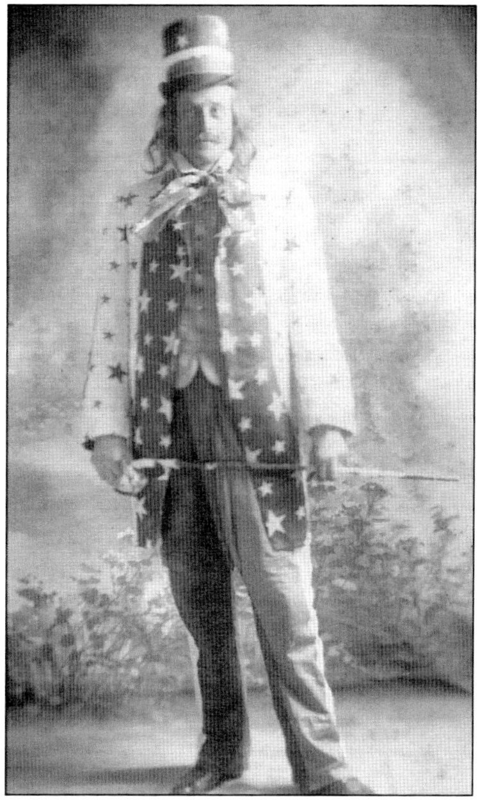

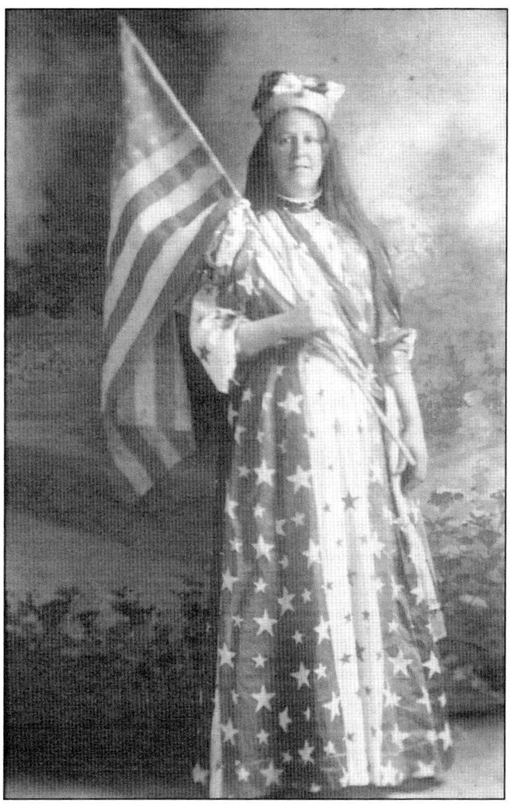

Margaret Barry dressed as "Mrs. Liberty" for the 1905 celebration. James and Margaret Barry were married on August 28, 1894 and built the house on South Westfield Street (see page 60). They had four children: Kathryn, who served on the board of managers of the Hampden County Improvement League; James, who was active in the Barry Coal Company and served in the 279th Aero Squad and served in France during World War I; Ruth; and Philip, who was also active in the coal company. (Courtesy of Jay and Mary Barry.)

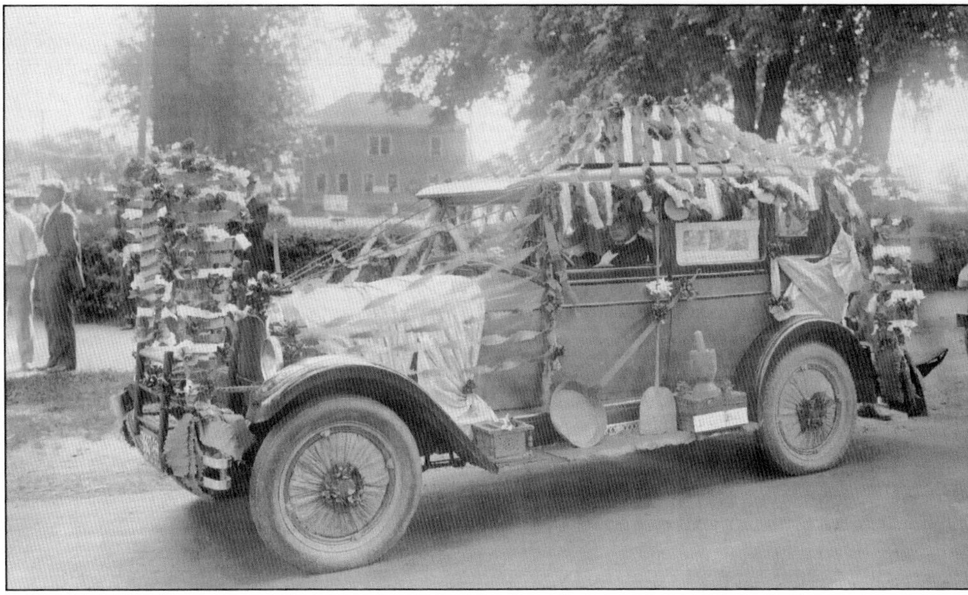

At the town meeting on March 8, 1930, the town voted to "appropriate the sum of one thousand dollars for the celebration of the 75th anniversary of the incorporation of the Town," which included a parade. Mr. and Mrs. Herbert Bamforth of Feeding Hills entered this float entitled "An Entry from the Old Griswold Home" (see page 55). It was the winning float, and Mrs. Bamforth was presented a $20 gold piece by Charles Hull, father of the late Agawam historian Edith Hull LaFrancis. (Agawam Historical Association collection.)

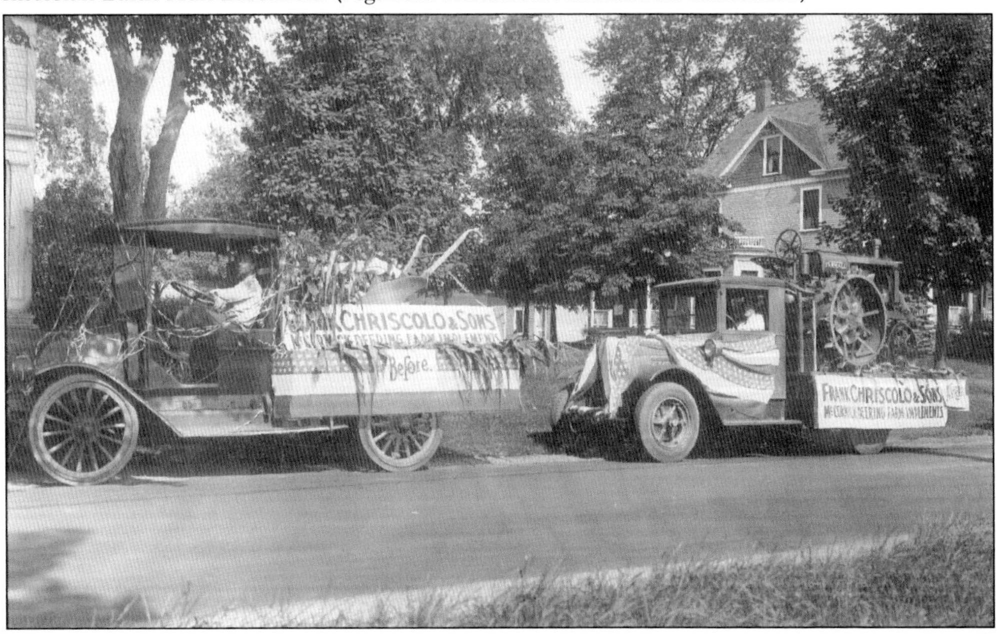

Andrew and Frank Chriscola Jr. (see page 83) also took part in the parade. Their two-truck float for Frank Chriscolo & Sons presented the "old" and "new" ways to farm. Agawam farmers were hesitant to purchase the tricycle-style Farmall tractor shown on the right. Frank Chriscola Jr. remembers that it sat in their shed until 1932, when Louis DePalma of Feeding Hills bought the first Farmall tractor in Agawam. (Courtesy of Frank Chriscola Jr.)

In September 1938, the Labb family gathered to celebrate Abraham and Anna Labb's 50th and their daughter Lena and son-in-law Sam Morrison's 25th wedding anniversaries. This Labor Day reunion became a family tradition that continues to this day. Shown are four generations of the Labb family. They are, clockwise from right, as follows: Anna Labb, with her first great-granddaughter Myrna Gail Kaufman, daughter Ida Davidson, and granddaughter Agnes Kaufman. (Courtesy of Evalyn Baron, grandaughter of Anna Labb.)

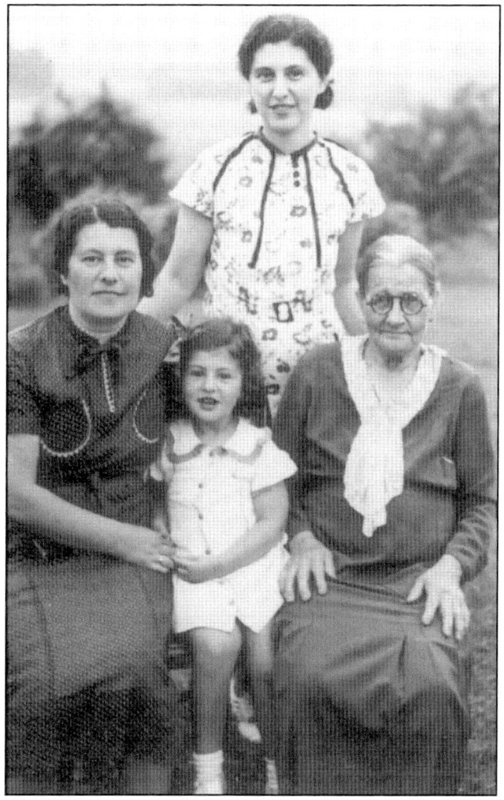

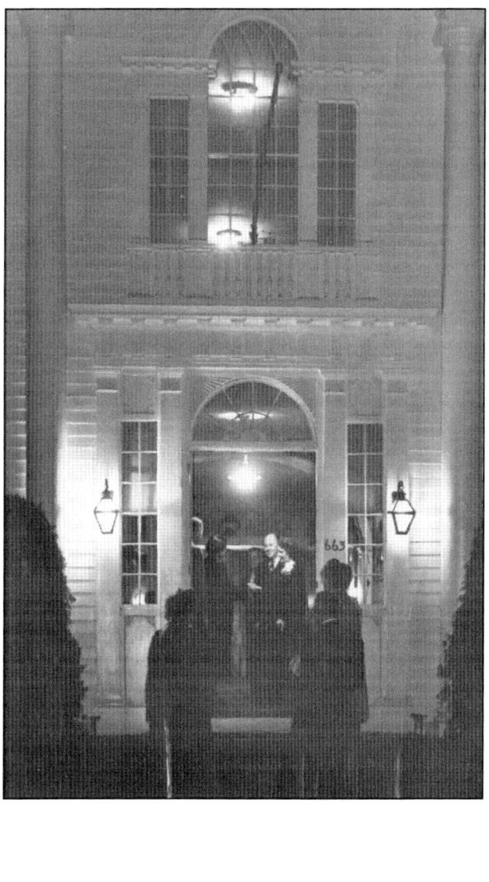

After a year of renovation and restoration by Mrs. Minerva Davis, the Captain Charles Leonard House (see page 10), located at 663 Main Street, was opened to the public as a community house in September 1939. At that time, the board of trustees included the following: Mrs. Minerva J. Davis, owner of the house; Mrs. Ralph D. Pond, president of the Agawam Women's Club; Mrs. Percival V. Hastings, president of the Ladies Aid Society of First Baptist Church and past president of the Agawam Women's Club; Mrs. H. Preston Worden, writer of children's books; Sidney F. Moore, teller at the Union Trust Company; William R. Walker, county agent for 4-H clubs; and Edwin Stewart, superintendent of the General Fibre Box Company. Here, members of the board receive guests on opening night. (Courtesy of the Board of Trustees of the Captain Charles Leonard House.)

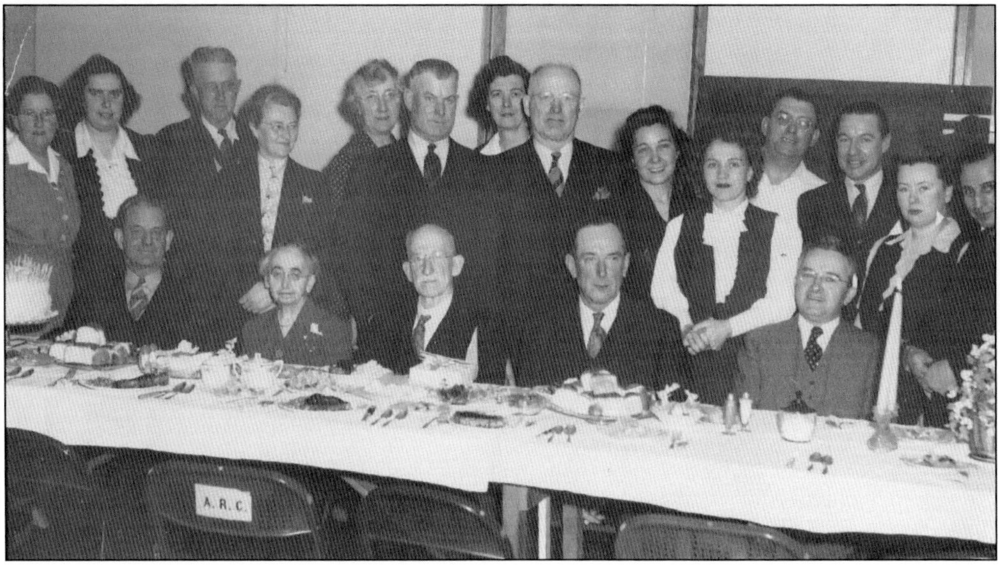

Henry E. Bodurtha was appointed town clerk and treasurer of Agawam in 1912 and held the position for more than 30 years. Shown at his 79th birthday on March 15, 1944, are, from left to right, the following: (front row, seated) Herman Cordes, Belle Bodurtha, Henry Bodurtha, Giles Halladay (see page 75), and Joe Borgatti; (back row) Clara Williams, Jean Goss, Stuart Kibbe, Minnie Barden, Leafie Maynard, Walter S. Kerr, Mary O'Brien, Perly Hewey, Fran Pedula, Margaret Ferranti, Steve Carlisto, John Malley, Camillo Baerdi, and (?) Roy Founier. Cordes, Halladay, and Borgatti were town selectmen. (Courtesy of Mr. and Mrs. Norman Roberts.)

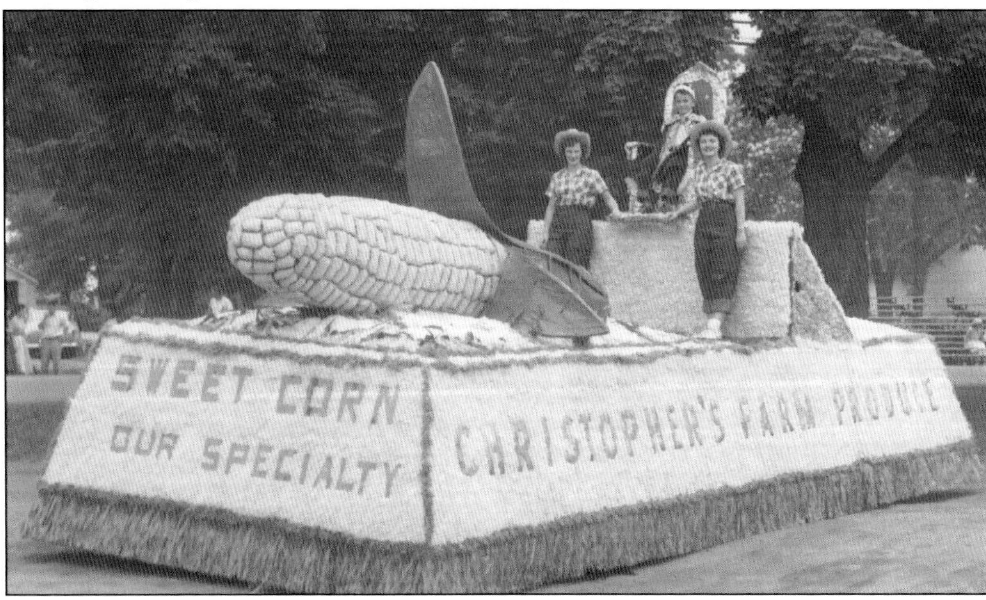

A four-day centennial celebration was held from June 16 to June 19, 1955. On Sunday afternoon, June 19, the centennial parade headed north up Main Street from Phelps School for the then new Agawam Shopping Center at the corner of Walnut and Springfield Streets. A stand was set up at the town hall to review the floats. Albert "Corn King" Christopher (see page 76) entered this float with 10-year-old son, Tommy Christopher, on the throne. (Courtesy of Jenny Christopher.)

Seven

When the Train Came to Town

Rail service through Feeding Hills had been discussed as early as 1841, and even though there was much excitement regarding the creation of the Springfield and Farmington Railroad in 1856, nothing ever became of their plans to come through Feeding Hills Center. It was 1903 before the Central New England Railroad (CNE) began regular rail service from Tariffville, Connecticut, through Feeding Hills Center to Springfield. By then, trolley service and in the coming years, the automobile, diminished demand for train service. The Great Depression further complicated matters, and by 1938, the last train left the Feeding Hills station.

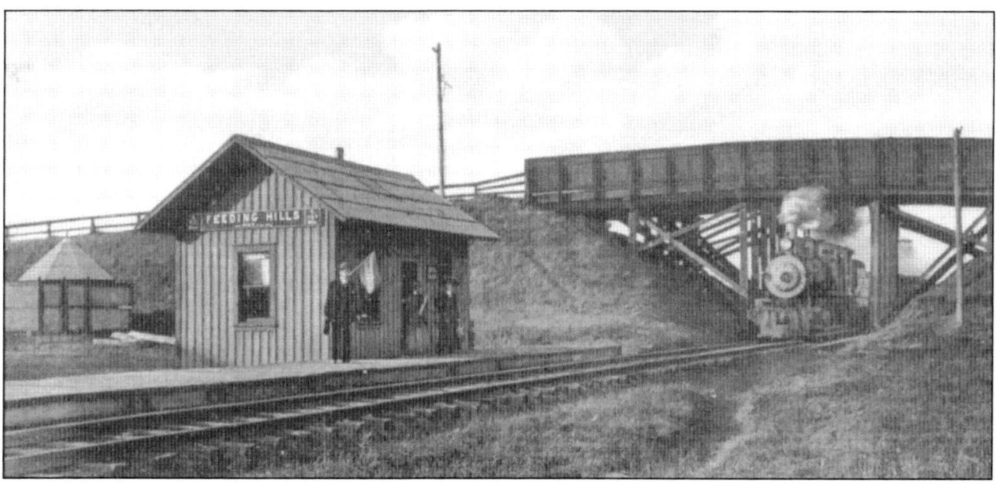

The first railroad station in Feeding Hills burned. The CNE then brought in an old boxcar to serve as the station, which was replaced with the station seen here in this rare postcard from 1911. The tracks were located approximately where the driveway to the Agawam Junior High School on Springfield Street is located. The station was later moved out of town for use as a cabin. (Courtesy of Rick Bellico.)

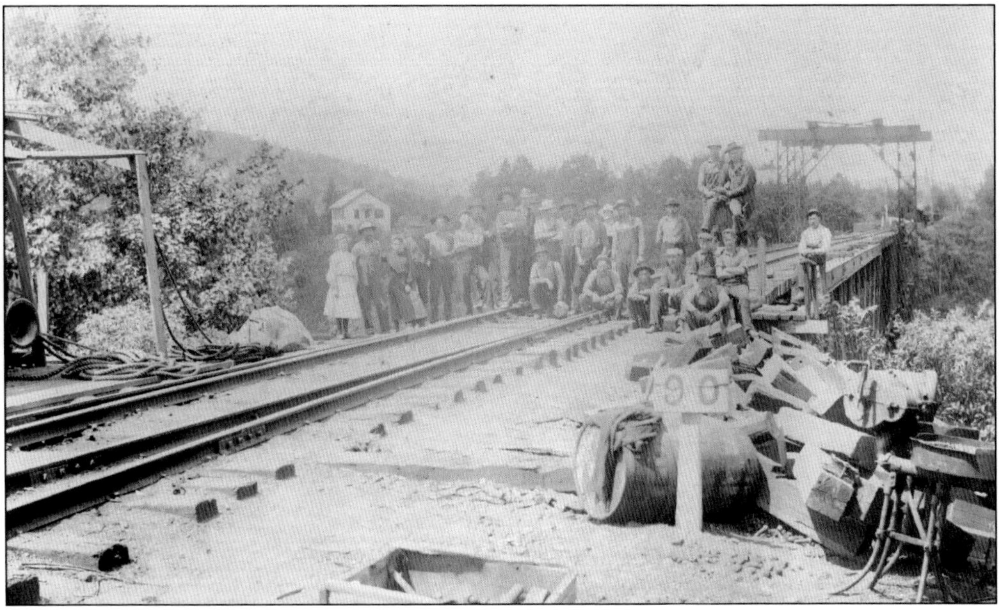

Although regular rail service through Feeding Hills did not begin until 1903, work began on the trestle crossing the Agawam River (see page 48) much earlier, with work completed by 1899. From Feeding Hills Center, the railroad headed north through what is now Robinson State Park, across the Agawam River to Agawam Junction in West Springfield, and then via the Boston & Albany right-of-way to Springfield, Massachusetts. Here, the trestle construction crew takes a break for the camera. (Agawam Historical Association collection.)

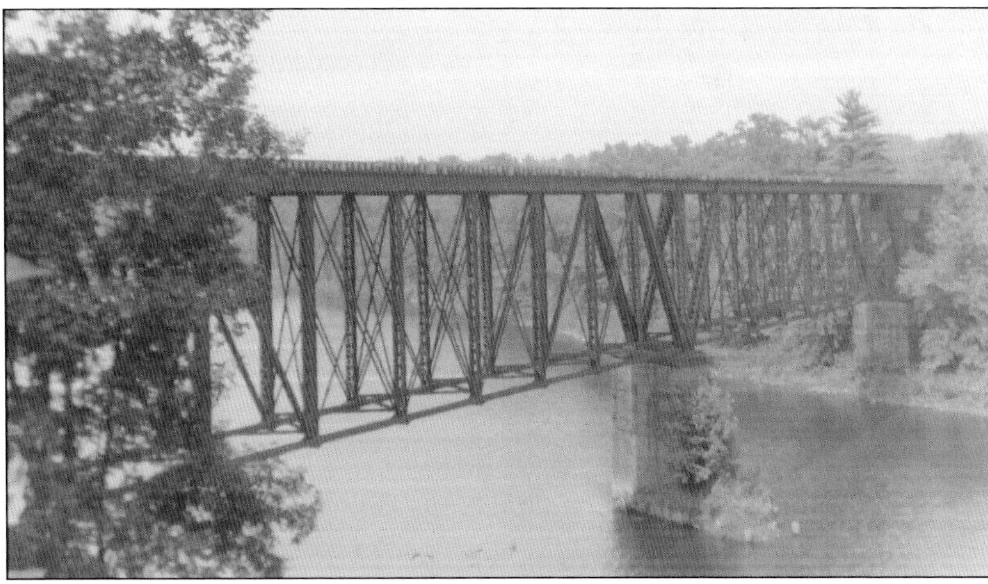

Service north of Feeding Hills Center to Springfield ended in 1921. The CNE then stored empty boxcars on the tracks north of the center until 1938. Al Kellogg Jr. remembers as a youth that the row of boxcars was broken only where a farmer had a right-of-way over the tracks. During the Great Depression, more than a few hobos inhabited the empty cars, sometimes accidentally setting them ablaze with their cooking fires. The trestle was eventually dismantled, although the stone pier in the middle of the river remains. (Agawam Historical Association collection.)

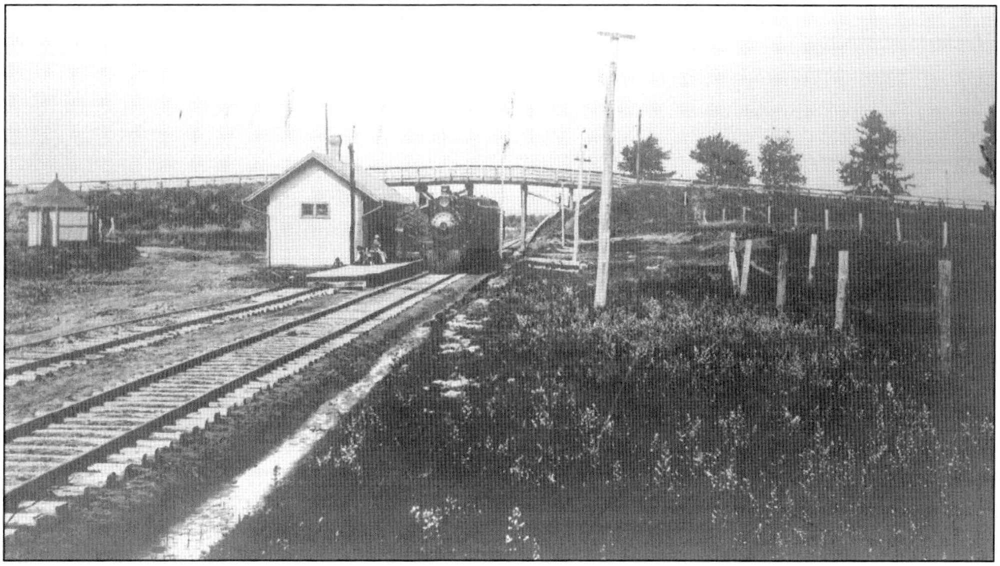

Engine No. 16 appears photographed at the Feeding Hills station, *c*. 1907. This is most likely the original station in Feeding Hills that burned, later replaced by the station pictured on page 91. The first train to run through Feeding Hills was an inspection train on September 8, 1902. Aboard were Connecticut Railroad commissioners, Alice Sheldon Barton of West Suffield, and her father. (Agawam Historical Association collection.)

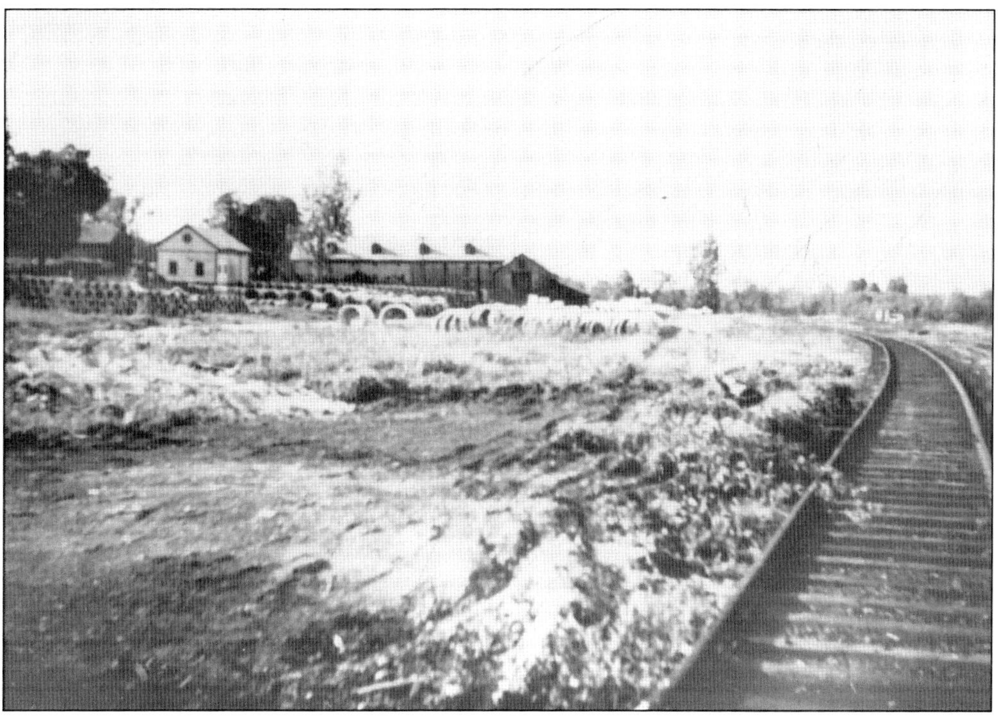

The N.E. Conrete Pipe Company was located on the east side of South Westfield Street approximately where Route 57 ends. After the CNE ended service, the company moved to Union Street in Westfield, Massachusetts. (Gift of the East Granby, Connecticut, Public Library to the Agawam Historical Commission.)

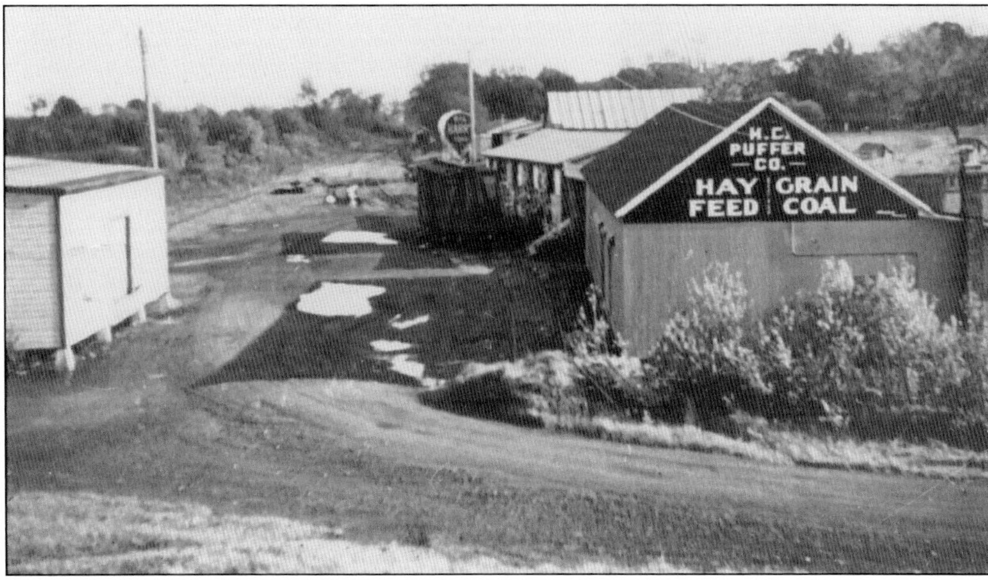

E.A. Kellogg & Sons (see page 63) sold their grain business to H.C. Puffer in the 1920s. The business then relocated to the south side of Springfield Street and a rail spur was built to service them. H.C. Puffer employee Prentiss Jenks (see page 60) was among those on hand in July 1938 to witness the last train leave the Feeding Hills station. (Gift of the East Granby, Connecticut, Public Library to the Agawam Historical Commission.)

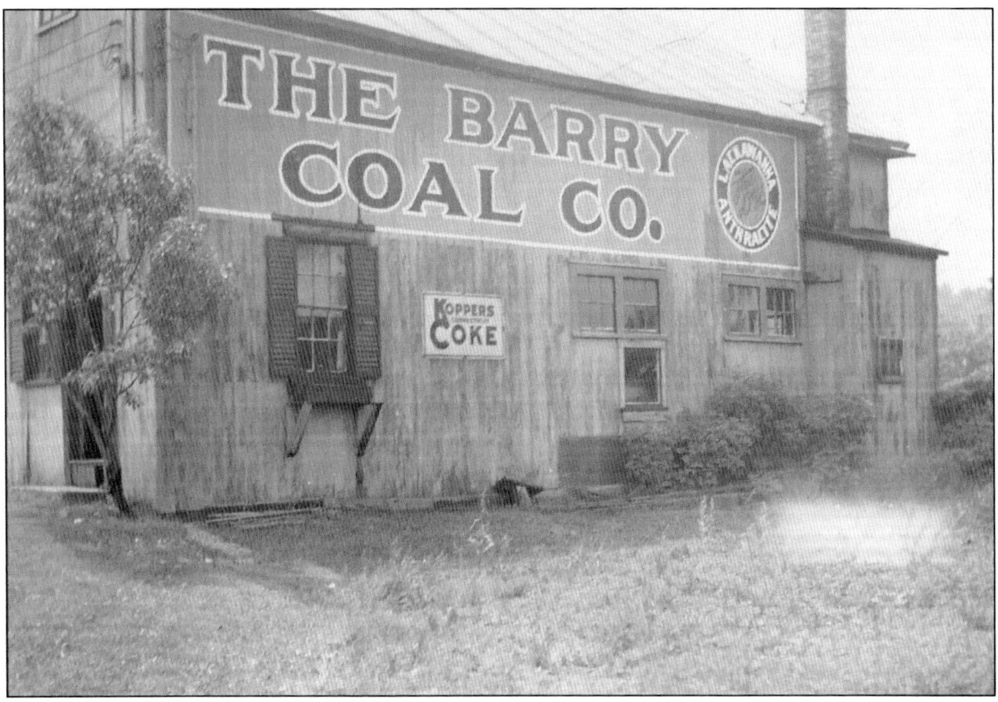

The Barry Coal Company was founded by James Barry (see page 60) in 1902 when the CNE began rail service to Feeding Hills Center. The business was moved to Union Street in West Springfield upon the abandonment of the railroad line to Feeding Hills. (Gift of the East Granby, Connecticut, Public Library to the Agawam Historical Commission.)

Eight

AIRPLANES AND HORSES

Newer residents of town are often surprised to learn that Agawam had an airport; some who have lived in town for decades are equally surprised to learn that there was also a horse-racing track in town, located on the site of one of the airports. In fact, over the years, airplanes have operated out of six separate locations in town: three land-based and three water-based. The last airport in operation was Bowles Airport, which closed in 1982 and is now the site of the Agawam Regional Industrial Park.

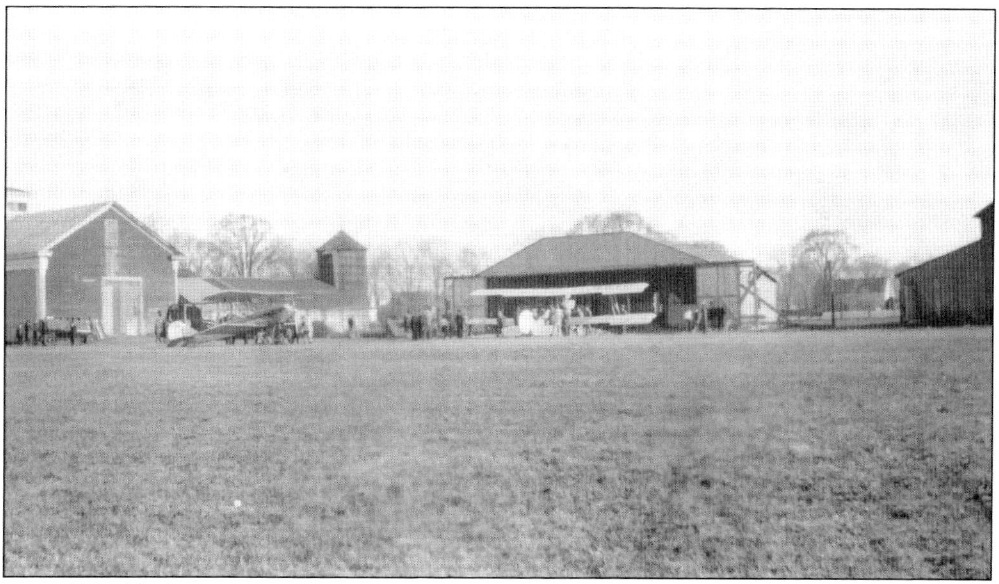

Randall Field, shown in 1929, was located on part of the Randall Brothers horse farm at 530 Main Street. Their motto was, "Selling Horses that Do Not Come Back to Customers Who Do." The north–south runway ran parallel to Main Street where the Bethany Assembly of God is now located. The east–west runway occupied the land where Route 57 now runs. Opened in 1926, the airport closed shortly after the opening of Bowles Field, though the last plane to fly from the field was in 1940. (Courtesy of Mr. and Mrs. Alvord Hutchinson.)

In 1928, Rep. Henry Bowles purchased more than 300 acres from the Cuba Connecticut Tobacco Company (see page 68) with the intention to create a first-class air center for New England. Upon its opening in 1930, Bowles Airport was just that, consisting of four 1,000-foot runways, a fireproof hangar (see page 97), and administration building on Silver Street. On May 27, 1930, 30 planes left Springfield Airport as part of the New England Air Tour to show the feasibility of establishing permanent air routes. They arrived at Bowles Airport on May 30 for the dedication ceremonies. Springfield native Maude Tait, the first licensed woman pilot in Massachusetts, was first to land. (Author's collection.)

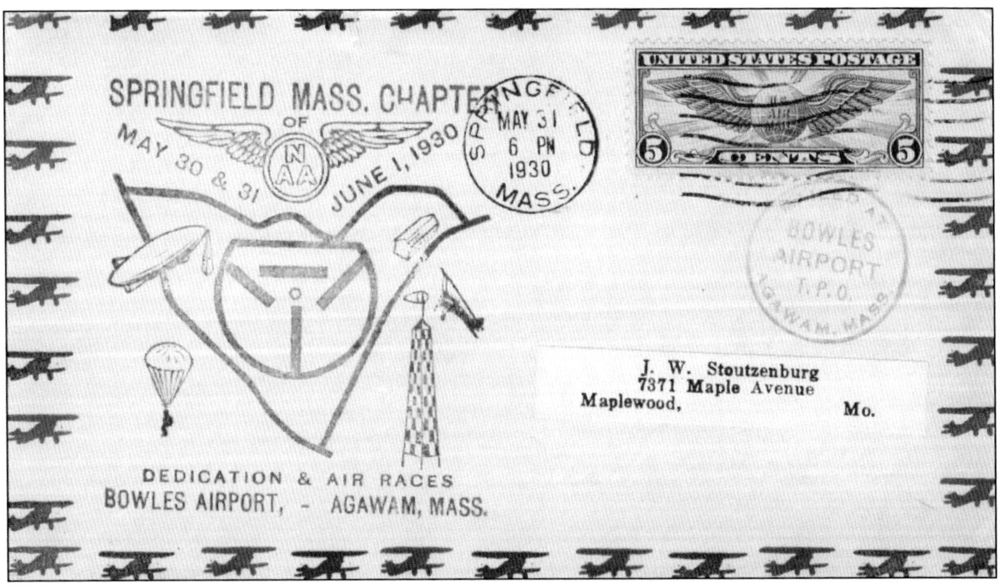

The dedication of Bowles Airport in 1930 saw over 15,000 people witness air races, stunt flying, formation flying, and other events. In attendance were former Pres. Calvin Coolidge and Amelia Earhart, who commented "As I look upon this beautiful field my only regret is that I did not bring my ship with me." (She had arrived via automobile.) This first day cover, commemorating the dedication, shows the layout of Bowles Airport when it opened. (Author's collection.)

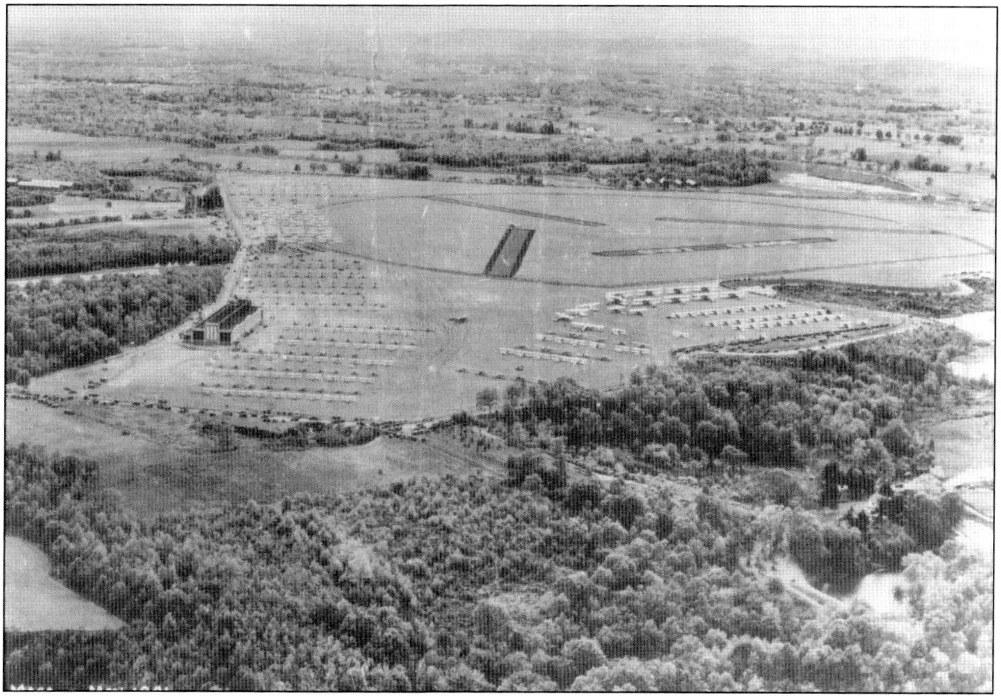

In 1931, the Army Air Corp held the Eastern Air Maneuvers. On May 25 that year, 750 planes took off from Dayton, Ohio en route to Washington, D.C., via Chicago, Cleveland, Hartford, Agawam–Springfield, Boston, Providence, New York City, Philadelphia, and Baltimore. Bowles Airport was the only airport in the area large enough to accommodate the fleet. The commanding officer, Gen. Benjamin Foulais remarked that Bowles was "the finest field the Division has struck to date." (Courtesy of Leslie and Dale Melanson.)

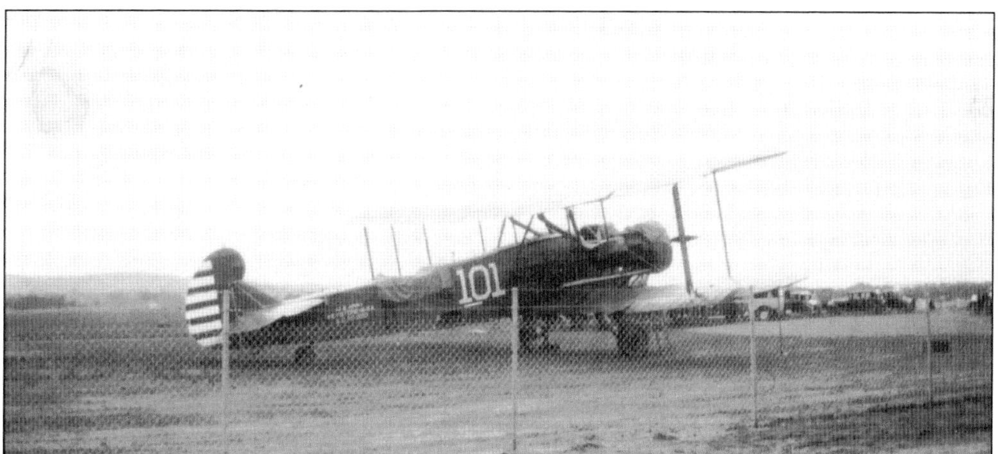

During the Eastern Air Maneuvers, more than 400 planes ranging from small pursuit and observation planes to large Keystone bombers, such as the one shown, spent the night at Bowles before taking off for Boston the next morning. Thousands of spectators were on hand to view the largest force of military planes gathered up to that time. (Courtesy of John Bitgood.)

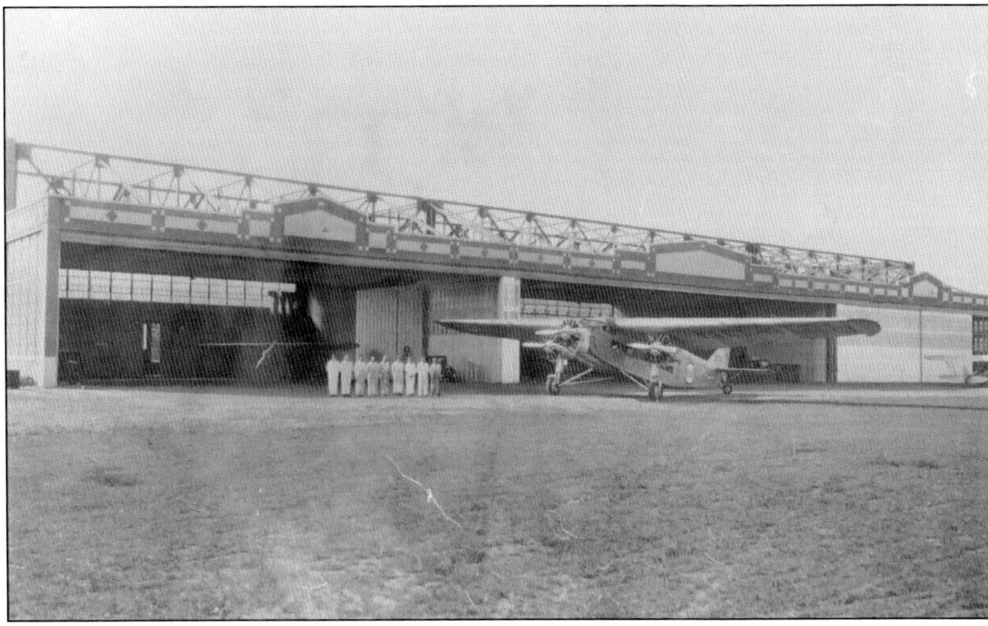

This photograph shows the 300-foot-long fireproof Art Deco hangar that was built along Silver Street. It was divided into three bays, and could accommodate up to 60 planes. When Bowles Airport closed for good in 1982 to make way for the Industrial Park, three of the six decorative lintels over the doors were saved; one was shipped to the National Air and Space Museum at the Smithsonian in Washington, D.C. (Courtesy of Leslie and Dale Melanson.)

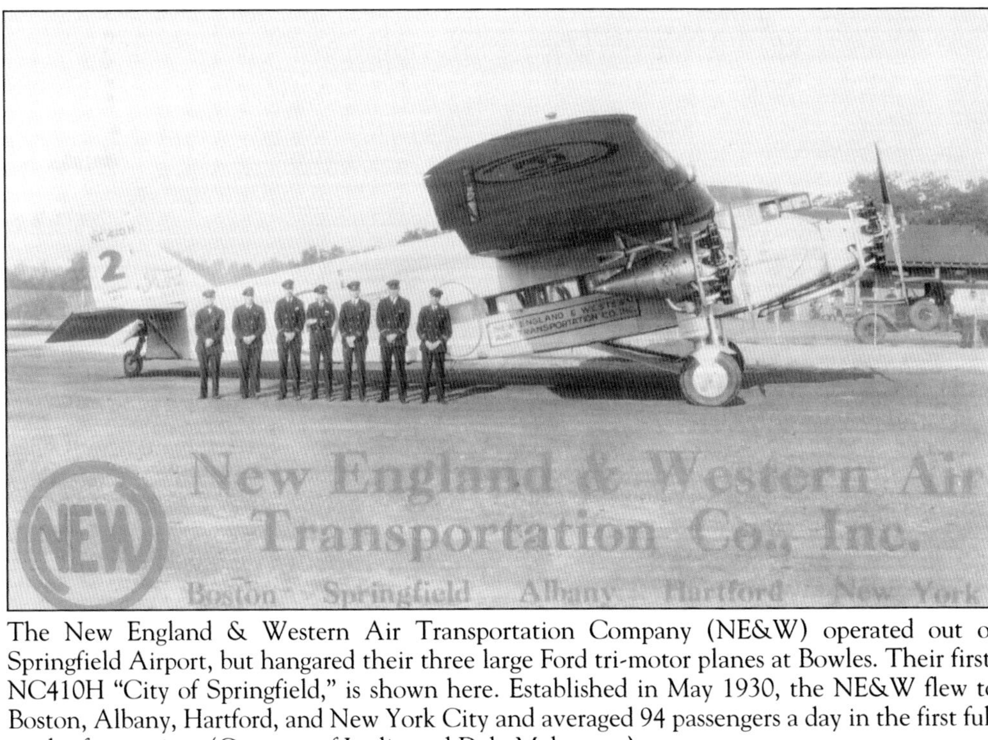

The New England & Western Air Transportation Company (NE&W) operated out of Springfield Airport, but hangared their three large Ford tri-motor planes at Bowles. Their first, NC410H "City of Springfield," is shown here. Established in May 1930, the NE&W flew to Boston, Albany, Hartford, and New York City and averaged 94 passengers a day in the first full week of operation. (Courtesy of Leslie and Dale Melanson.)

Miss Katharine McIntire—who was later the town historian for West Springfield, Massachusetts—is shown leaning against a Ford Tri Motor at Bowles Airport during the 1930s. This plane is the NE&W "City of Chicopee," shown on page 97. (Courtesy of Katharine McIntire.)

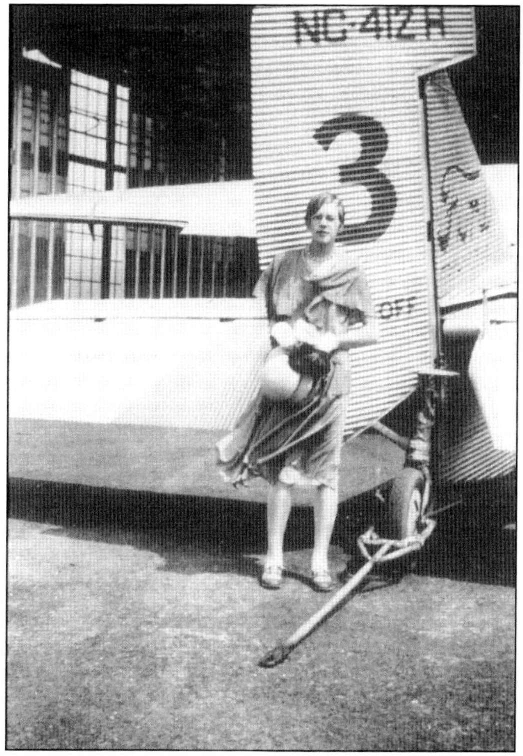

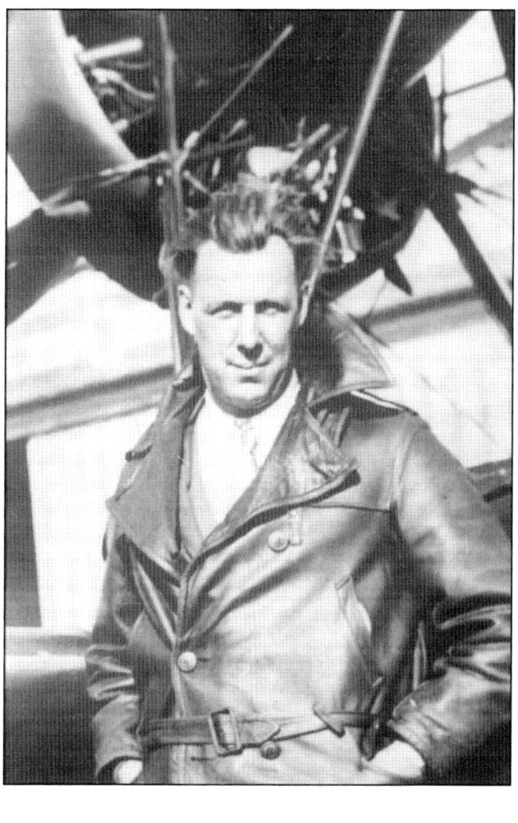

Lowell Bayles poses in front of the Bowles Airport hangar. Bayles was a relief pilot for the NE&W and a local test pilot who flew for the Granville Brothers, makers of the famous "Gee Bee" racers. Although the Granvilles were based at Springfield Airport, they often landed their planes on Bowles's longer runways and trucked the craft back to Springfield. Bayles set an unofficial airspeed record of 267 mph on September 1, 1931, in the Gee Bee Model Z at the Cleveland Air Races. He was killed on December 5, 1931, when his Model Z crashed at Wayne County Airport in Detroit while trying to break the record. (Courtesy of Leslie and Dale Melanson.)

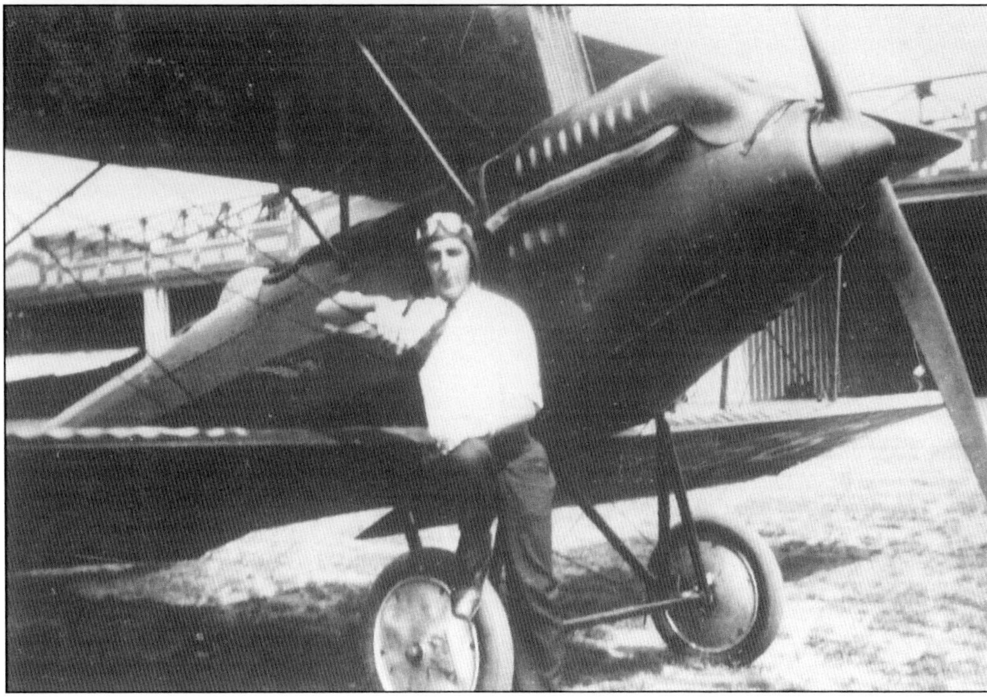

Charles Antaya was one of the many pilots who flew out of Bowles Airport during its long history. (Courtesy of Katharine McIntire.)

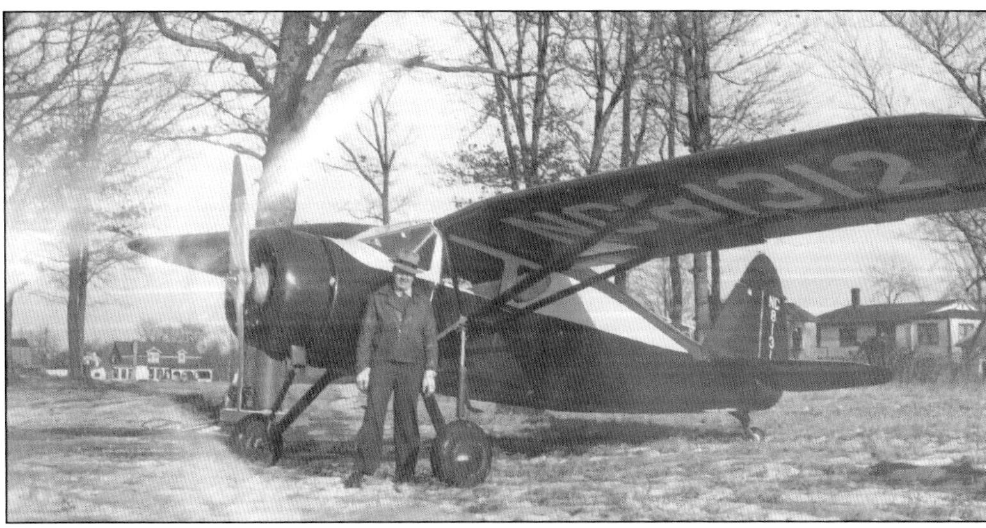

Walter O'Connor established the Northeast Airmotive Corporation in 1941, flying seaplanes from his base at 1000 River Road. He later moved to the combination sea and land base at the Campbell property (see page 101), further down River Road pictured here. He returned to his original base in 1948. O'Connor flew passengers for more than 40 years to destinations as far as Washington, D.C., and Newfoundland. His seaplane and many aircraft parts may still be seen on River Road at the foot of School Street. (Courtesy of Leslie and Dale Melanson.)

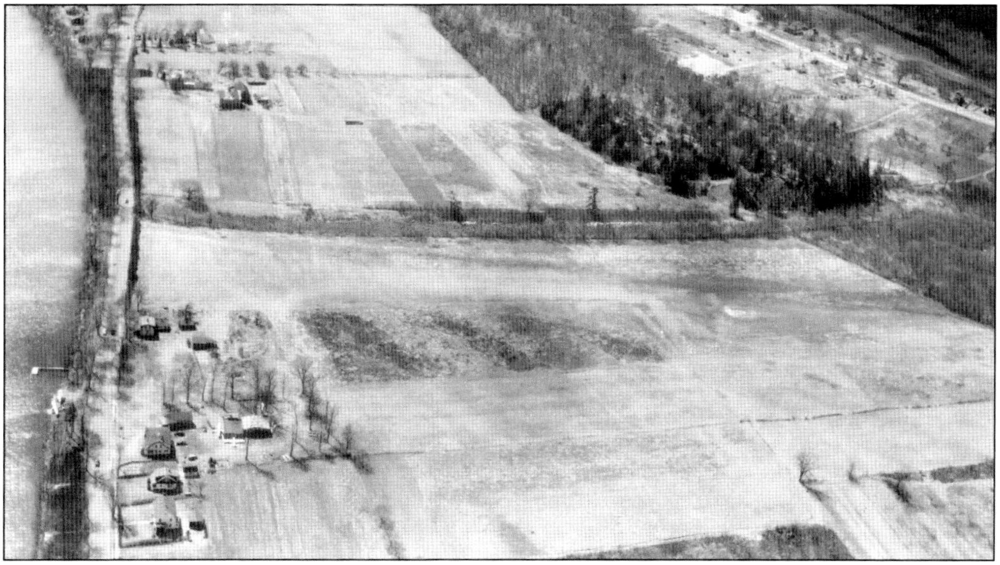

The Campbell sea and land base on River Road (where Channel, Campbell, and Florida Drives are now located) is shown in this image looking south along River Road. The Town of Agawam closed the Campbell airbase due to improper zoning in 1948. The third building from the bottom was the Green Gables bar and grill, which is the site of the current Los Dorados Mexican restaurant on River Road. Note the two seaplanes on the riverbank and the three land-based planes around the garage. (Courtesy of Leslie and Dale Melanson.)

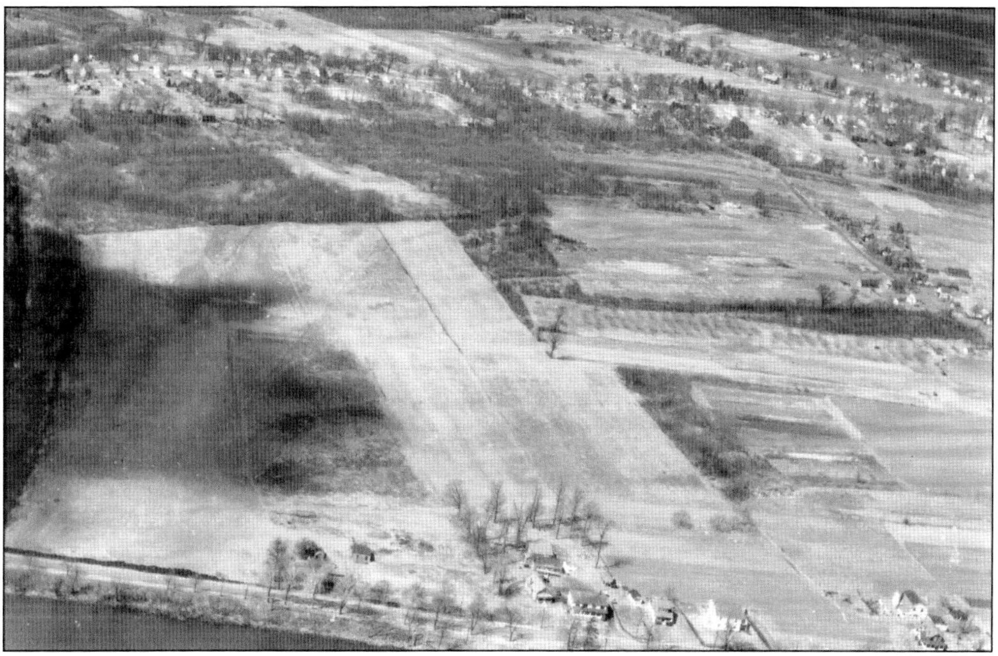

The Campbell sea and land base on River Road is shown in this view looking west toward Main Street. Leonard Street descends from Main Street at the right. The Agawam Company woolen mill on Elm Street can be seen at top center. At this point in the town's history, there were still many acres of farmland on River Road. Nearly all of what can be seen here has been developed. (Courtesy of Leslie and Dale Melanson.)

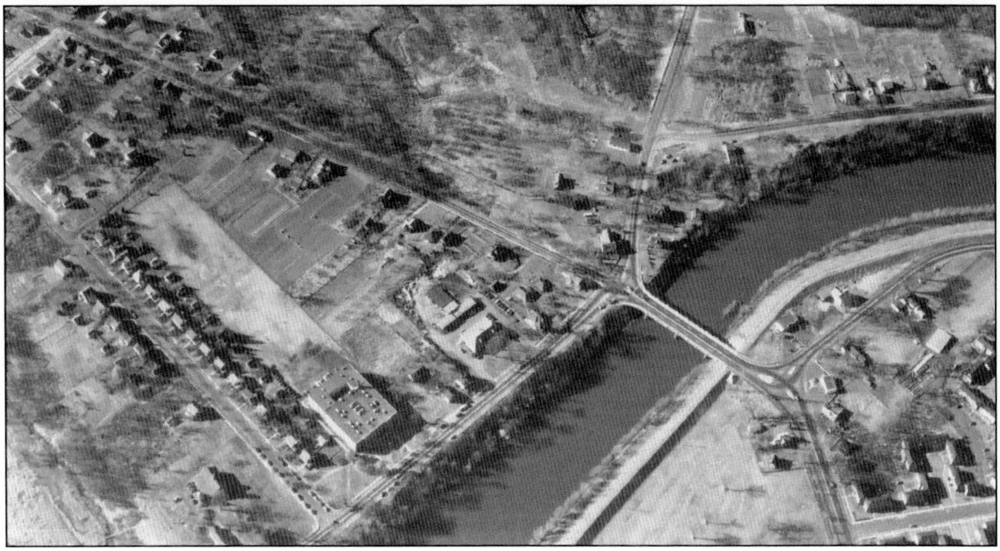

This photograph and the one below were taken in the late 1940s/early 1950s as part of the site selection process for the new high school which was built on Cooper Street in 1955. This photograph was taken over the Agawam River at the foot of Main, Suffield, and Springfield Streets. At the lower left is what was then the Agawam High Schoo (now the Agawam Middle School), built in 1922. The Agawam Town Hall is just to the right of it. Reed Street is at the bottom left. Also visible is the Pliny Leonard–Worden House (see page 39) at the corner of Suffield and Springfield Streets before it was moved to the corner of Walnut and Springfield Streets. Keefe Florist on Walnut Street (see page 73) is also shown at above right. (Courtesy of Esther Reynolds.)

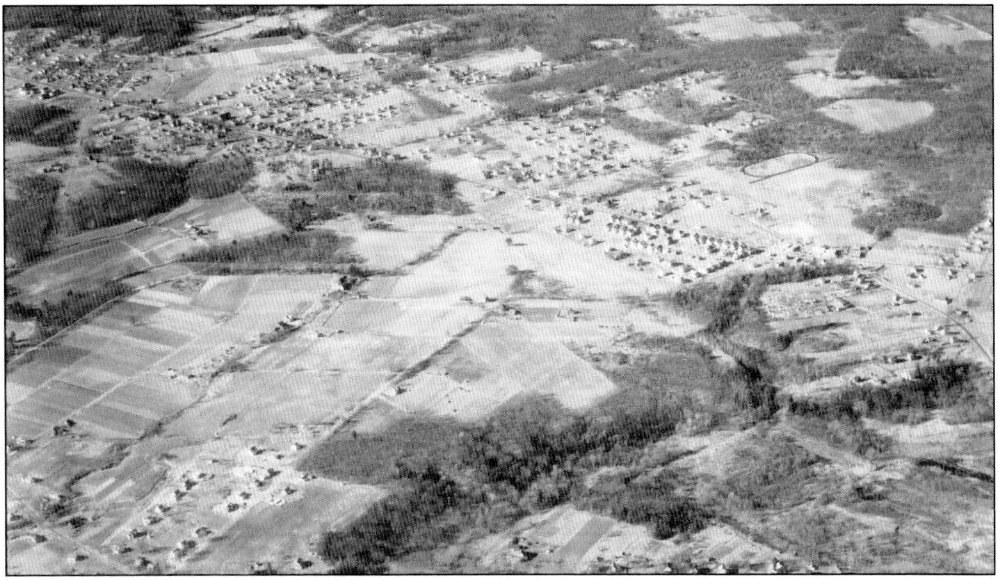

This photograph was taken looking north from just above Suffield Street, which runs along the bottom of the photograph. Rowley Street runs up the middle of the photograph, connecting Suffield Street and Springfield Street, which runs left to right across the middle of the photograph. O'Brien's Corner is shown at middle right, with "Lemon City" just to the left. (Courtesy of Esther Reynolds.)

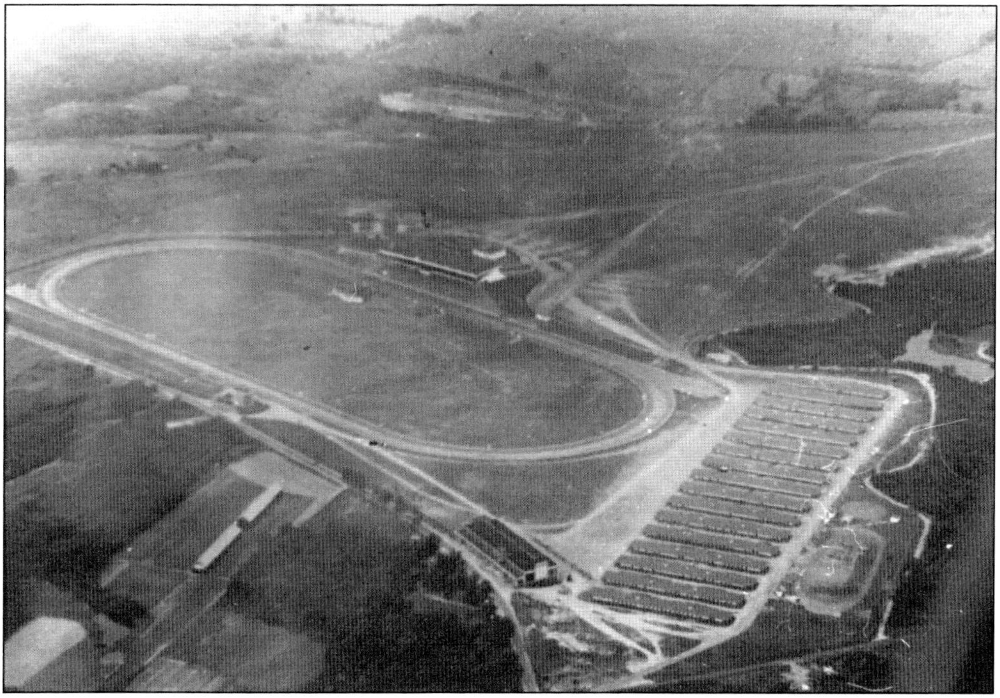

When it opened in 1930, Bowles Airport was one of the finest in the country, but by 1935 it was apparent it would not survive the Great Depression. That same year, the State Racing Commission granted a horse racing license to the Agawam Racing and Breeders' Association. This photograph shows the racetrack, located where runways stood a few years earlier. A grandstand was built (center), and 17 horse barns were constructed along the eastern edge of the property. The hangar was used for hay storage. (Courtesy of Leslie and Dale Melanson.)

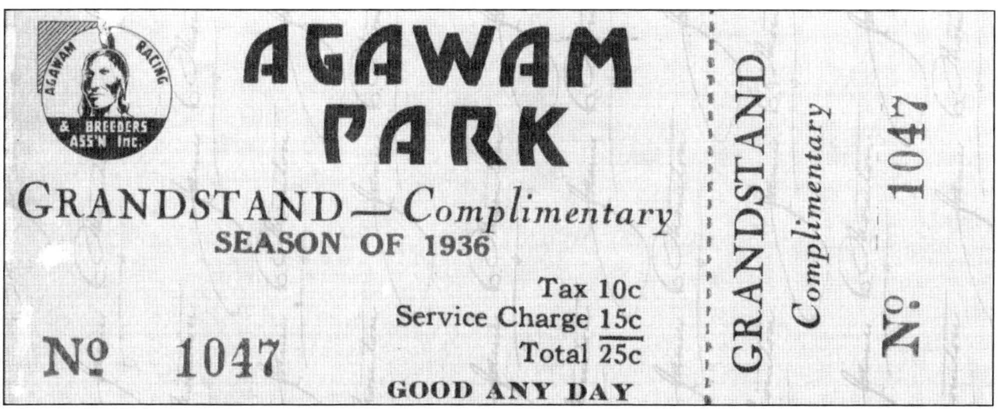

On opening day at Agawam Park in 1935, more than 15,000 people were in attendance for the first race, which the long shot Playaway won, paying $26.40. Later that season 30,000 people—more than four times the town's population—broke all attendance records by attending the Columbus Day holiday program. (Courtesy of Clyde Pomeroy.)

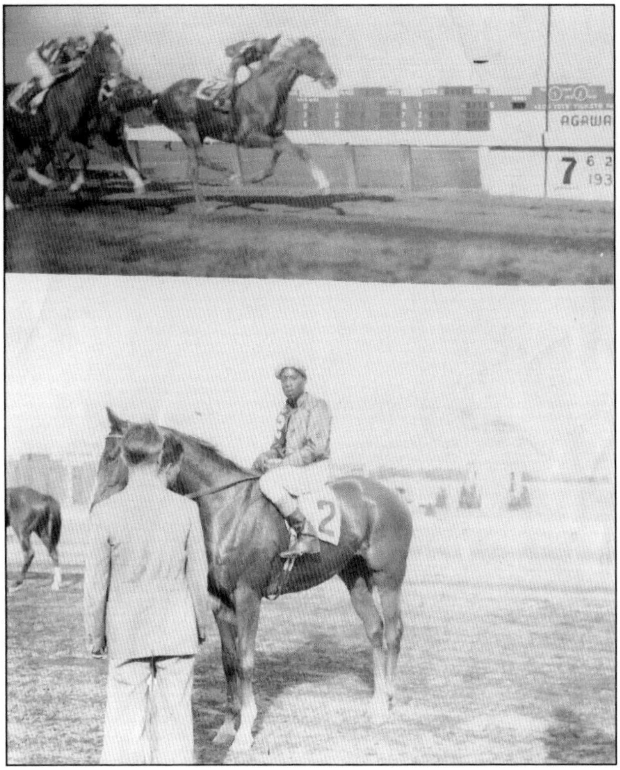

Horse racing was voted out of Hampden County in 1938, the last season at Agawam Park. This photograph was taken after the seventh race, June 22, 1938. The winner was Wedding Ring (by Golden Broom out of War Darling by Man o' War), who was born 1930. Wedding Ring placed in one stakes as a two-year old, raced 112 times, and won 20 races. The jockey is identified only as Johnson. This is a rare photograph from an era when black jockeys were few and far between. (Author's collection, with special thanks to Robin Bledsoe.)

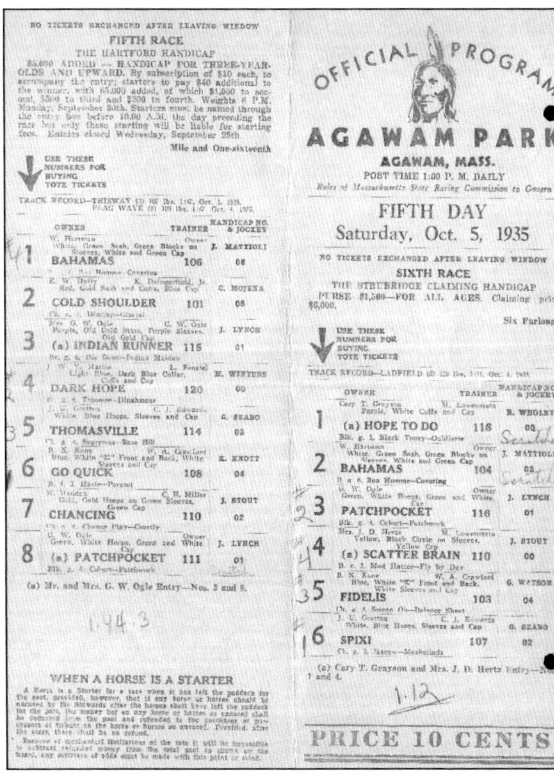

NO TICKETS EXCHANGED AFTER LEAVING WINDOW

FIFTH RACE

THE HARTFORD HANDICAP

$5,000 ADDED — HANDICAP FOR THREE-YEAR-OLDS AND UPWARD. By subscription of $10 each, to accompany the entry; starters to pay $40 additional to the winner, with $5,000 added, of which $1,000 to second, $500 to third and $300 to fourth. Weights 6 P.M. Monday, September 30th. Starters must be named through the entry box before 10.00 A.M. the day preceding the race but only those starting will be liable for starting fees. Entries closed Wednesday, September 25th.

Mile and One-sixteenth

USE THESE NUMBERS FOR BUYING TOTE TICKETS

TRACK RECORD—THISWAY (3) 107 lbs. 1:47, Oct. 1, 1935.
FLAG WAVE (8) 109 lbs. 1:47 Oct. 4, 1935.

	OWNER	TRAINER	HANDICAP NO. & JOCKEY
1	W. Harriman — White, Green Sash, Green Blocks on Sleeves, White and Green Cap	Owner	J. MATTIOLI
	BAHAMAS	106	06
2	E. W. Duffy — Red, Gold Sash and Cuffs, Blue Cap	K. Daingerfield, Jr.	C. MOJENA
	COLD SHOULDER	101	05
3	Mrs. G. W. Ogle — Purple, Old Gold Stars, Purple Sleeves, Old Gold Cap	C. W. Ogle	J. LYNCH
	(a) INDIAN RUNNER	115	01
4	Light Blue, Dark Blue Collar, Cuffs and Cap	L. Feustel	M. WINTERS
	DARK HOPE	120	00
5	J. U. Gratton — White, Blue Hoops, Sleeves and Cap	C. J. Edwards	G. SEABO
	THOMASVILLE	114	03
6	B. N. Kane — Blue, White "K" Front and Back, White Sleeves and Cap	W. A. Crawford	K. KNOTT
	GO QUICK	108	04
7	Gold, Gold Hoops on Green Sleeves, Green Cap	C. H. Miller	J. STOUT
	CHANCING	110	02
8	G. W. Ogle — Green, White Hoops, Green and White Cap	Owner	J. LYNCH
	(a) PATCHPOCKET	111	01

(a) Mr. and Mrs. G. W. Ogle Entry—Nos. 3 and 8.

WHEN A HORSE IS A STARTER

A Horse is a Starter for a race when it has left the paddock for the post, provided, however, that if any horse or horses should be excused by the Stewards after the horses shall have left the paddock for the post, the money bet on any horse or horses so excused shall be deducted from the pool and refunded to the purchaser or purchasers of tickets on the horse or horses so excused. Provided, after the start, there shall be no refund.

Because of mechanical limitations of the tote it will be impossible to subtract refunded money from the total pool as shown on the board, any estimate of odds must be made with this point in mind.

OFFICIAL PROGRAM

AGAWAM PARK

AGAWAM, MASS.

POST TIME 1:30 P. M. DAILY

Rules of Massachusetts State Racing Commission to Govern

FIFTH DAY

Saturday, Oct. 5, 1935

NO TICKETS EXCHANGED AFTER LEAVING WINDOW

SIXTH RACE

THE STURBRIDGE CLAIMING HANDICAP

PURSE $1,500—FOR ALL AGES. Claiming price $6,000.

Six Furlongs

USE THESE NUMBERS FOR BUYING TOTE TICKETS

TRACK RECORD—LADFIELD (6) 128 lbs. 1:11, Oct. 1, 1935

	OWNER	TRAINER	HANDICAP NO. & JOCKEY
1	Cary T. Grayson — Purple, White Cuffs and Cap	M. Lowenstein	R. WHOLEY
	(a) HOPE TO DO	116	00
2	W. Harriman — White, Green Sash, Green Blocks on Sleeves, White and Green Cap	Owner	J. MATTIOLI
	BAHAMAS	104	03
3	G. W. Ogle — Green, White Hoops, Green and White Cap	Owner	J. LYNCH
	PATCHPOCKET	116	01
4	Mrs. J. D. Hertz — Yellow, Black Circle on Sleeves, Yellow Cap	M. Lowenstein	J. STOUT
	(a) SCATTER BRAIN	110	00
5	B. N. Kane — Blue, White "K" Front and Back, White Sleeves and Cap	W. A. Crawford	G. WATSON
	FIDELIS	103	04
6	J. U. Gratton — White, Blue Hoops, Sleeves and Cap	C. J. Edwards	G. SEABO
	SPIXI	107	02

(a) Cary T. Grayson and Mrs. J. D. Hertz Entry—Nos. 1 and 4.

PRICE 10 CENTS

This program is from the fifth day of racing, Saturday, October 5, 1935. After the track closed, the Agawam Racing and Breeders' Association failed to pay 1938 taxes, and the Town eventually took the land. In 1954, it was sold, and the Republican Company reopened the property as an airport. The grandstand stood for decades until it was destroyed by fire. As many as 65 planes operated from the new Bowles Airport until the Agawam Regional Industrial Park was built on the site in the 1980s. (Author's collection.)

Nine

SCHOOL TIME

Before 1869, the district school system was in place in Agawam, dividing the town into ten school districts: (1) Agawam Center; (2) Feeding Hills Center; (3) Main Street and River Road; (4) Shoemaker Lane and South Westfield Street; (5) Cooper Street, south side; (6) North Westfield Street; (7) River Road, south of School Street; (8) South West Street; (9) North West Street; and (10) North Agawam. Many of the former schoolhouses have been moved and are still in use as residences.

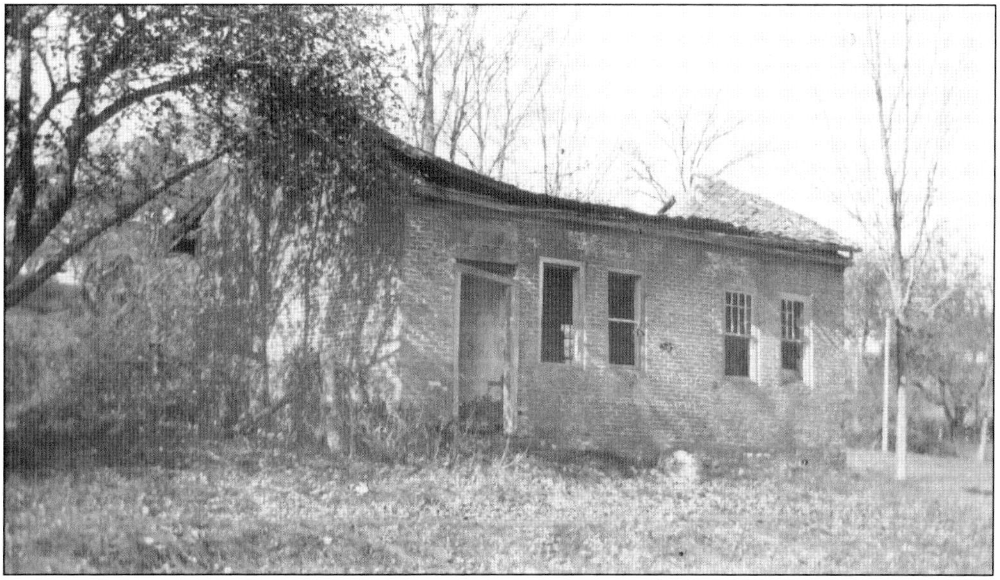

The "Old Brick School" was built in 1787 on South Westfield Street. This was the schoolhouse that Benjamin Wade attended as a child before his family moved to Ohio. He later became U.S. senator from that state and was president of the Senate during Andrew Johnson's term as president. This photograph was taken on November 6, 1906, after it had fallen into disrepair. It was later rebuilt and used as a wheelwright shop until it was demolished in 1913. (Courtesy of Donald Goss.)

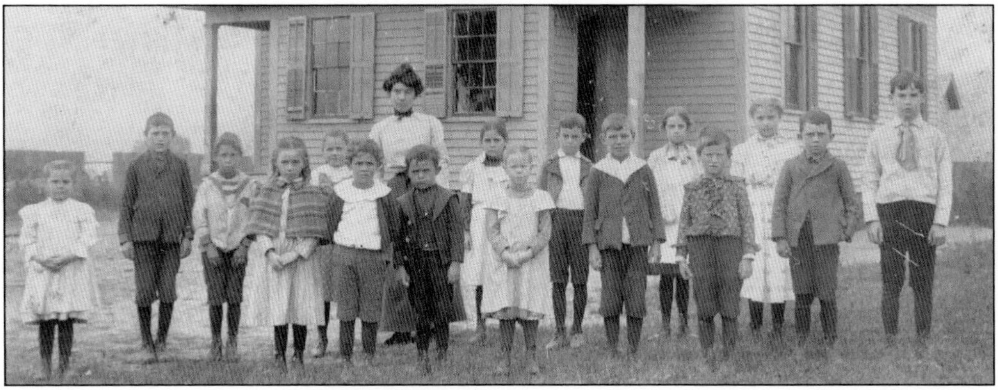

West Street School (now the Grange Hall on North West Street) is shown *c.* 1901. Shown, from left to right, are Doris Mecum, Joseph Schmantz, Thomas Ahearn, Theresa Sullivan, Blanche Mecum, Andrew Sweatland, Edward Sullivan, Flora Sweatland, Gladys Steere, Thomas Roache, William Schmantz, May Roache, unidentified, Mildred Smith, William Sullivan, and Walter Sullivan. Etta Taylor was the teacher. (Agawam Historical Association collection.)

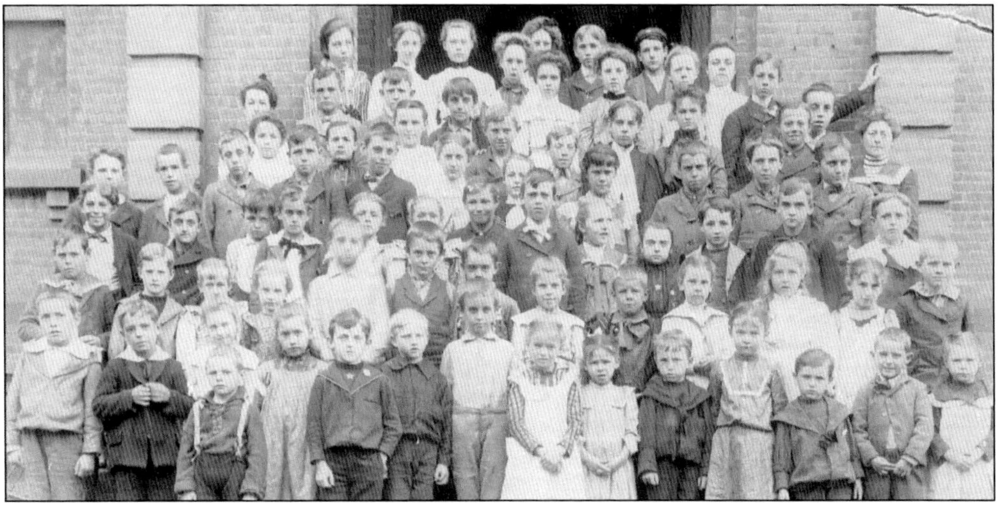

Shown at the Feeding Hills Center School *c.* 1901 are, from left to right, the following: (first row) Raymond Cleary, Edward Cordes, Julia Huntley standing behind Harold Hellpold, Helen Cleary, Chandler Garfield, unidentified, Fay Noble, Edith Granger, Ida Morse, unidentified, Jeanette Taylor, David Kasef, Evelyn Cordes, and Robena Hellpold; (second row) unidentified, Herbert Taylor, Lena Fuller, Esther Cesan, Walter Noble, Daniel Cesan, James Cesan, Myrtle Huntley, Bertley Jenks (see page 60), Julia Halladay, Ernestine Arnold, Myrtle Brooks, and Jack Shea; (third row) Herman Cordes, Perley Fuller, Ed Marse, Richard Fuller, Lillian Fish, Lara Fuller, Thaddeus Johnson, Arthure Taylor, Ethel Snow, Helen Hastings, William O'Connor, Percy Fuller, and Arthur Spear; (fourth row) Harry Spear, Miner Robinson, Guy Fuller, Tom Marse, James Cleary, Cara Wiggins, Flora White, Winnie Scanlon, Fred Robinson, Giles Halladay (see page 75), and Leslie Wiggins; (fifth row) Lillian Spear, Dorothy Arnold, Minnie O'Brien, Patrick Shea, Clarence Rice, Louise Cordes, unidentified, Harry Johnson, Lewis Robinson, and Miss Carr; (sixth row) Miss Richards, unidentified, Carroll O'Connor, Harry Sanborn, Eva Spear, Edna Taylor, Edna Steere, Miss Hermanse, and Raymond Belleville; (seventh row) Louise Taylor, Edna Moore, Cara McIntyre, Ruby Belleville, Elsie Othick, Howard Smith, and Phillip Hastings. The Clifford M. Granger Elementary School now occupies this location. (Courtesy of Patrica Noble.)

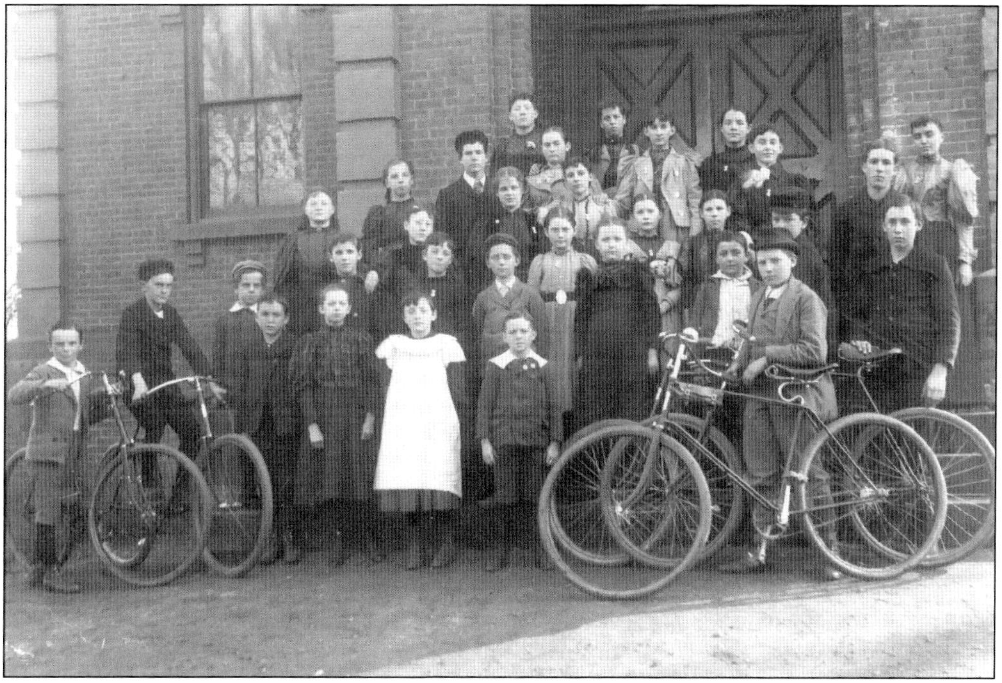

This Feeding Hills Center School photograph from the early 1900s includes members of the Kerr, Kellogg, and Taylor families. (Courtesy of Roberta Cesan.)

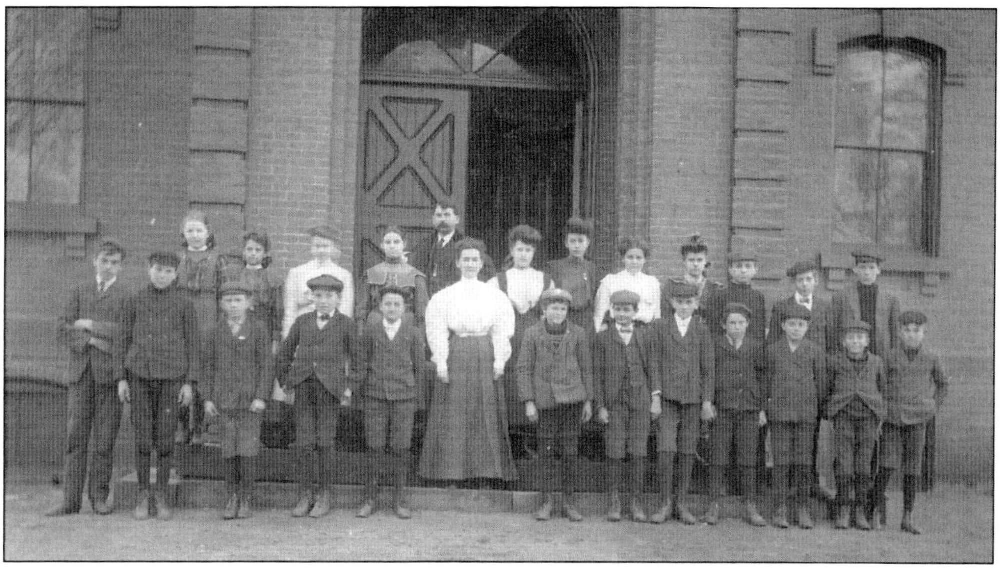

Shown at the Feeding Hills Center School *c.* 1905 are, from left to right, the following: (front row) James Cleary, Giles Halladay (see page 75), William Sullivan, Raymond Cleary, Perley Fuller, Miss Emerson, Silas Westcott, Maurice Clark, Percy Fuller, Thomas Ahearn, James Cesan, William Schmantz, and Jack Shea; (back row) Ethel Snow (see page 65), Ida Dix, Julia Huntley, May Roche, Mr. Gushee, Ruby Miller, Minnie Martin, Flora Sweatland, Charlotte Miller, Walter Noble, Edward Noble, and Sydney Tarbox. Many of these students are pictured on the previous page. Clifford M. Granger Elementary School now occupies this location. (Courtesy of Patricia Noble.)

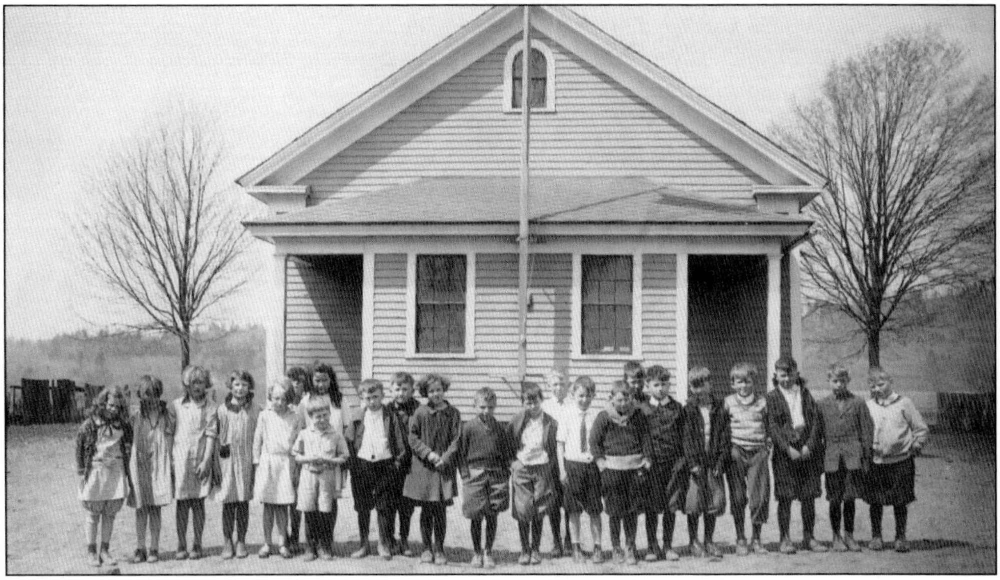

This photograph of the West Street School (now the Grange Hall on North West Street) from the 1930s includes Ruth Brown, Edith Cesan, Celia Jerski, Ruth Kerr, J. Carleton Kerr, Albert Brown, and Jean Peirson. (Courtesy of Roberta Cesan.)

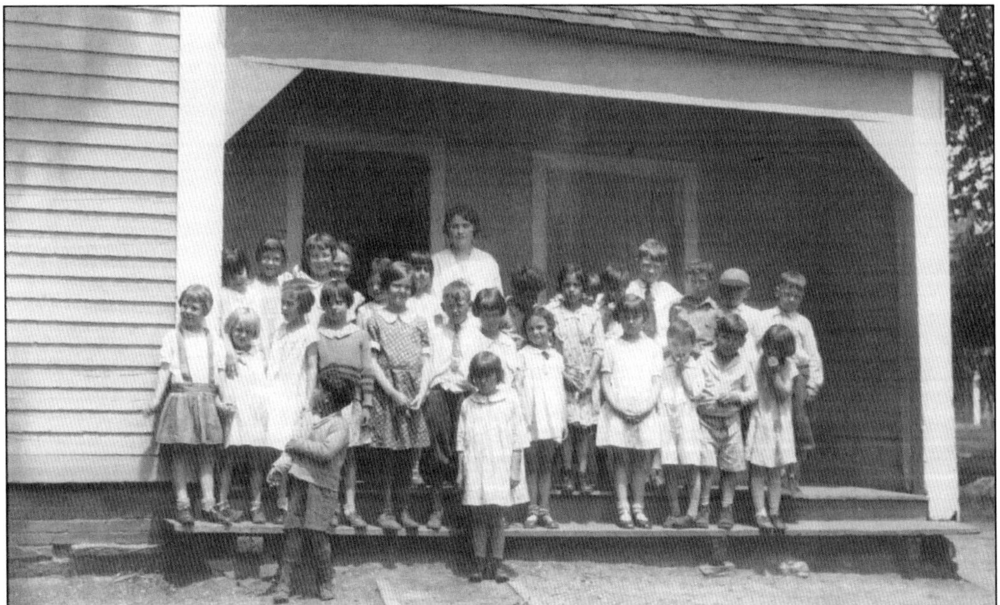

The South Agawam or South Main Street School stood at the intersection of River Road and Main Street until 1932. Photographed are, from left to right, the following: (front row) Larry Maiolo and Vera Diduk; (middle row) Claire Barden, Doris Stone, June Hale, Virginia Brinker, Shirley French, George La Violette, unidentified, Nellie Buoy, Kenneth Cowles, unidentified, unidentified; (back row) Janet Wheeler, Rosie Meyer, Lois Barden, Doris Stone, Barbara Wheeler, Columbine Frogameni, Miss Weeks, Carmen Cirillo, Rose Maiolo, unidentified, Albert Jackson, Warren Roberts, John Diduk, Gilbert Fields, and Frank Maiolo. (Courtesy of June [Hale] Cook.)

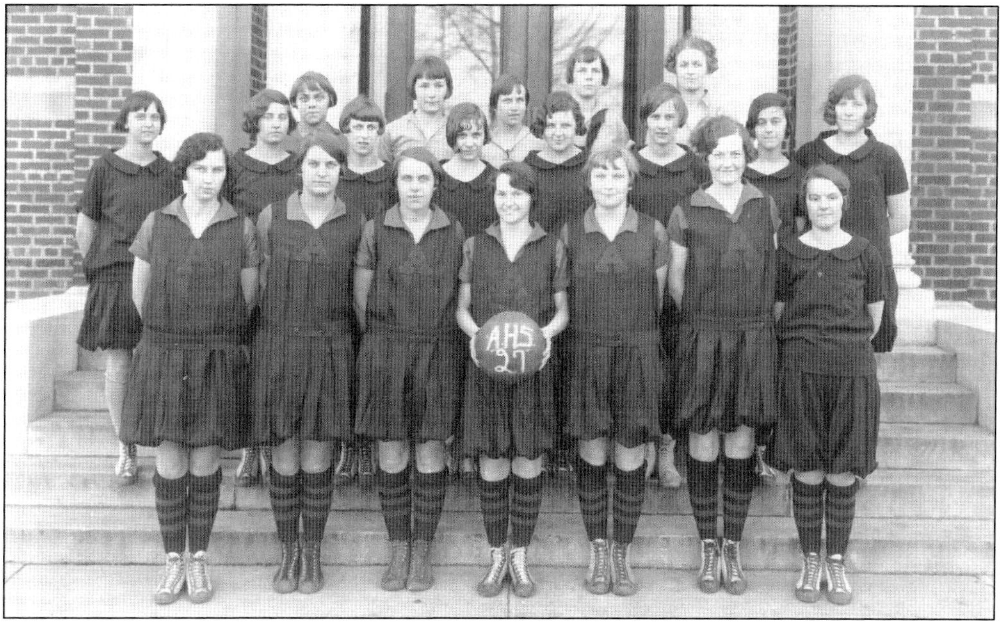

The 1925 Agawam High School girl's basketball team included, from left to right, the following: (front row) Catherine Burke, Grace Pond, Esther Schwartz, Audrey Phillips, Esther Pond, Dorothy Skinner, and Helen Rudman; (middle row) Inez Lucardi, Lottie Voisallo, Nellie White, Ruthie Renton, Marie Bozenhard, Grace Merrill, and unidentified; (back row) Josie Novelli (manager), Kahtleen Grimes, unidentified, Dot Hastings, and Betty Pond. (Courtesy of Esther [Schwartz] Reynolds.)

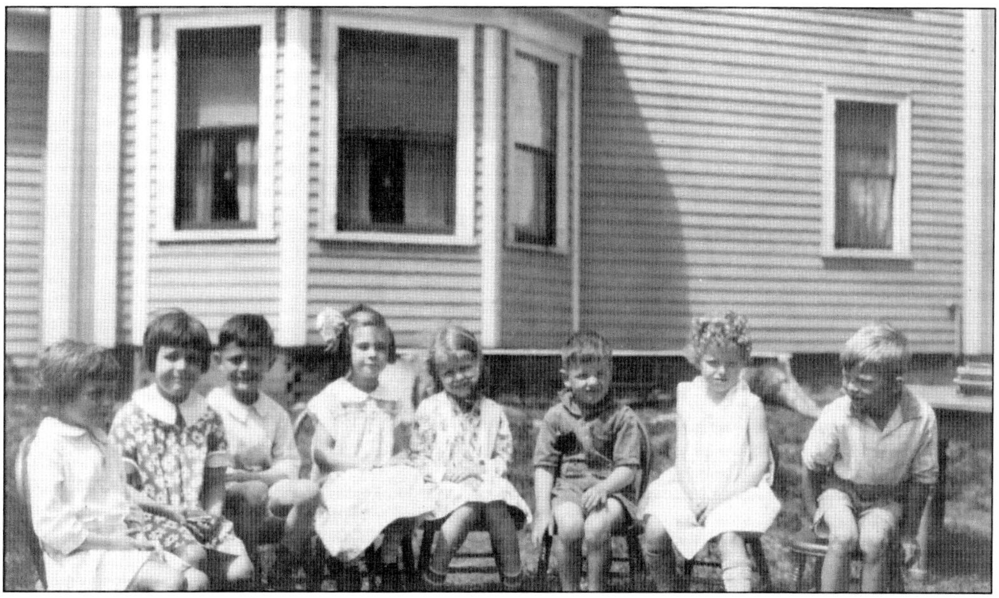

Verna Meyer provided the first kindergarten classes in town in her Elm Street home. This class is from the early 1930s. Shown, from left to right, are the following: unidentified, Jean Shaylor, Kenneth Cowles, June Hale, unidentified, Ralph Barker, Grace Shaylor, and unidentified. Many of these students later attended the River Road School and are pictured on the previous page. (Courtesy of June [Hale] Cook.)

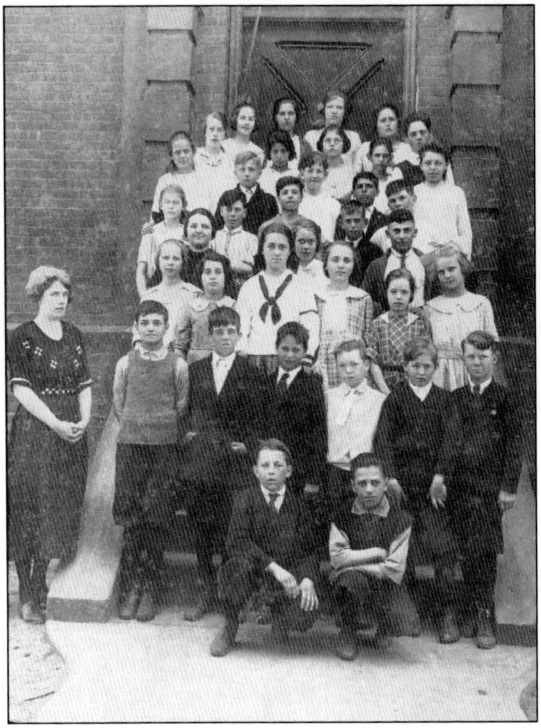

The teacher at the Agawam Center School, c. 1921, was Minta Maxwell. Esther Schwartz is in the center. The two boys kneeling in front are George Reynolds (left, see page 44) and Tommy Cascio. Esther Schwartz, who later married George Reynolds, remembers on the day this photograph was taken, George and Tommy were playing baseball in the field behind the school and would not come to get their pictures taken. It was only at the last minute that they ran up and kneeled in the front as the shutter was clicked. (Courtesy of Esther [Schwartz] Reynolds.)

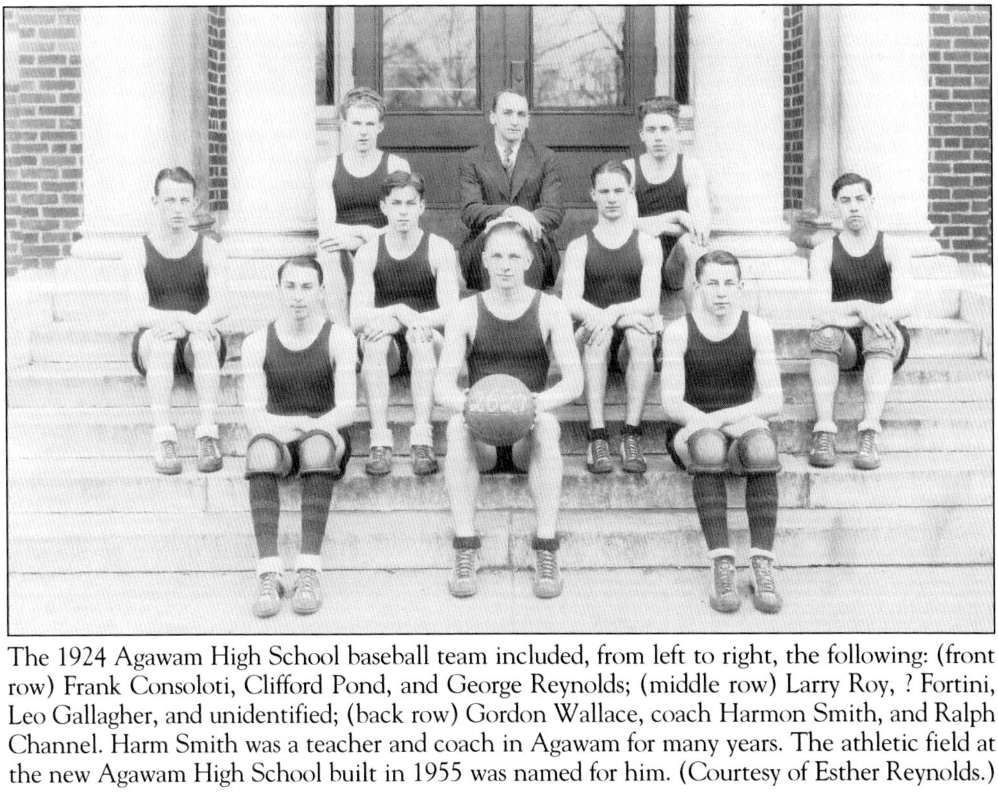

The 1924 Agawam High School baseball team included, from left to right, the following: (front row) Frank Consoloti, Clifford Pond, and George Reynolds; (middle row) Larry Roy, ? Fortini, Leo Gallagher, and unidentified; (back row) Gordon Wallace, coach Harmon Smith, and Ralph Channel. Harm Smith was a teacher and coach in Agawam for many years. The athletic field at the new Agawam High School built in 1955 was named for him. (Courtesy of Esther Reynolds.)

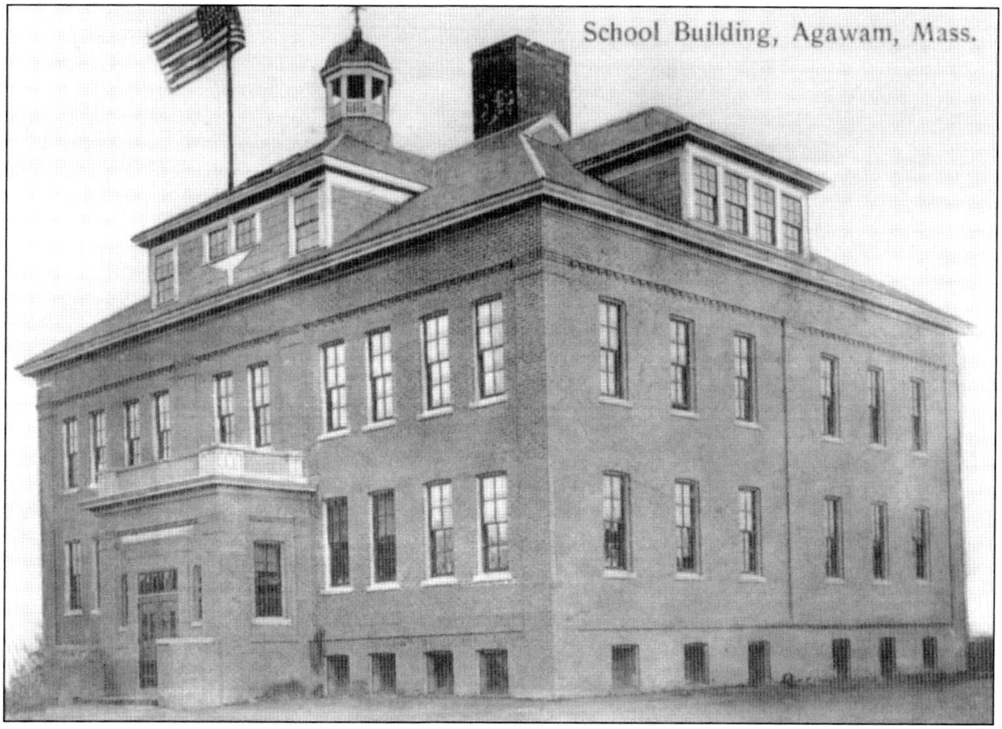

The original Maple Street or Mittineague School was built in 1862 and was in use until 1895, when a new school was built. It was struck by lightning and burned to the ground in 1904. The school pictured here was then constructed. It was later renamed the Katherine G. Danahy School after the longtime principal (1899–1947). The building was in use until the 1980s, when it was converted to housing for the elderly. The bell from the school is housed in a replica of its cupola at Veteran's Green at the Benjamin Phelps School (see below) in Agawam Center. (Author's collection.)

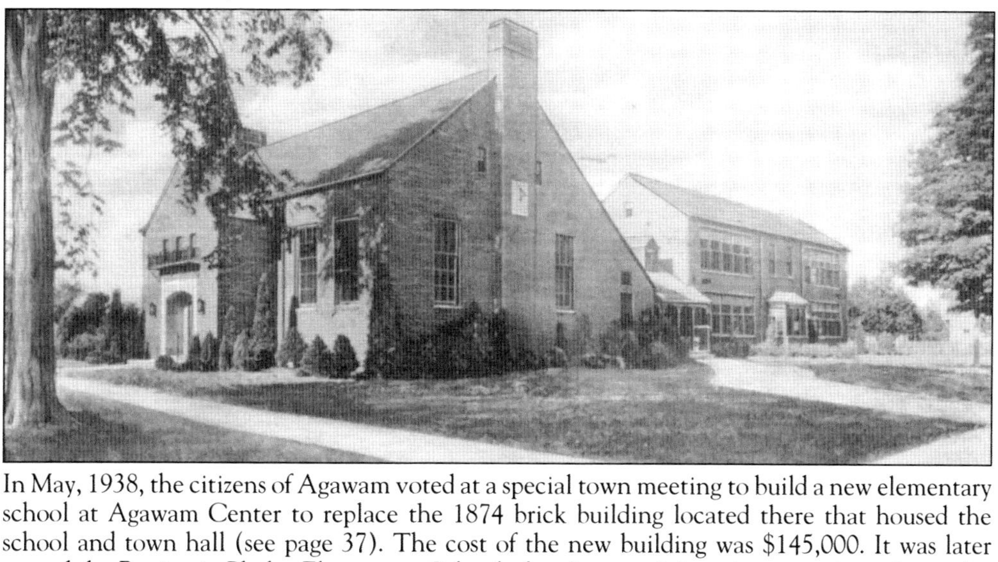

In May, 1938, the citizens of Agawam voted at a special town meeting to build a new elementary school at Agawam Center to replace the 1874 brick building located there that housed the school and town hall (see page 37). The cost of the new building was $145,000. It was later named the Benjamin Phelps Elementary School after Agawam's longtime superintendent, who was killed in an automobile accident in 1946. (Courtesy of Rick Bellico.)

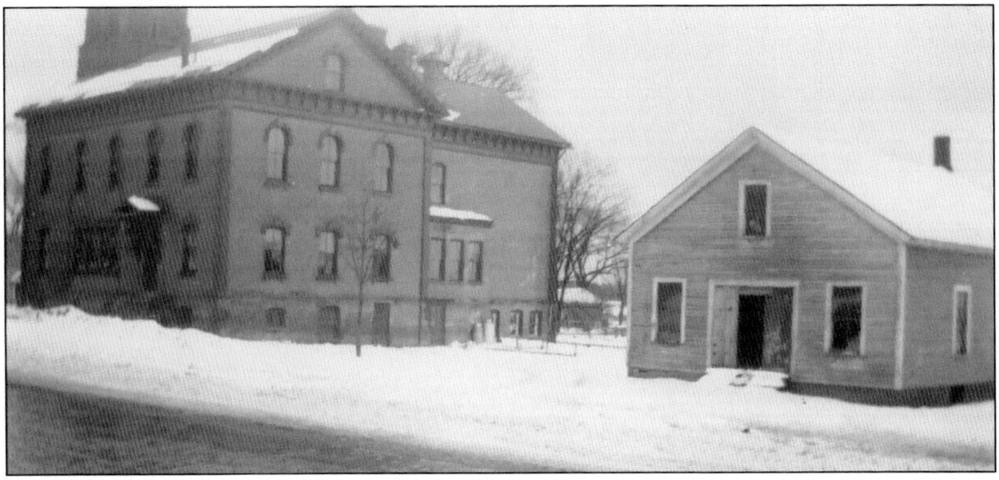

In 1949, preparations were being made to construct a new elementary school in Feeding Hills Center. The town hall (see page 51) was to be torn down, and the former primary school, located to the south, was purchased by James Kerr and moved via sled to 548 North West Street in March of that year for use as a residence, where it still stands. On January 7, 1950, the new Clifford M. Granger School was dedicated in honor of the longtime school committee member, who had died in 1946. (Courtesy of Roberta Cesan.)

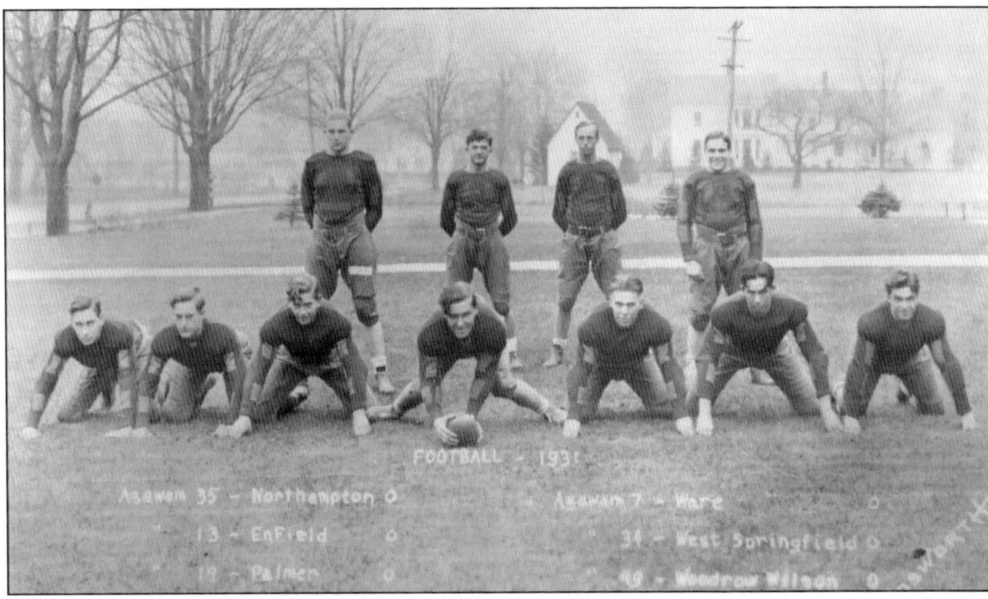

The 1931 Agawam High School football team was undefeated, untied, and unscored upon. Teams like this come around once in a lifetime. Team members shown in this photograph are, from left to right, as follows: (front row) Walter Mosely, Everett Pond, Norman Roberts, Creighton Abrams, Edward Parent, Robert Raymond, and "Squeaks" Mutti; (back row) Charles Benoit, Sam Provo, Clark Jones, and Merrill Tisdel. Scores that season were: Agawam 35–Northampton 0; Agawam 13–Enfield 0; Agawam 19–Palmer 0; Agawam 7–Ware 0; Agawam 34–West Springfield 0; Agawam 49–Woodrow Wilson 0. Team captain Creighton Abrams grew up on North Westfield Street, attended West Point, commanded the 4th Armored Division during World War II, and was appointed chief of staff of the U.S. Army on October 12, 1972. (Courtesy of Mr. and Mrs. Norman Roberts.)

Ten

THE AGAWAM FIRE DEPARTMENT

The Agawam Fire Department did not exist as such until the early part of the 20th century, when a volunteer fire department was organized. Three companies of 20 men each were assigned to the three precincts in town: (1) North Agawam; (2) Feeding Hills; and (3) Agawam.

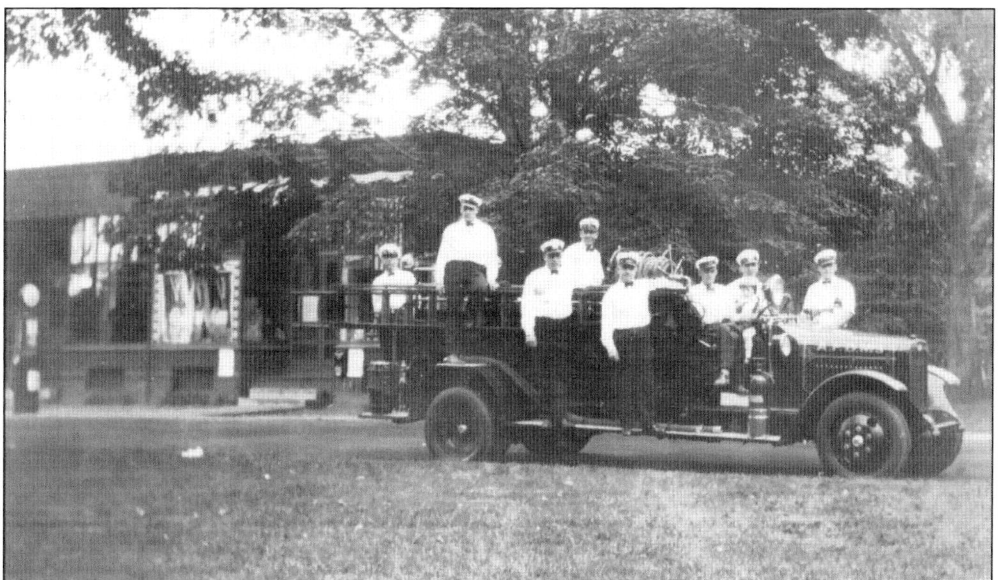

Agawam Center did not have a permanent fire station until 1918. Before that, space was rented for apparatus in the Congregational Church's horse shed. In this photograph, taken on Main Street, is the 1929 International belonging to Station No. 3 (Agawam Center). (Courtesy of Esther Reynolds.)

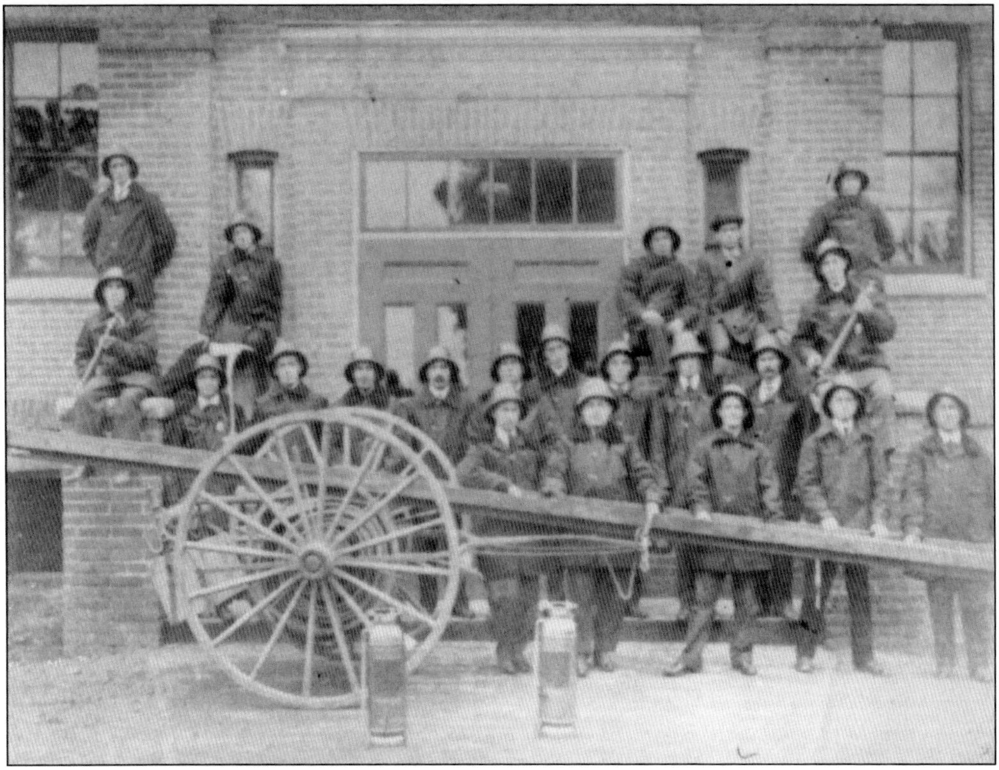

The Mittineague Volunteer Firemen pose in front of the new Mittineague School (see page 111) before the establishment of the Agawam Fire Department's North Agawam station (Station No. 1). (Agawam Historical Association collection.)

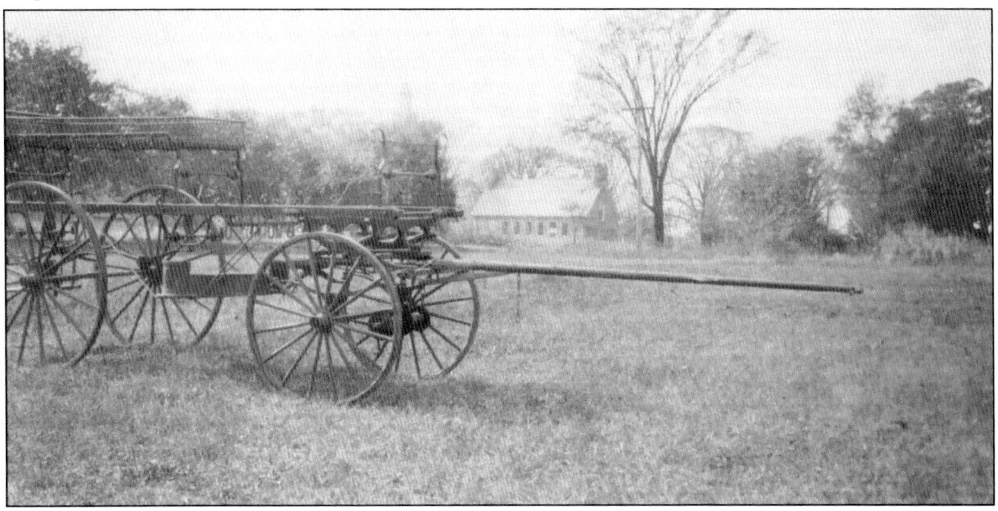

In 1913, an American LaFrance ladder wagon was purchased by the Town for $300. This piece of apparatus could be horse- or hand-drawn. This photograph was taken after 1924, as the Agawam Center Public Library that Mrs. Minerva Davis deeded to the Town in that year can be seen in the background. The old Agawam Congregational church can also be seen. The photograph was taken from a vantage point between Monroe and School Streets. (Courtesy of Ray Pond.)

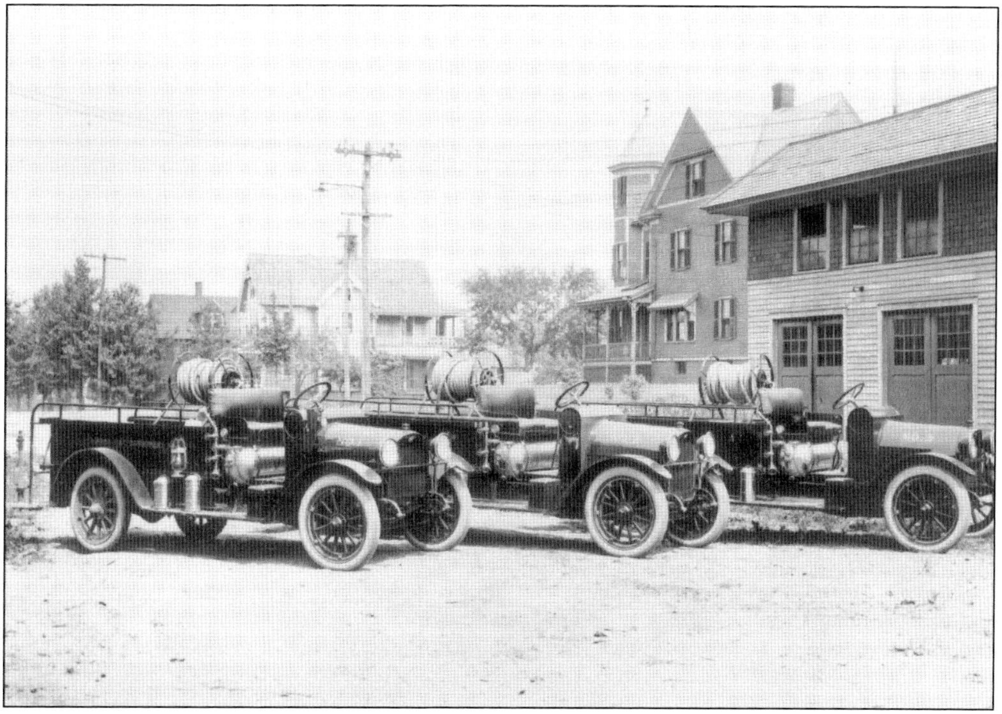

In 1919, the Town voted to "appropriate the sum of six thousand dollars for the purchase of three fire trucks." Three identical REO hose and chemical trucks—one each for the Agawam, North Agawam, and Feeding Hills stations—were purchased that year. This photograph was taken in front of Station No. 1 (North Agawam) on Ottowa Street. (Courtesy of Ray Pond.)

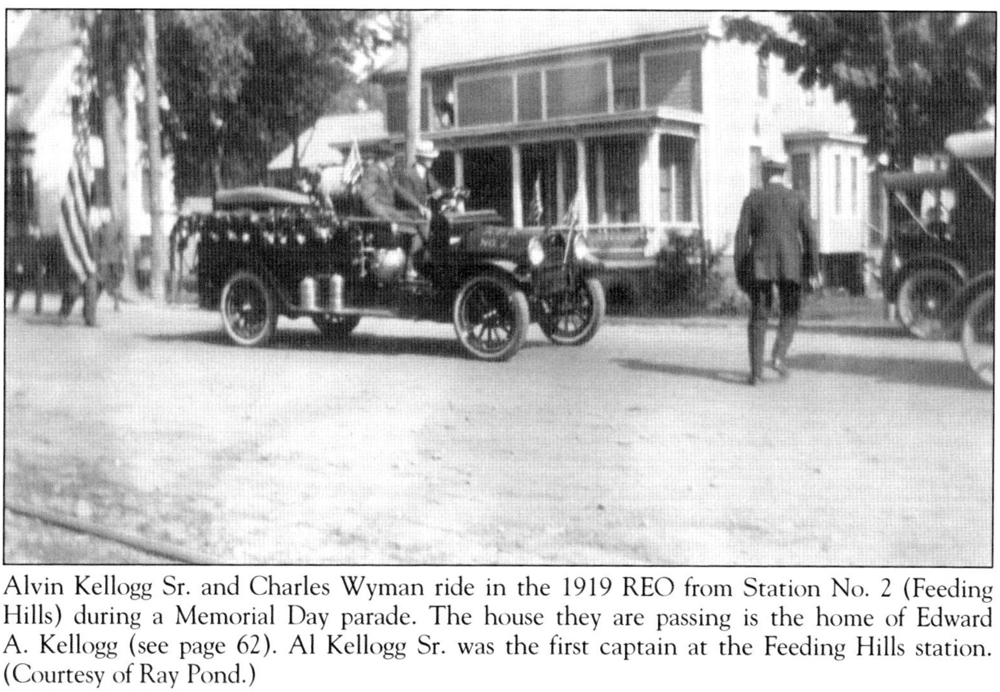

Alvin Kellogg Sr. and Charles Wyman ride in the 1919 REO from Station No. 2 (Feeding Hills) during a Memorial Day parade. The house they are passing is the home of Edward A. Kellogg (see page 62). Al Kellogg Sr. was the first captain at the Feeding Hills station. (Courtesy of Ray Pond.)

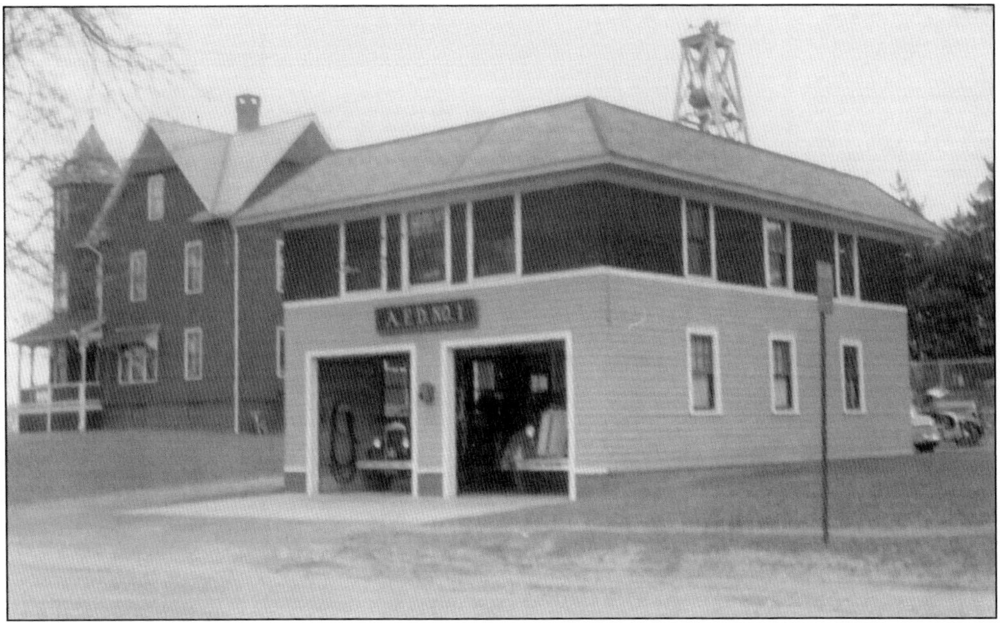

In 1916, Station No. 1 was built on Ottowa Street to replace North Agawam's first fire station, a rented barn. The station cost $1,904.80 to build, broken down as follows: Rita Savioli, land, $525; M.B. Harding, architect, $60.00; J.N. Trudeau, contractor, $1,200; J.A. Roy, supplies, $9.29; and grading payroll, $110.51. The station was decommissioned in October 1978, but it stood until the 1990s, when it was demolished. This photograph was taken in the 1950s. (Agawam Historical Association collection.)

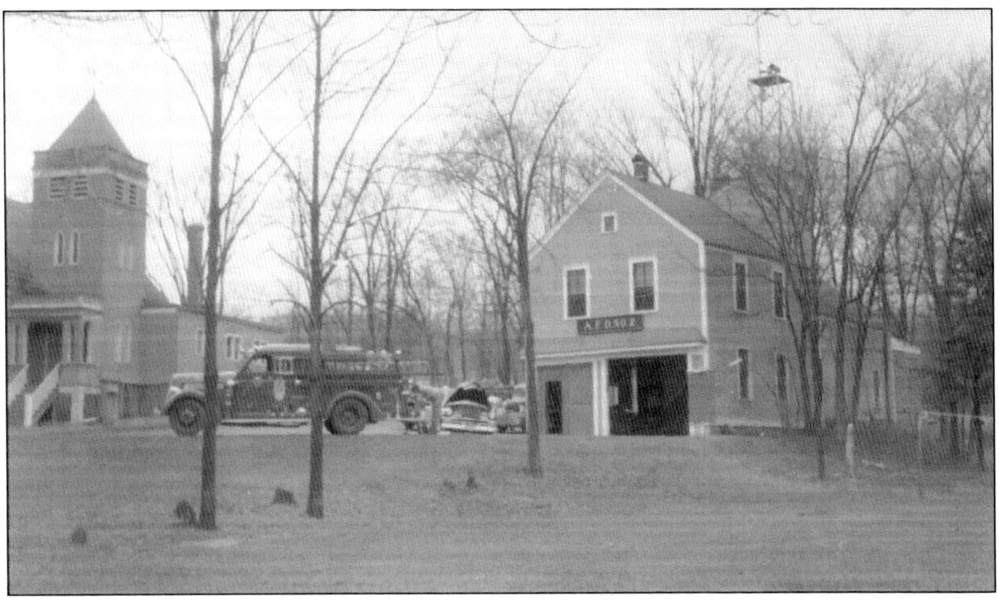

The Feeding Hills's fire station was quartered in a building that previously housed the highway department's horses. It was located on South Westfield Street directly behind the Halladay Library (see page 65). A new building was eventually constructed on Springfield Street, and Station No. 2 moved into its new quarters in 1967. (Agawam Historical Association collection.)

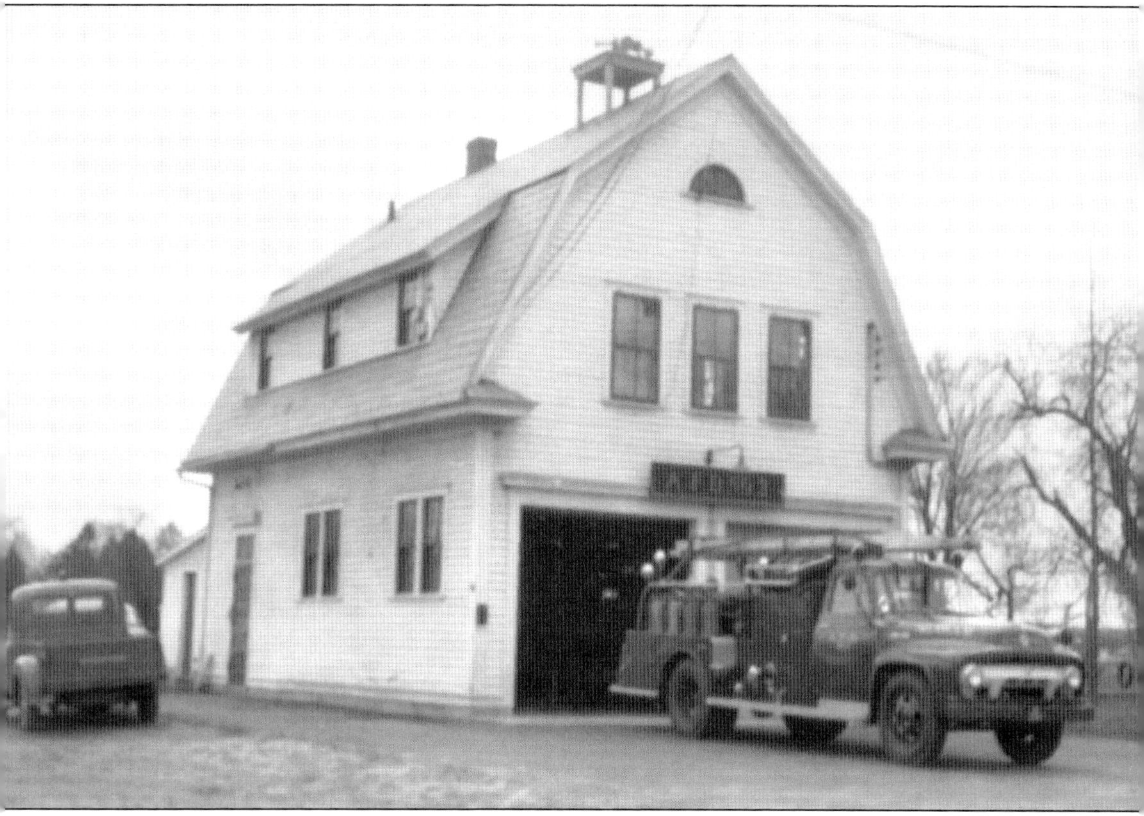

At a special town meeting on September 26, 1917, the "Special Committee on Fire Department Needs in Agawam Center reported advising the building of a hose house." It was voted that day "that the town take a lot of land situated on the Southerly side of Elm Street belonging to the heirs of Edward K. Bodurtha, described substantially as follows: Beginning at the northwest corner of land of the First Baptist Church of Agawam, and running Westerly on said street 75 feet; thence Southerly 65 feet; thence Easterly 48 feet; then Northerly on land of said church 75 feet to point of beginning, for the purpose of erecting a hose house thereon." It was also voted "that the Moderator appoint a committee of three to secure plans, advertise for bids and erect a suitable hose house at Agawam Center on the aforementioned lot, and that the Treasurer is hereby authorized and directed to borrow for the term of one year with the approval of the Selectmen, a sum of money not exceeding thirty-six hundred dollars ($3600) for the payment of same." The actual cost of the Elm Street fire station (Station No. 3) was $4,638.23, broken down as follows: Norman F. Winter, architect, $219.98; Amos Gosselin, contractor, $4,398.85; Springfield Gas Light Company, connection, $18.50. This was the first fire station in Agawam to be built specifically for motorized apparatus. Construction was finished in 1918, and the station was in service for more than 75 years. The station was moved 186 feet west on Elm Street from its original location to its current location so that the Baptist Church could build an addition. The truck on the right is a 1954 Seagrave-Ford 500 GPM triple combination pumper. The International pickup truck on the left belonged to Russell "Rusty" Jenks, who was appointed the first deputy chief in 1975. He was later appointed chief and served in that capacity for many years. Decommissioned in 1996, when the new Agawam Fire Headquarters opened around the corner on Main Street, the station is soon to be the home of the Agawam Historical and Fire House Museum. Rusty Jenks is currently a member of the Agawam Historical Association Board of Directors, which raised over $35,000 for the renovation of the station into the Agawam Historical and Fire House Museum. (Agawam Historical Association collection.)

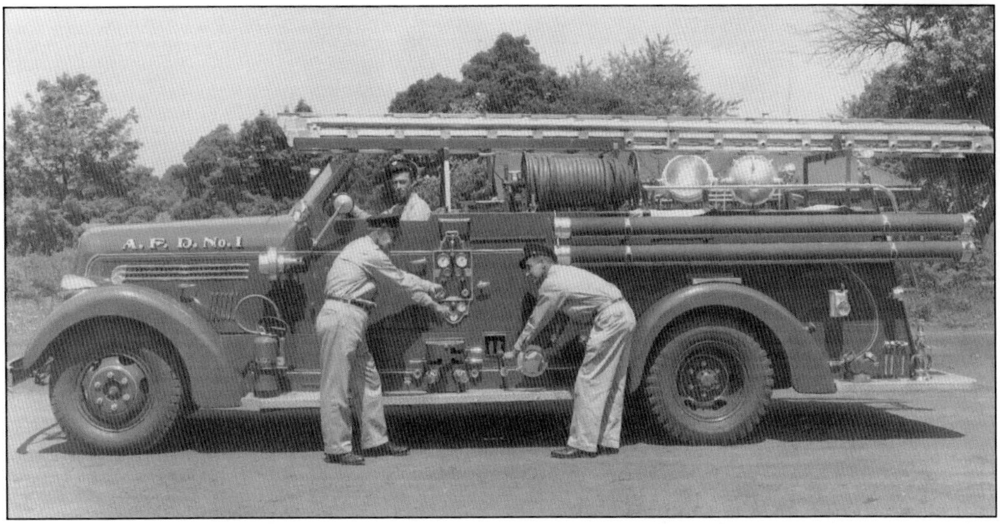

The 1949 Seagrave 750 GPM pump truck from Station No. 1 (North Agawam) appears in this c. 1951 photograph. Bill DeForge is at the wheel. Riley Farnsworth is standing on the left with Johnny Duggan. (Courtesy of Merwyn Farnsworth.)

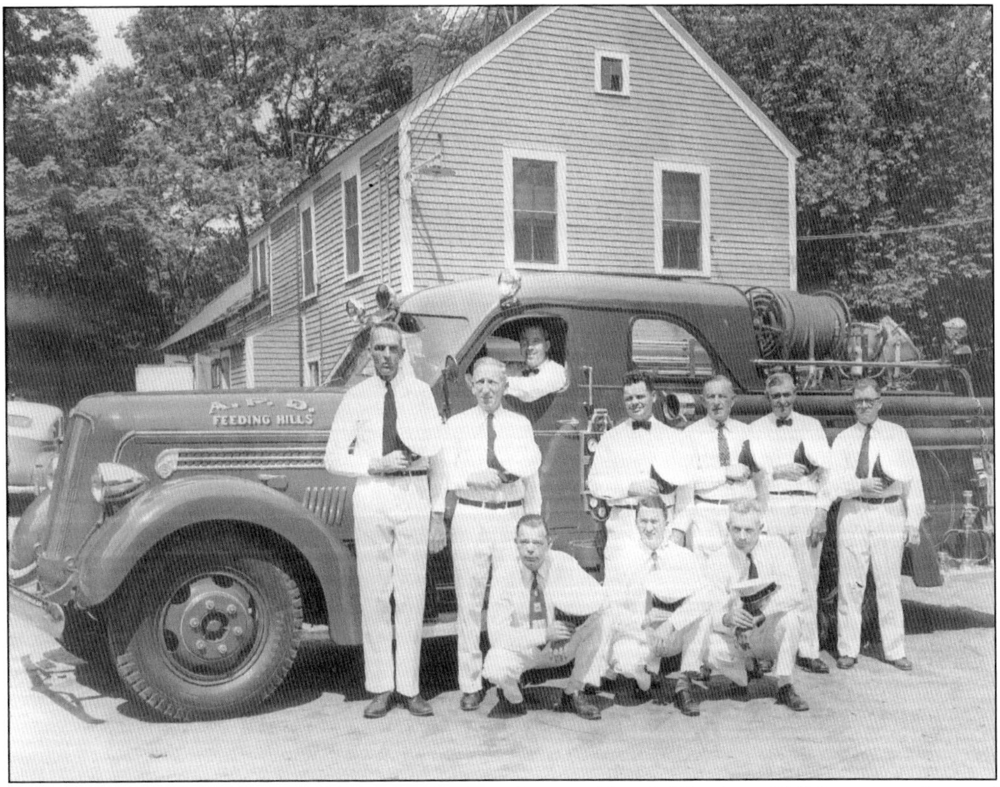

The 1948 Seagrave 750 GPM pump truck from Station No. 2 (Feeding Hills) rests in front of the old Feeding Hills station, c. 1951. The firefighters in this photograph are, from left to right, as follows: (kneeling) Dick Kellogg, Eddie Johnson, and Frank Crichton; (standing) Lloyd Major, Harold Davis, Hollis Kane, George Riley, Riley Farnsworth, and Oel Blodgett. Ken Burton is in the truck. (Courtesy of Merwyn Farnsworth.)

Eleven

Riverside Park

The land at the south end of Main Street was used for recreation long before Six Flags moved into town. As early as the 1840s, picnics were held at what was then known as Gallup's Grove (see page 32). John Gallup sold the land to Harvey Porter in 1881, who in turn sold it to Henry Smith, who changed the name to Riverside. His son, Elmer, sold the property to Henry J. Perkins in 1912. It was Henry Perkins who transformed the property from a picnic grove into an amusement park.

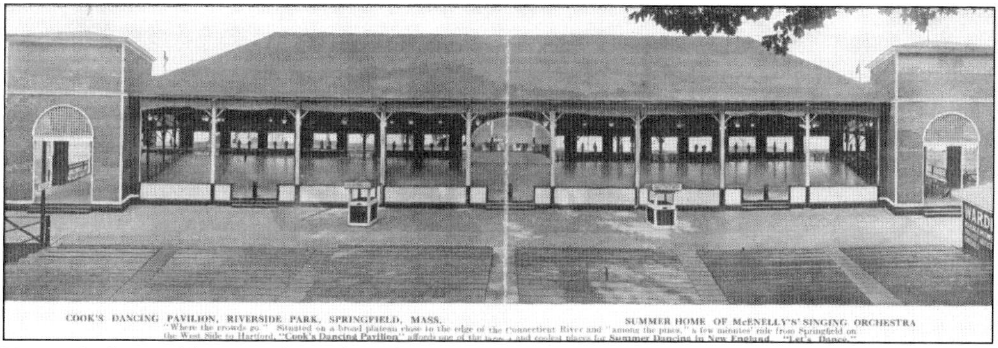

Henry Perkins sold Riverside Park to the W.J. Cook Amusement Company. This is the layout of Cook's Dancing Pavillion at Riverside Park, c. 1920, the "summer home of McEnelly's Singing Orchestra." The 70-by-160-foot dance floor was "situated on a broad plateau close to the edge of the Connecticut River and among the pines" and afforded "one of the largest and coolest places for Summer Dancing in New England." (Courtesy of Leslie and Dale Melanson.)

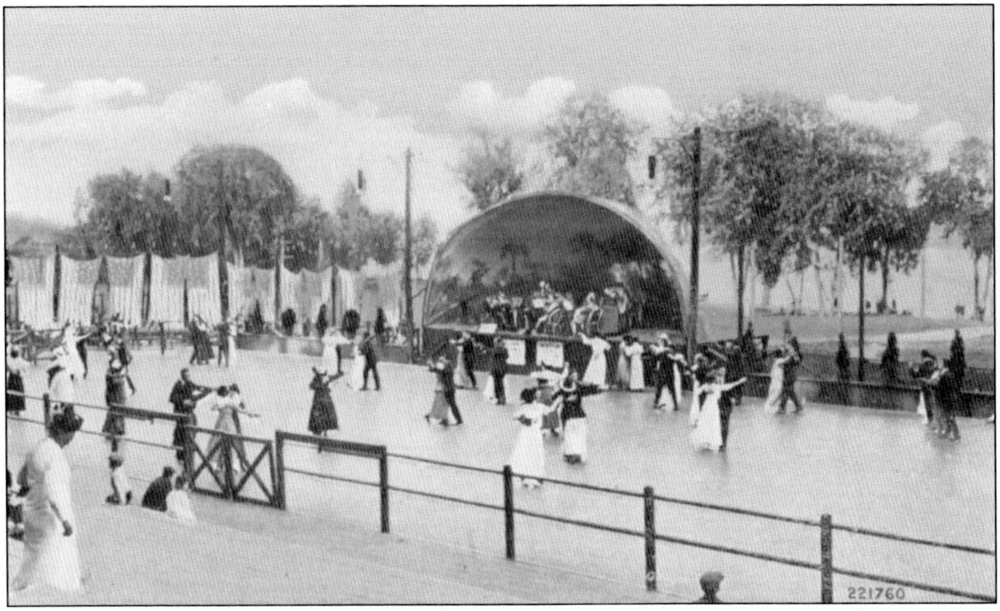

The caption of this postcard reads, "Dancing Pavillion at Riverside Park. The Park or Grove is located three miles down the Connecticut River and is the City's principal pleasure grounds. Easily accessible by small river steamers. Its dancing pavillion is a favorite rendezvous for the young people. As many as 40,000 people visit this resort on a pleasant day." In the 1940s, the Dance Pavillion was replaced with a stock car racing track, which was removed in 1999. The "Superman Ride of Steel" roller coaster now occupies the site. (Courtesy of Leslie and Dale Melanson.)

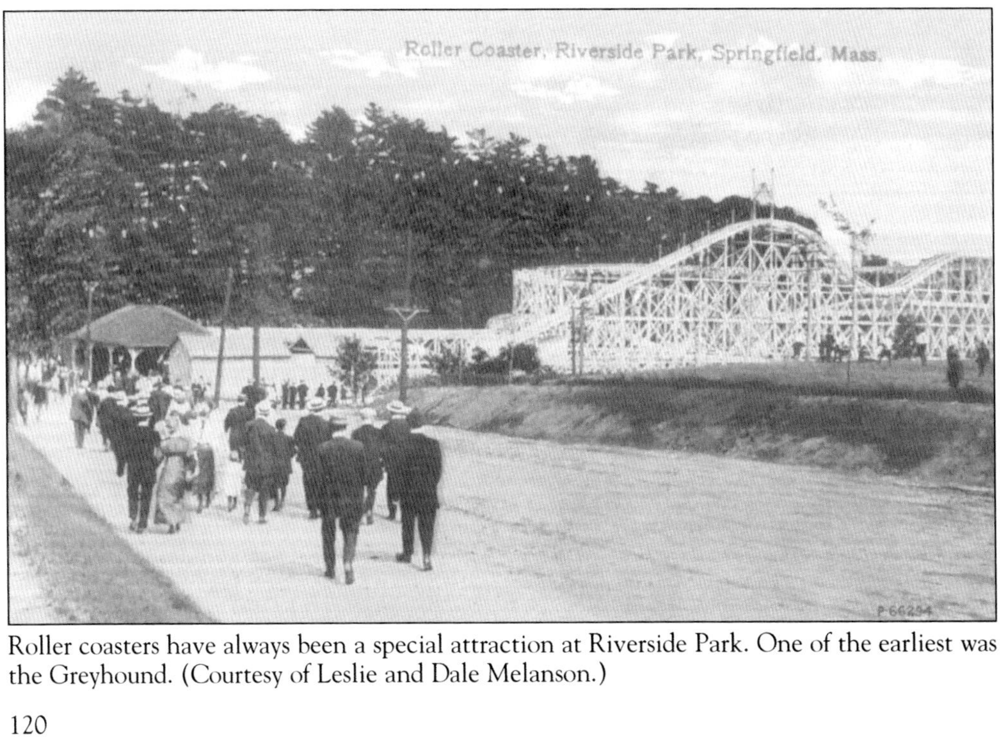

Roller coasters have always been a special attraction at Riverside Park. One of the earliest was the Greyhound. (Courtesy of Leslie and Dale Melanson.)

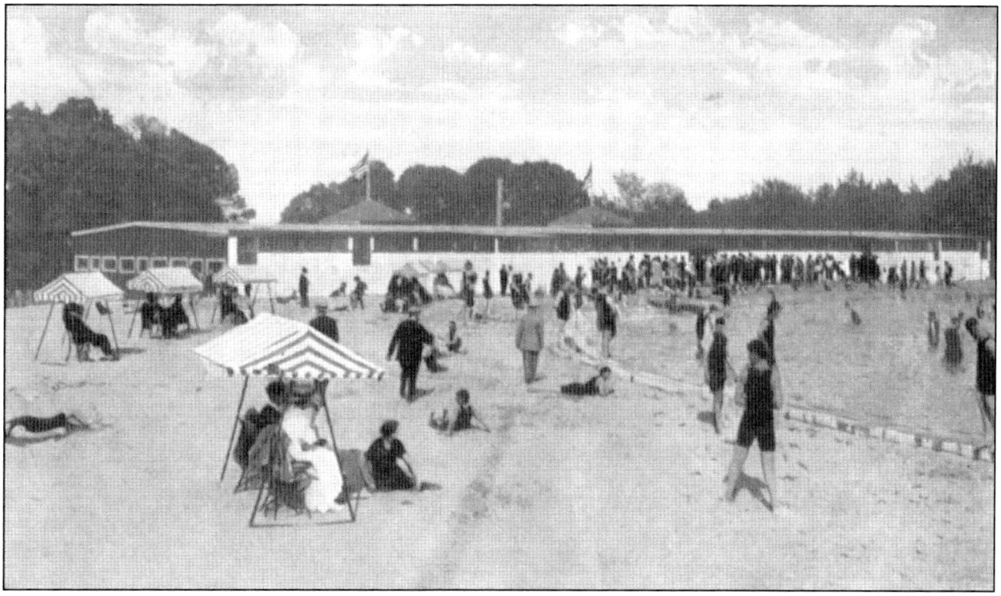

Six Flags New England's water park is located where Riverside Park's natatorium stood for many years in the 1920s and 1930s. Also known as Lake Takadip, it was touted as "the most sanitary bathing pool in the world; 300 feet in diameter; filtered water 98 percent pure, 3,000 gallons per minute flowing in and out of the pool." The pool was later filled in to provide parking. (Author's collection.)

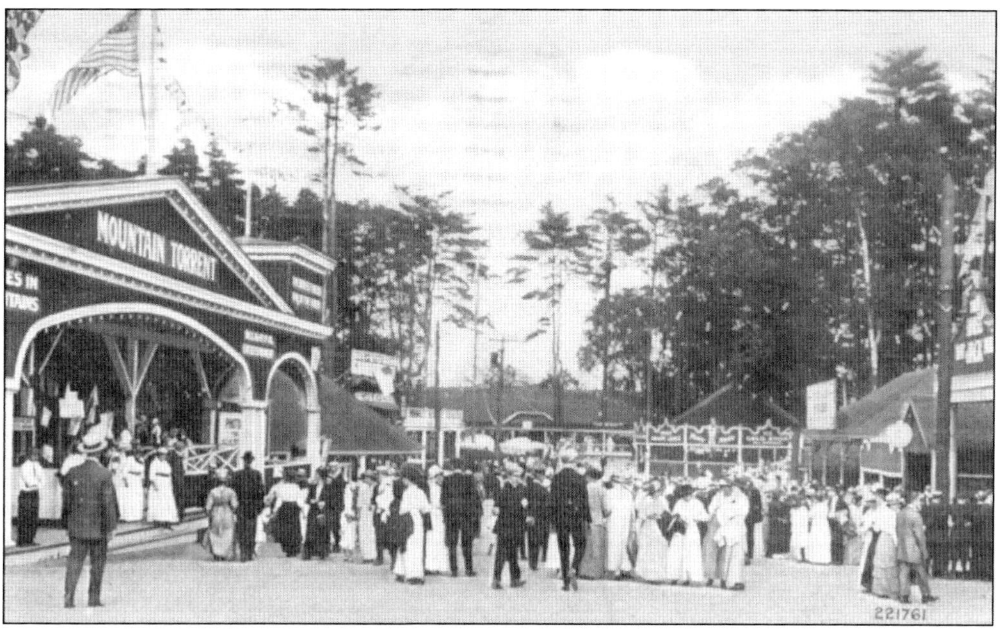

In July 1920, as now, the midway at Riverside Park "is constantly crowded with pleasure seekers." (Courtesy of Leslie and Dale Melanson.)

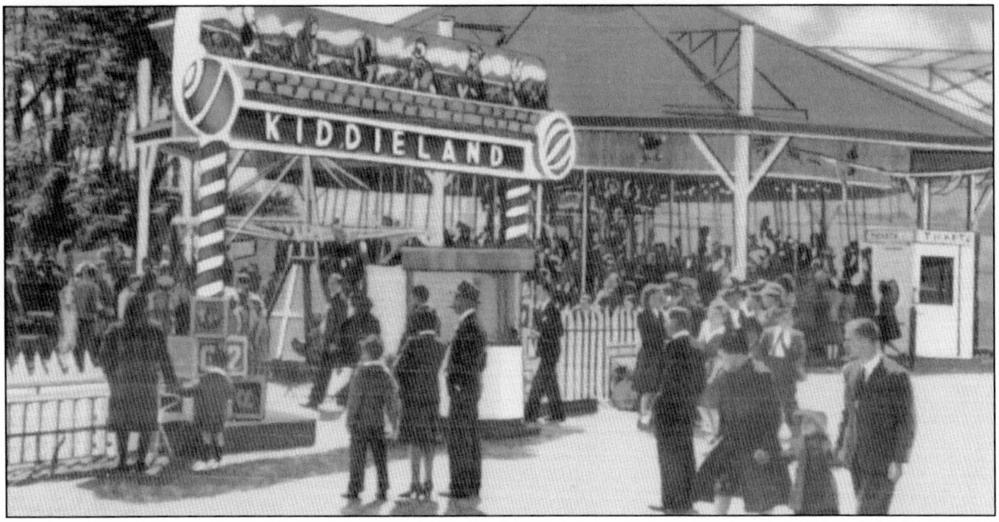

The caption on this 1940s postcard reads, "Kiddieland at Riverside Park is the delight of the youngsters. It is one of the 50 amusement features at the popular 'Playground of the Connecticut Valley,' on Route 5-A in Agawam, Massachusetts. In addition to the gay midway, Riverside Park has midget auto racing, outdoor shows, dance gardens, private picnic and clambake groves, etc. Edward J. Carroll is Owner-Manager of the famous resort." Riverside Park was bought in 1939 by the Stuart Amusement Company under the management of Edward Carroll. The Carroll family owned Riverside until Premier Parks purchased the property in 1997. (Author's collection.)

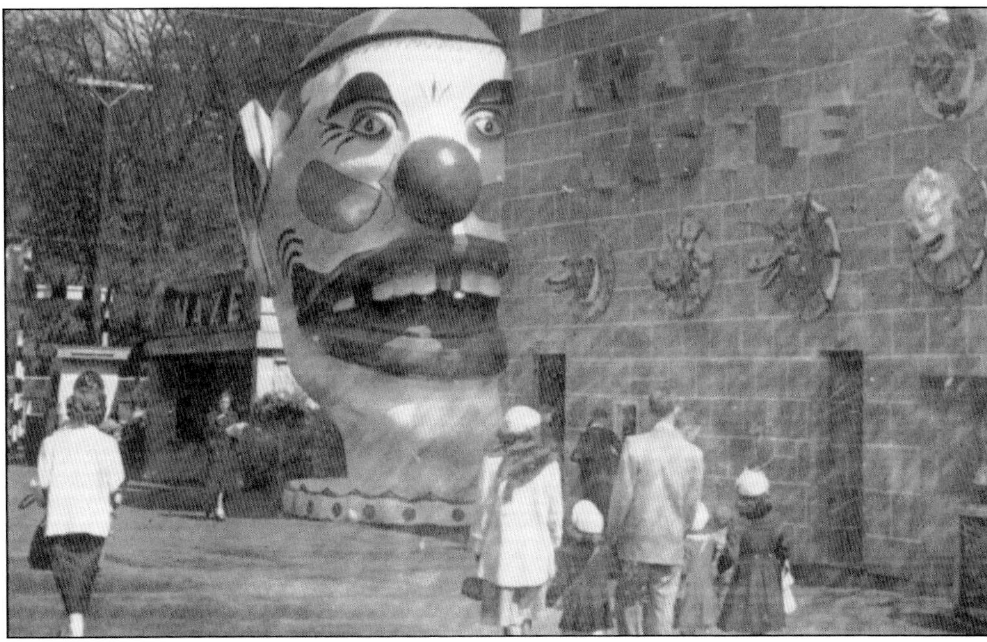

The caption of this postcard reads, "Picture shows the huge clown head, built in 1954, at Riverside Park, Agawam, Massachusetts, located on route 5-A between Hartford and Springfield. Riverside Park is one of the greatest amusement parks in the East with many thrilling rides, picnic groves, free shows, fireworks, auto racing and many other attractions." (Author's collection.)

Twelve

WHAT'S IN A NAME?

Although the Native American word *agaam*, or *agawam*, meaning "crooked river" or "low meadow land," is not very common, it is nonetheless seen in a number of places outside of town. The town of Ipswich was called Agawam for a short time in its early history, and the river near there is still called the Agawam River. The Agawam Diner on Route 1 in Peabody, Massachusetts, is still in operation. There is an Agawam Realty and Lake Agawam in the Hamptons on Long Island and an Agawam Hunt Club in East Providence, Rhode Island. The town of Agawam, Montana, was named by a Milwaukee Railroad worker in 1912 after his hometown in Massachusetts. The Agawam Copper Mine is located in the Lake Superior region. Two naval vessels also bore the name—one a gunboat during the Civil War, the other a World War II oiler named after the Agawam River.

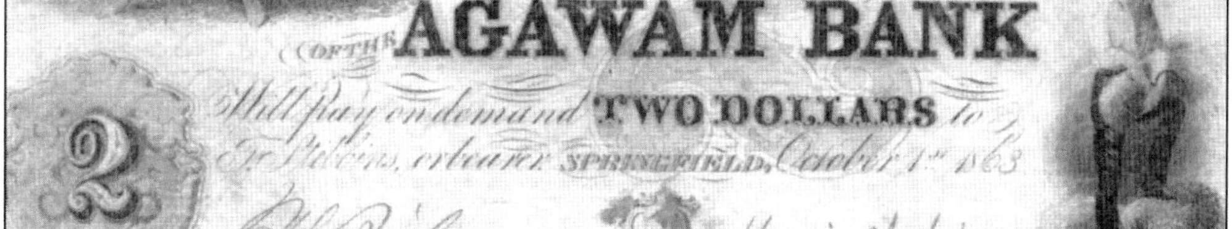

The Agawam Bank was founded in 1846 in Springfield, Massachusetts, and was named after the town where William Pynchon stopped in 1635 before founding Springfield in 1636. Manin Chapin was president. Printed on one side only, this $2 note from 1863 may in fact be counterfeit; the author owns an identical note stamped so by a Virginia bank. (Author's collection.)

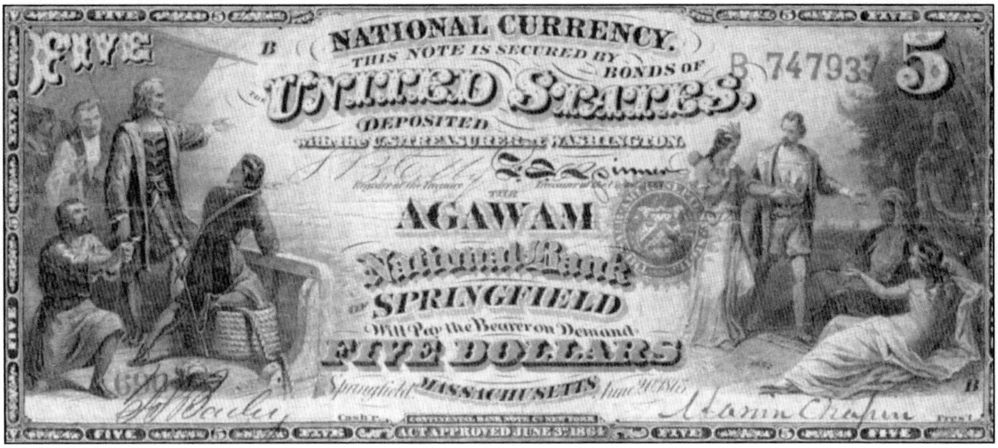

The Agawam Bank became the Agawam National Bank on April 26, 1865, and was eventually located at the corner of Main and Lyman Streets in Springfield. This $5 note from 1865 features scenes of Christopher Columbus. (Agawam Historical Association collection.)

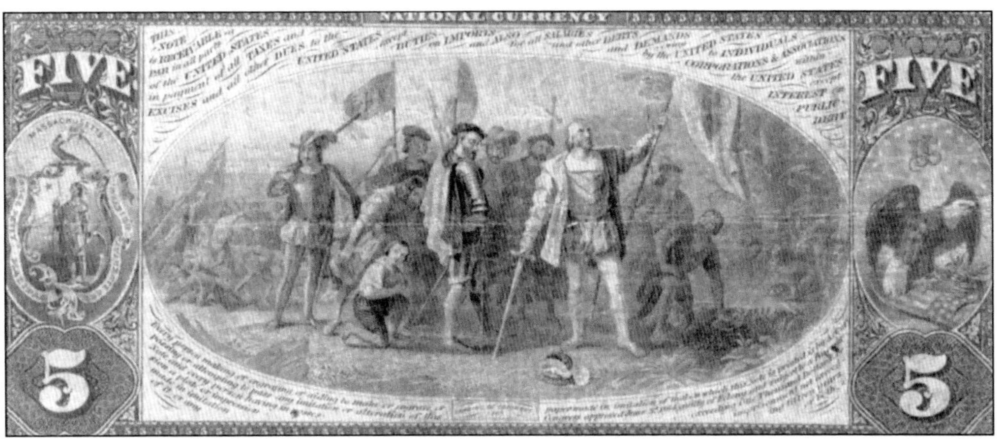

The reverse of the $5 note above features the "Landing of Columbus, 1492." The fine print at the bottom reads, "Every person making or engraving or aiding to make or engrave or passing or attempting to pass any imitation or alteration of this Note, and every person having in possession a plate or impression made in imitation of it or any paper made in imitation of than on which this Note is printed is by Act of Congress approved June 3rd, 1864 guilty of Felony and subject to a fine not exceeding One Thousand dollars or imprisonment not exceeding fifteen years, or both." Perhaps this was included in response to some previous incidents. (Agawam Historical Association collection.)

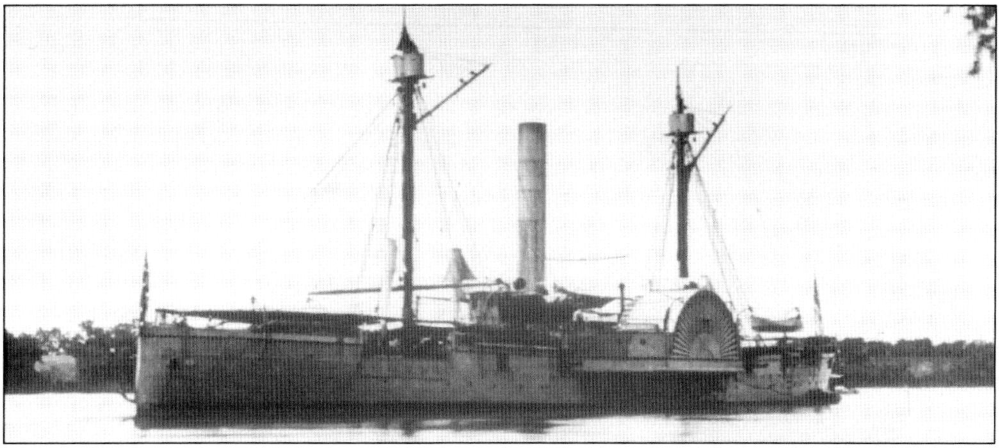

There were 27 "Sassacus" class double-ended side-wheeler gunboats in service during the Civil War. This class of boats was named after towns with Native American names. The USS *Agawam* was launched in Portland, Maine, on April 21, 1863, and was commissioned on March 9, 1864. Armament consisted of two 100-pound rifled cannons, four 9-inch smoothbore cannons, two 24-pound smoothbore cannons, one 12-pound rifled cannon, and one 12-pound smoothbore cannon. Although she carried 200 crew members, no one from the town of Agawam served on her. She spent most of the war patrolling the James River in Virginia. She was decommissioned in 1867. (Agawam Historical Association collection.)

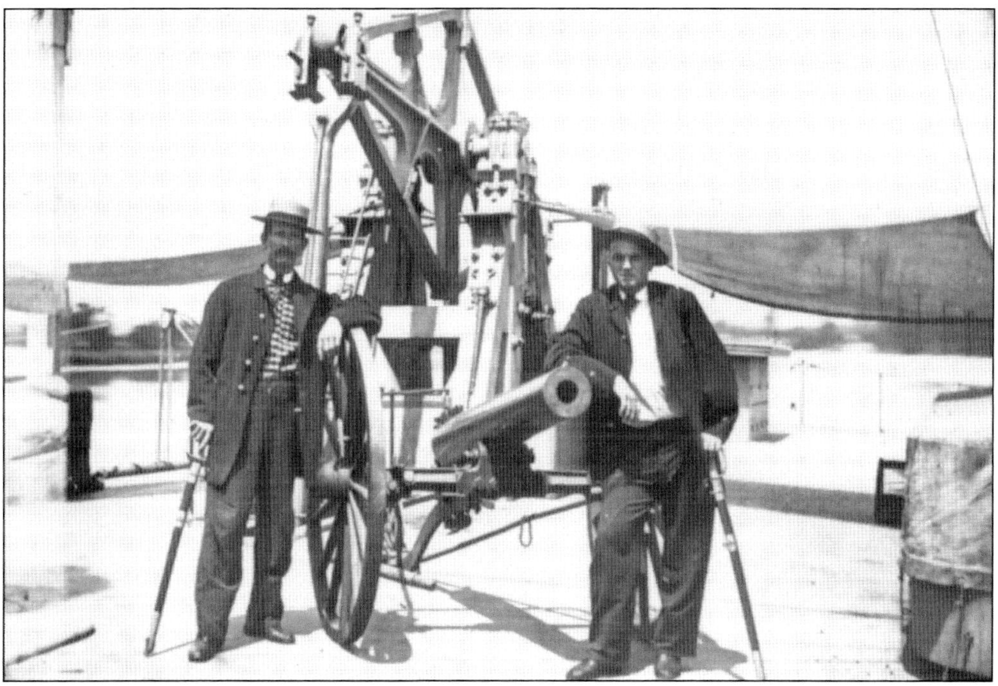

This photograph from the National Archives was taken in spring 1864 aboard the USS *Agawam*. The acting ensign is at the left. Listed as serving aboard the ship at that time in the rank of acting ensign were the following: Charles M. Anthony of Dartmouth, Massachusetts; Samuel Sherwood Bissell of Fairfield, Connecticut; Ely M. Boggs; Peter Howard of France; Clinton Wiley of New York; and Charles L. Willcomb of Massachusetts. This photograph could show of any one of them. (Author's collection.)

The Agawam Historical Association

The Agawam Historical Association was founded on November 15, 1962. It is a nonprofit, tax-exempt organization. Its stated purpose and objectives are as follows:

> To encourage an interest in the collection and preservation of historic materials, documents, and landmarks pertaining to the town of Agawam, Massachusetts, so as to be available for the enjoyment of present and future generations.
>
> To provide educational opportunities for the dissemination and understanding of facts concerning Agawam's history and the cultivation of civic pride in Agawam's heritage.
>
> To provide facilities for the proper storage, preservation, and public display of historic artifacts and documents.

The Agawam Historical Association hosts informative and interesting speakers at its four meetings each year, with one fall meeting, a winter meeting, and two spring meetings, one of which incorporates the association's annual meeting.

Membership is open to all, and there is an affordable dues schedule with rates for individuals, families, and seniors. Please send inquiries regarding membership to the Agawam Historical Association, P.O. Box 552, Agawam, Massachusetts, 01001.

The Agawam Historical Association will also operate the Agawam Historical and Fire House Museum upon its opening in spring 2001. As a volunteer organization, the Agawam Historical Association is always interested in anyone willing to donate their time, artifacts or resources. Please contact us at the address above.

THE AGAWAM HISTORICAL AND FIRE HOUSE MUSEUM

Plans for the Agawam Historical and Fire House Museum began in 1995 during construction of the new Agawam Fire Department headquarters on Main Street. The 1918 Elm Street station (see page 117) was scheduled for decommissioning upon the dedication of the new station. Then-mayor Christopher Johnson brought together the Agawam Historical Commission, the Agawam Historical Association, and the Agawam Fire Department to discuss the feasibility of renovating the building and opening it as a museum. The Town would retain ownership of the property, and the Historical Association would raise the funds necessary for materials. The Agawam Historical Association then embarked on a three-year fundraising campaign that raised more than $35,000. Much of the renovation cost went into the addition built at the rear of the building, which houses a chairlift, making the museum fully handicapped accessible.

The dayroom on the second floor has been completely renovated to look as it did in 1918. The Historical Association hopes to have both permanent and revolving displays housed there. The kitchen area has been renovated as well to look as it did at the time the station was built. The old gas stove located in the kitchen is not original to the station; it was a prop from the movie *The Cider House Rules* that was bought for use in the museum.

The first-floor apparatus bay will house displays pertaining to the Agawam Fire Department, including the International fire truck (purchased by the Town in 1930) after it is restored.

Future plans for the museum include having period doors built that would be similar to what was once found on the old Ottowa Street fire station (see page 115). These doors would replace the overhead doors currently in place on the front of the museum.

The Agawam Historical and Fire House Museum will be the first historical museum in the town's 350-plus years of existence. The Historical Association has in its possession many artifacts of the town's past, including much of the collection of the late Edith LaFrancis, Agawam's town historian for many years, who died in 1999.

Royalties from the sale of this book will be used for the operation of the Agawam Historical Association and Agawam Historical and Fire House Museum. Anyone interested in donating artifacts to the museum should contact: Archivist, Agawam Historical Association, P.O. Box 552, Agawam, Massachusetts, 01001.

BIBLIOGRAPHY

The information accompanying the photographs in this book was collected from many sources.

1985 Inventory of Historic Structures, Greg Farmer and the Agawam Office of Planning and Community Development.

75th anniversary, Agawam, Massachusetts, souvenir booklet.

Agawam, Massachusetts: Over the Span of a Century, 1855–1955. Centennial souvenir booklet

Annual Reports of the Town of Agawam, 1903–1970s. Collection of Walter T. Kerr, courtesy of the family of Walter T. Kerr.

Raymond Louis, Raymond Carl and Alfred Robert Casella. *Some Old Homes of the Lower Connecticut Valley*. Copyright 1988

Encyclopedia of Massachusetts, Biographical–Genealogical. The American Historical Society.

Everts, Louis H. *History of the Connecticut Valley in Massachusetts*, Vol. II, 1879.

The website of Terry Foenander.

Labb family history by Evalyn Baron and Bill Labb

LaFrancis, Edith. *Agawam, Massachusetts*. Copyright, Town of Agawam, Massachusetts.

The Little Chronicle, Vol. 1, No. 10, February 1928. The West Springfield Trust Company.

The aviation collection of Leslie and Dale Melanson.

Agawam Center National Register Historic District Nomination Form, Bonnie Parsons, Tammy Peters, Pioneer Valley Planning Commission.

The scrapbook of Clyde Pomeroy, containing many newspaper photographs and articles from the 1920s and 1930s.

Springfield Suburban Directory. Copyright 1928, the H.A. Manning Company.

Superior Facts, Vol. 3, No. 6, December 1929. Copyright 1929, the Paper Makers Chemical Corporation.

Please submit photographs for future volumes of Agawam and Feeding Hills to the Agawam Historical Association, P.O. Box 552, Agawam, Massachusetts, 01001, attn: David Cecchi.